hotels • villas • restaurants • shops • galleries • spas

balichic

For regular updates on our special offers, register at

www.thechiccollection.com

hotels • villas • restaurants • shops • galleries • spas

balichic

text susi johnston

thechiccollection

executive editor
melisa teo

senior editor
laura jeanne gobal

assistant editors
ong li ling • janice ruth de belen

designers
nelani jinadasa • wong hean meng

production manager
sin kam cheong

editions didier millet pte ltd
121 telok ayer street, #03-01
singapore 068590
email: edm@edmbooks.com.sg
website: www.edmbooks.com

first published 2004 • reprinted 2005
second edition 2007 • third edition 2008
© 2004, 2007, 2008 editions didier millet pte ltd

Printed in Singapore.

All rights reserved. No part of this publication may be reproduced, stored in a retrieval system, or transmitted in any form or by any means, electronic, electrostatic, magnetic tape, mechanical, photocopying, recording or otherwise, without prior written permission from the publisher.

isbn-13: 978-981-4217-10-1

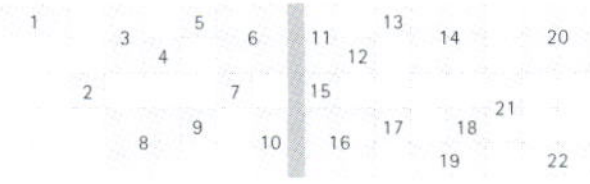

COVER CAPTIONS:
1: *The pool at Simona Oasis + Spa*
2: *An outdoor living room at Simona Oasis + Spa*
3: *Pura Luhur Uluwatu*
4: *A bedroom at Simona Oasis + Spa*
5: *A treatment room at COMO Shambhala Resort at Begawan Giri*
6: *Kites take flight in Kuta*
7: *Exquisite jewellery from Treasures*
8: *Outdoor dining at KU DE TA*
9: *Balinese cuisine at Warung Enak*
10: *A daybed at COMO Shambhala Estate at Begawan Giri*
11: *Bali's tropical greenery*
12: *Natural ingredients used in spa therapies*
13: *Wayang kulit puppet*
14: *Master bedroom at COMO Shambhala Estate at Begawan Giri*
15: *Traditional masks at Toko Antique*
16: *A pool at COMO Shambhala Estate at Begawan Giri*
17: *Daybeds at Bulgari Resort*
18: *The gender, a metallophone*
19: *Nampu restaurant at Grand Hyatt Bali*
20: *A view of Jimbaran Bay*
21: *A bedroom at Four Seasons Resort Bali at Jimbaran Bay*
22: *A one-bedroom villa at the Four Seasons Resort Bali at Jimbaran Bay*

PAGES 2, 4, 5 AND 6: *COMO Shambhala Estate at Begawan Giri*

PAGES 8 AND 9: *Meru shrines at dusk, Besakih*

contents

maps of bali 10 • introduction 12 • dining in bali 38 • night fever 40 • being beautiful in bali 42 • the art of life 44 • island shopping 48 • the best views of bali 52

54 ubud+surroundings

COMO Shambhala Estate at Begawan Giri 68 • Four Seasons Resort Bali at Sayan 70 • Komaneka Resort at Monkey Forest 72 • Komaneka Resort at Tanggayuda 76 • Majapahit Beach Villas 80 • Pita Maha Resort + Spa 82 • The Royal Pita Maha 84 • Ubud Hanging Gardens 86 • Vajra Villas 88 • Ary's Warung 92 • Café des Artists 96 • Lamak Restaurant + Bar 98 • Mozaic 100 • Warung Enak Bali 102 • Gaya Fusion 104 • Macan Tidur 108 • Toko Antique 110 • Treasures 112

114 sanur

Villa Casis 124 • Carlo 128 • Island Arts 132 • Uluwatu Handmade Balinese Lace 134

138 bukitpeninsula+jimbaran

Conrad Bali Resort + Spa 152 • Four Seasons Resort Bali at Jimbaran Bay 154 • Grand Hyatt Bali 156 • Heavenly Residence 160 • Indah Manis 164 • InterContinental Resort 166 • Club InterContinental 168 • The Istana 170 • Jamahal Private Resort + Spa 174 • Jimbaran Puri Bali 176 • Kayumanis Jimbaran 178 • The Shaba 182 • Villa Balquisse 184 • Tirtha Luhur 186 • Tirtha Uluwatu 188 • Warisan Casa 190

192 kuta+southwestcoast

The Dusun Hotel 208 • Hotel Tugu Bali 210 • Jajaliluna 212 • The Oberoi, Bali 214 • Simona Oasis + Spa 218 • Sitara Padi Villas 222 • Kafe Warisan 226 • KU DE TA 230 • The Living Room 234 • Ma Joly 236 • The Wave 238 • Haveli 242 • IO + CO 244 • Milo's 246 • Warisan Gallery 248

index 250 • picture credits 252 • directory 254

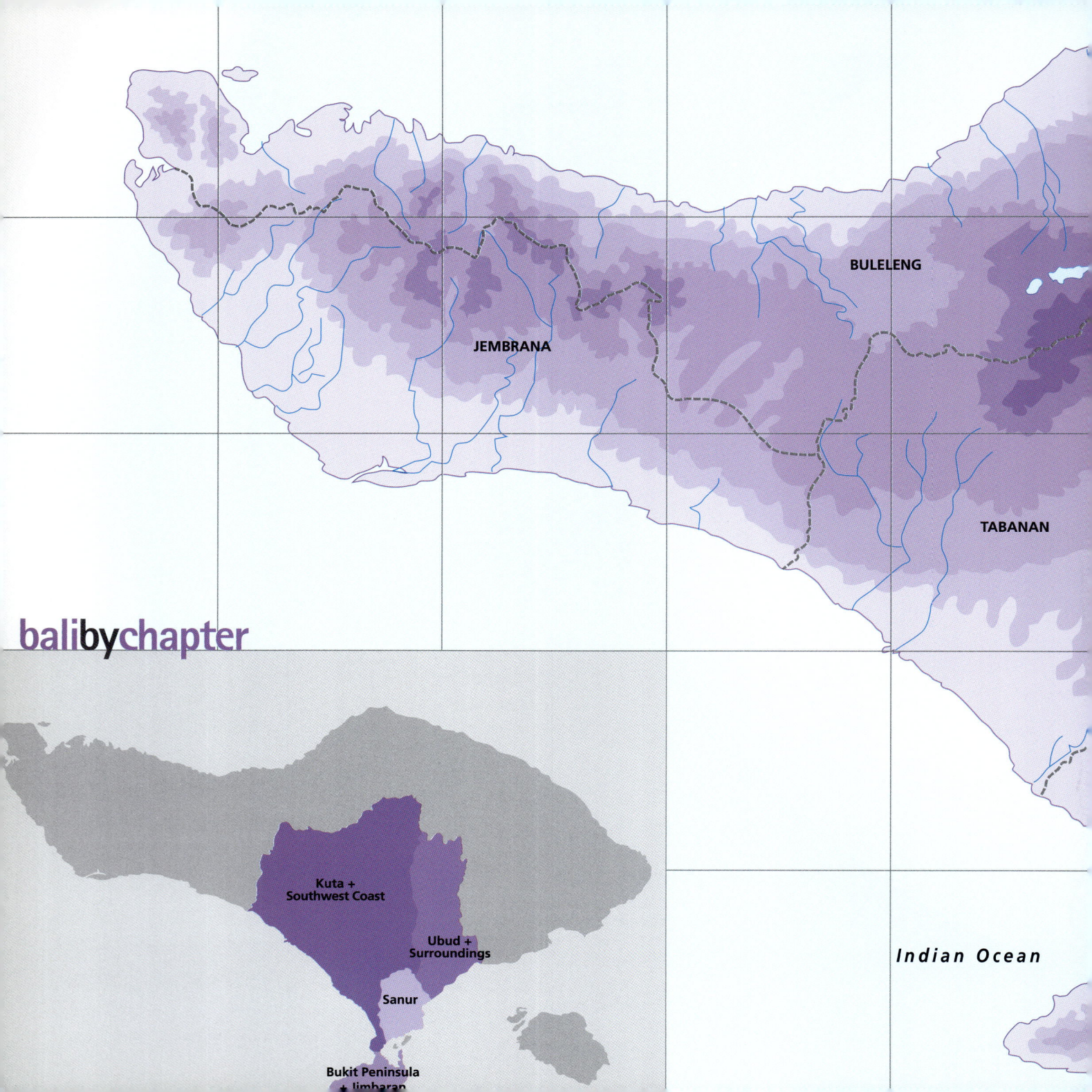

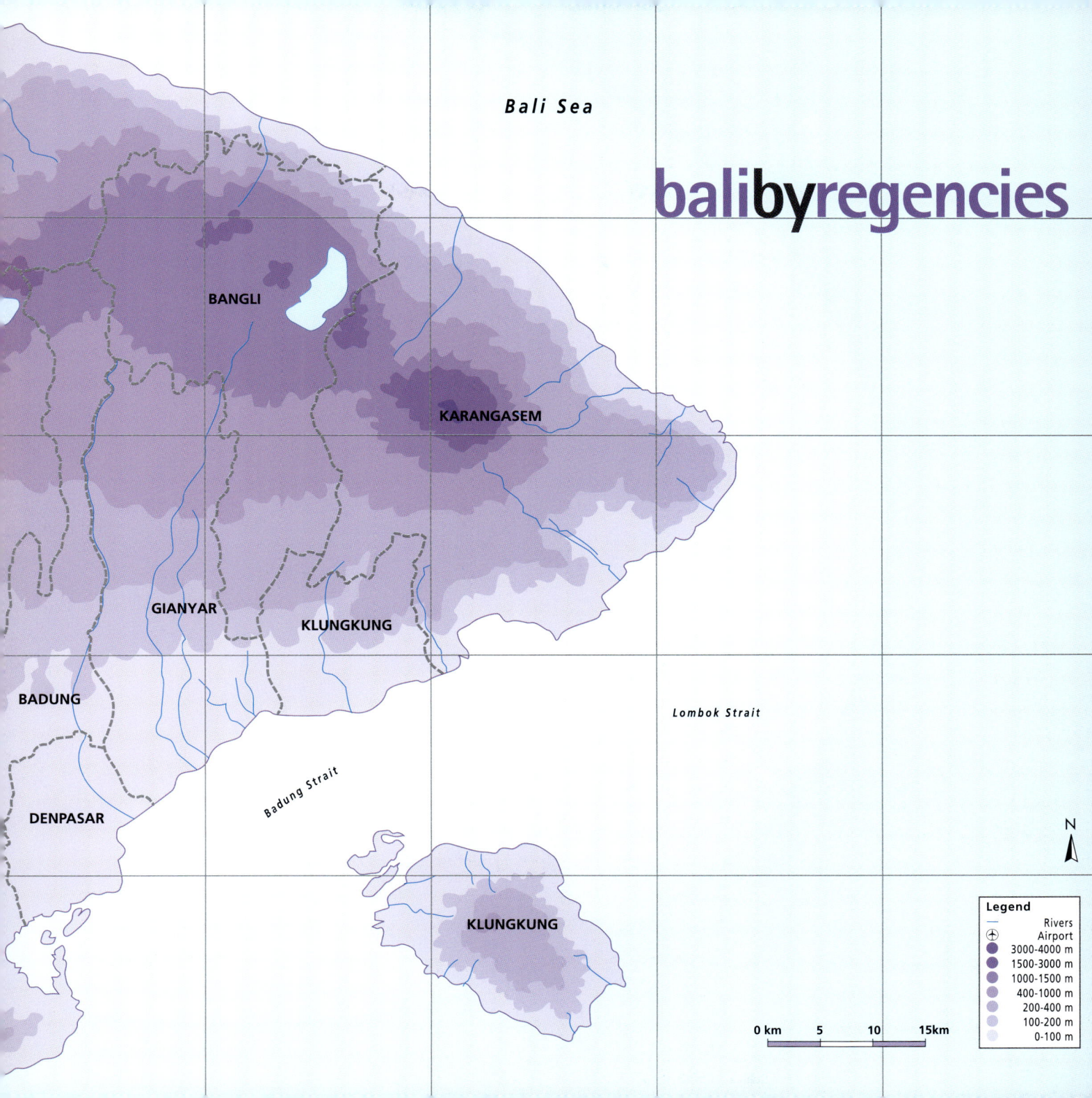

introduction

a small island with a big reputation

Bali has been called 'The Island of the Gods', 'The Last Paradise', 'The Ultimate Island' and 'The Island of a Thousand Temples'. It is a place that inspires enthusiastic, even zealous, praise and has done so for centuries. It is probably the most written-about island in the world, and the most mythologised. There are numerous books expounding at length about every aspect of Bali, or fictionalising it. Not to mention scholarly dissertations and articles, of which there are thousands upon thousands. A keyword search for Bali on Amazon.com turns up over 20,000 titles—more than Tahiti, Ibiza, Capri, Kona, Maui, Mauritius, the Seychelles or Sardinia!

With so much written about Bali, one might assume it is big. In fact it is one of the smaller island-provinces of Indonesia, located 8° south of the equator and just to the east of Java. From north to south it spans a mere 85 km (53 miles) and from east to west, 140 km (87 miles). Sri Lanka is 12 times bigger. Jamaica is twice as big. This brings us to one of the reasons Bali is so popular and so beloved by sophisticated travellers. It is an island of a very manageable size and, therefore, easy to explore.

Almost all of Bali's modern facilities and most of its population are intensely concentrated in the southern quarter. The rest of the island is largely undeveloped and harbours the so-called 'real Bali'. Every corner of the island can be reached from the most developed areas in a few hours by road and in less than an hour by helicopter. This means that visitors can stay where the action is, surrounded by world-class luxuries, and still enjoy the richness of the island's traditional culture and natural scenery without sacrificing comfort and style.

diversity

Bali offers a wealth of cultural and natural delights, with plenty of variety. In the centre are mountains covered with forests, fields, scenic roads and paths for walks on the wild side. The middle elevations in the south and east are the richest in culture, dotted with traditional villages, rice terraces, temples and palaces. The north of Bali is dry,

THIS PAGE: *The beaches of Bali are one of its most popular features, many of them sandy and pleasant, as in this aerial view of Sanur.*

OPPOSITE: *Morning mist rises from the farms and forests of central Bali. Beyond the main centres of tourism the island remains much the same as it has for centuries.*

mostly wild and a bit rough, with black-sand beaches and lush marine life under crystal-clear water. The west of Bali is vast and rarely explored, with plenty of deserted beaches, rainforests and farming villages to explore. The south of Bali is intense, dense and mostly urban. This is the centre of nightlife and beach culture, and the streets are filled with people from all over the world, shopping, eating and playing.

The island of Bali is home to nearly 4 million people, most of whom practice Hinduism, a minority religion in Indonesia. Half of the population lives in or around Denpasar, the capital. It is a city to miss, unless there is some urgent and specific reason to dive into its churning confusion of traffic, noise, heat and dirt. As in other urban areas of Indonesia, Denpasar's population is more diverse than elsewhere. A recent government survey indicates that less than half of Denpasar's population are Balinese Hindus, making for a colourful, polyglot mix.

Expatriates make up a growing section of Bali's population and they are concentrated mostly in communities around the southern coast. To talk of an expatriate community, however, is misleading as they are an individualistic bunch. Most are too busy doing their own thing with their own set of like-minded folk or interacting with the local community. Among them, the French, Italians, Australians, Japanese and Brazilians have the most numbers in Bali. With its expatriate population now topping 10,000, Bali is, more than ever, an island with a vibrant, multicultural community.

culture

Since tourism began taking off in the 1920s, Bali's big claim to fame has been its unique culture. Say 'Bali' and images immediately come to mind of colourful religious festivals, exotic dances, shadow puppet theatre, mysterious temples and dramatic cremation ceremonies. The culture that won over the world and inspired so many books and articles years ago is just as alive now as it was back then. Floral offerings, incense, ceremonies, processions, dances and the rich mythologies of Balinese Hinduism still colour daily life in cities, resort towns and remote villages alike.

Modernisation and globalisation have not uprooted the living culture of Bali in the least. To the Balinese there is no implied contradiction between modern life and tradition. A Balinese real estate developer may have wi-fi in his house, fly first class, stay connected by Blackberry, and arrive at a meeting with a flower behind his ear and rice grains on his forehead, having just received a temple blessing. After the meeting, he might be called upon by his community to take part in a trance ritual, performing a masked dance in which he 'becomes' Rangda, a personification of Durga, the goddess of death and chaos. He may speak in tongues while in trance, but the next day he speaks perfect English to a Singaporean architect on a work site.

The Balinese have a reputation for being kind people, gracious, hospitable, and lovers of beauty, decoration, laughter and camaraderie. This reputation is not undeserved and many visitors find themselves charmed by the people more than by the island itself. English is spoken widely and the national language, Bahasa Indonesia, is easy to pick up, which means communication is rarely a problem. Foreigners are welcomed into local culture and given ample opportunity to learn, appreciate and enjoy life as it is lived by the Balinese. The level of service travellers discover in Bali is another reflection of the culture. In Balinese society, there is no stigma attached to serving other people. In fact, it is quite the opposite—being of service is seen as an honour and a pleasure even, when the person being attended to is a complete stranger, and there is no obligation to assist. First-time visitors are surprised to find that offers to help from strangers they encounter on the street or in the countryside are genuine and come with no strings attached. The Balinese really do enjoy caring for others. In this day and age, that may seem impossible, but in Bali it is true. There is no greater joy than simply letting go in Bali, letting the wonderful people share and explain their extraordinary island culture. And they do so with great pleasure.

THIS PAGE: *Temple anniversaries are festive occasions. Colourful offerings are presented to the gods and the whole community comes together in ritual, prayer, music, dance and drama.*

OPPOSITE: *A parade of demon effigies takes place all over Bali on the day before Nyepi, the annual day of silence.*

everyone's bali is different

With such a welcoming culture, Bali has become a favourite travel destination for people from all walks of life and from all around the world. Many come again and again, stay longer each time, and eventually make Bali their first or second home. The result is a buzzing international social scene centred in the coastal south and around Ubud. This, in turn, is attracting more and more diverse and accomplished people to the island. It is now, and has long been, a cool island adored by cool people, and for good reasons. It is exotic, but relatively safe and healthy, so it is the perfect place for a holiday, a long sabbatical or a lifetime.

Bali is a land of legends, some of them true, others wildly exaggerated. Bali is also a land of mysteries, many still unsolved, so no authority can know it all. And Bali is a land of dreams, a place people visit to make their fantasies real. Others find surprises beyond their wildest dreams, or get swept away by it all.

This should help explain the draw of Bali. Everyone's Bali is a different Bali, because it is an experience as much as it is a place. Bali is not a frozen museum diorama or a contrived tableau with smiling natives playing their roles in a theme park. The island is culturally alive, multicultural and constantly changing.

a history as idiosyncratic as the island itself

Islands are by nature idiosyncratic, and Bali is certainly no exception. Island histories tend to be a bit bizarre, since evolution takes place in relative isolation. Bali is no exception either. It is a world unto itself and has been since it became permanently separated from the Sunda peninsula some 15,000 years ago. Around 3000 BCE, when people began to settle on Bali, they began a history which has followed a peculiar storyline, eventually bringing us to the current chapter—the Bali of today.

Bali was strongly influenced by Indian culture. Sanskrit inscriptions from the first millennium refer to it as Balidwipa, 'the land of sacred offerings', and describe a landscape of terraced wet rice fields. Some things have not changed apparently. During Europe's Dark Ages, Bali was entangled in a complex web of trade and politics with the early Hindu and Buddhist kingdoms of Southeast Asia. Voyagers from as far as China, India, the Arab world and even Rome, knew of Balidwipa. Tales from this time are full of intrigue and espionage, kings and mystics. It is thrilling stuff, just begging to be made into a Hollywood epic.

THIS PAGE: *Bingin beach on the rugged Bukit Peninsula is reached via a dramatic path that cuts through this rocky cliff.*

OPPOSITE: *In the river valleys and on the high ridges of central Bali, lush vegetation gives the landscape an otherworldly feeling.*

introduction 17

THIS PAGE: Wayang kulit shadow puppets are one of the many ancient art forms that still thrive in the heartland, around Ubud.

OPPOSITE: The rocky reefs dotting Bali's coastline are an excellent habitat for marine life and offer superb snorkelling opportunities as well.

When Europe entered the Middle Ages, Balinese kings were jockeying for position among themselves for a safe place amid the power struggles of Java's great empires—Singhosari and, later, Majapahit. More thrilling tales of warrior princesses, sorcerers, golden treasures, super priests and others were put down in writing. Some of this ancient literature is still heard today, recited in droning tones during temple ceremonies in Bali. It is sung in Kawi, an extinct language of the Majapahit court. Only literary scholars and puppetmasters understand the language now, but that does not seem to bother anyone much.

Bali always remained a bit marginal to the main events of the region. It was a small island and kept its own company, to some degree—it still is and does. When Java was converted to Islam, the Balinese did not care to, and so they didn't. Then, Europeans started showing up in the 16th century and some of them loved Bali so much that they stayed. The Dutch soon swept the Indonesian archipelago into its collection of colonies, but had a hard time with Bali. The kings would not recognise Dutch rule and some fantastic battles took place in north Bali in the mid-1800s, with Balinese warriors terrifying and surprising the well-equipped Dutch armies. The Dutch won the north but never managed to get a grip on the allied kingdoms of the rest of the island. In 1908, a Dutch army marched on Klungkung, the island's dominant kingdom, and the Balinese, in a characteristically contrary way, chose not to lose the battle. Instead, they 'won' it by killing themselves by the thousands—a dramatic gesture, and an effective one.

The Dutch, internationally embarrassed by the atrocity, put Bali on a long leash thereafter, allowing a great degree of autonomy and cultural integrity, until they lost the island during World War II. The ensuing Japanese Occupation was harrowing for the Balinese, yet they managed to maintain the authority of their palaces and priests, ensuring cultural continuity. Bali was returned to the Dutch in 1945, but the Balinese remained independent-minded island people nevertheless. They formed a league of freedom fighters and, following much derring-do, death and destruction, eventually participated in the founding of the Republic of Indonesia in 1950, as one of its constituent islands.

Although a part of the unfolding saga of Indonesia, Bali stays on the sidelines and continues to write its own story. It is a land with its own culture, distinct from the dominant one of the nation which contains it. Bali's culture has captured the imagination of the world and this is one of the reasons the island is the way it is today. From the 1920s, travellers adored it and spun tales of a magical paradise which was Bali as they perceived it.

Reality was somewhat different. The West's picture of Bali was hopelessly idealised, depicting a tropical scene of happy peasants and noble princes sharing a peaceful and perfect world, where time was devoted mostly to spiritual and artistic expression. But like any society, Bali's story has dark passages. Brutality, despotism and terror have left their mark, as they have in all histories on earth. Bali's idealised kingdoms, for instance, grew rich on slave labour—capturing able bodies to sell to traders was among the motivations for all their wars. Bali's beloved Galungan holiday celebrates a successful religious persecution which took place a millennium ago, when Hindu fiefdoms allied to destroy the ruling Buddhist dynasty. The island's history is not all so rosy, and plenty of facts have been conveniently forgotten.

The world prefers the paradise myth and the Balinese have, for decades, striven to make it real. To a large degree, they have succeeded, and that has made Bali what it is today: an idiosyncratic culture of great charm, on an island of great beauty.

THIS PAGE: *At the culmination of cremation ceremonies, the deceased is immolated in a decorated coffin taking the form of an animal, in this case, a black bull.*

OPPOSITE: *Pemangku (lay priests) survey the view at Pura Ulun Danu, which is perched at the rim of Mount Batur's crater.*

a rich religion that invites ideas and visitors inside

Balinese Hinduism blends together flavours of many faiths. Ancient animist beliefs are a key ingredient. These focus on reverence for ancestors and the forces of nature. Fertility and death rites are prominent, as are 'economic' approaches to dealing with deities. Through ritual and sacrifice, and by respecting taboos, the powers-that-be may be placated and balance maintained in the world. Many people underestimate the strength of these beliefs in Balinese Hinduism as practiced today. Simply look closer at common ceremonies and symbols to find the underlying elements which were here long before any Indian religions arrived.

For example, when a baby is born, the substances accompanying its exit from the mother's body are buried within the compound of the house, establishing a 'home base' for the child spiritually while it is on earth. The Dayaks of Borneo have similar customs. Shrines in every Balinese home contain male and female statues representing paired ancestors. These can house spirits or validate lineage and are fertility figures. Similar figures are essential to religions on other islands of Indonesia, including Flores and Timor, even today.

Hinduism and Buddhism began influencing Bali almost 2,000 years ago. They both took root, to varying degrees, were integrated into pre-existing belief systems, and evolved in relative isolation from India, taking a uniquely local course. Several different Hindu sects flourished in Bali and only came together for good in the 12th century. Tantric Buddhism also forms a large part of Balinese religion, with traces of Islam and Confucianism in the mix, too. The composite nature of this religion is due to a peculiarity of Balinese culture: it rarely replaces existing concepts with new ones, but subsumes them instead.

It is important to recognise that Balinese Hinduism varies from town to town, region to region, and even among families. It is more about practice and tradition than about religious philosophy. Although it is elaborate and finely structured, most people, including many priests, cannot elucidate on the deeper significance of

particular offerings, symbols and rituals. When asked why they perform a particular act, such as putting a set of smiley faces cut from palm leaves in a birthday ceremony offering, the Balinese usually respond with *mula keto*, which means, 'because it was always like that before.'

Just as the Balinese have welcomed new beliefs and practices over the years, they also welcome foreigners who wish to participate in their ceremonies. Any visitor with a sense of respect and decorum is drawn into the proceedings with great pleasure. Ceremonies take place almost constantly in homes, temples, even at crossroads and on beaches. Finding a Balinese participant who speaks one's language and can act as an advisor is usually all it takes to be ushered into the pageantry of Balinese religious life.

deep bali

Bali is known for its mystical side. Its religion and indigenous superstitions are based on a belief that there is more to the world than meets the eye—a lot more. Many practices in daily life and in ritual involve managing the forces of the unseen world. The

mystical roots of Balinese culture go very deep. The deepest level rests on prehistoric superstitions. Layered upon these are systems and practices of tantric Buddhism and several sects of Hinduism, which prevailed at different periods and in different areas of the island and were interpreted in unusual ways by the Balinese. The result is a web of mystical and magical practices, places and objects.

Some visitors are intrigued by these aspects of Balinese culture and take time to explore them. Others have no interest at all, yet experience things in Bali which they cannot easily explain, and which challenge them to re-examine their own beliefs. The best way to approach the unseen Bali is with the assistance of a guide or expert. Hotels are usually able to provide knowledgeable guides or offer recommendations.

Bali features many mystically powerful places: ancient temples, holy caves, sacred springs and mysterious archaeological remains. Many are not in any guidebook and some are known only to people who live nearby. Surprises await the curious, particularly those willing to do a bit of walking and scrambling. Bali is also filled with spiritually powerful people: *pedanda* (high priests), *pemangku* (lay priests) and *balian* (healers, shamans and paranormals) are a part of every Balinese community and they all deal in esoteric ways with unseen forces. Travellers sometimes choose to enrich their experience in Bali by visiting a spiritually charged place or person, or by taking part in rituals.

Visits to traditional healers to be treated or to observe them at work are not unusual. Some use plant medicines, others are 'seers' who can 'rearrange' things for clients on the spiritual level or reveal the source of a specific problem. Some are practitioners of very worldly magic, who create talismans to attract a lover, bother a business rival or banish an evil spirit. On the more orthodox side, some visitors to Bali appreciate the experience of a blessing with holy water, a 'cleansing' ritual conducted by a priest, or the opportunity to consult one to discuss metaphysical matters. Others, without intending to, find themselves witnessing the inexplicable, perhaps a revelation by a Balinese person in trance, or a seemingly miraculous talent. Their souvenir of Bali will not be just a sarong, but a new way of looking at the world and their place within it. Such experiences of Bali begin with an open mind, respect for the beliefs of others, and candid, but polite curiosity.

bohemian bali

Bali has attracted individuals with character since at least the 17th century. In the 1960s, when the world's hippies hit the road, tripping through Europe, the Middle East and Asia, Bali was not even an option because Indonesia was still in the throes of a coup d'état and suffering from bouts of unrest. When that began to settle down around 1970, Bali burst onto the bohemian world map. Artistic, unconventional and sybaritic characters discovered the island and told their friends. Fabulous freaks and offbeat intelligentsia began to stop in Bali during their peregrinations, between trips to Goa, Kathmandu, Sri Lanka and other exotic spots. Their alternative outlooks and irrepressible creativity have had a lasting influence on Bali. It still has a bit of a bohemian flavour and plenty of people with character to this day.

Many of the original arrivals from the 1970s are still here, and some have become prominent figures, particularly in creative fields: Milo Migliavacca has a fabulous fashion house and outrageous orchids; Linda Garland creates big bamboo and interior designs for the likes of David Bowie; and Lawrence Blair, a 'buccaneer' with a dashing black eyepatch, explored the remotest islands of Indonesia with his late brother Lorne in the 1970s—they spun their adventures into the award-winning documentary series and book, *Ring of Fire*. He still lives in the house he and his brother built in Bali way back then, and still produces documentaries in the wild places of the archipelago. There is also Jean-François Fichot, who, for decades, has made stunning artisanal jewellery in

THIS PAGE: *Offerings are placed every day at temples, houses, gardens, shops, rivers, and almost everywhere else in Bali.*

OPPOSITE: *A moment of prayer at dawn on the slopes of Mount Batur, which was the seat of an ancient Mahayana Buddhist kingdom that ruled the island.*

Ubud for elite clientele. He began on the beach in Goa, fashioning exotic body ornaments from shells, feathers and objets trouvé, then came to Bali during its hippy heyday. An art student by the name of John Hardy showed up in 1975 to work with local silversmiths and goldsmiths. Three decades later, his name is a global jewellery brand and he has turned his efforts to saving the planet and enlightening young minds. The names above are but a few of the creative non-conformists who arrived in the 1970s with bohemian dreams and left indelible traces behind.

Anyone who wants to know Bali should know about its pantheon of interesting old-timers. A good way to learn is through the publications and websites of one of the most beloved eccentrics on the island, Made Wijaya. This carrot-topped character arrived by shipwreck, or rather 'yacht wreck', in the 1970s with the name Michael White. He charmed his way into the hearts and homes of Balinese society, and into the flamboyant foreign social circles of Sanur. He has been there ever since, writing pithy columns and designing homes and gardens that have become synonymous with 'Bali style'. Start at strangerinparadise.com to get Made's take on Bali back then, and now.

living it up

Bali has become seriously chic. It is no longer just for bohemians, rat-race refugees and shaggy professor types. It is increasingly adored by the global elite and the tone of the island is moving steadily upscale. Roads once used only by farmers, foot traffic and sleeping dogs now see the occasional Hummer H3, Ferrari Testarossa or Jaguar. There is serious money here now, and some serious stuff to spend it on. More and more visitors to Bali come with taste, talent and big bank accounts, or at least with all the accessories to look the part. Important art, design and fashion figures are not only visiting, some are making Bali their second home or their primary one.

Luxury hotels are already as common as cremations in Bali. Now, ultra-luxurious ones are being built to outdo them. The most exclusive names, including Bulgari Hotels & Resorts and Christina Ong's COMO Shambhala have arrived, and others are sure to follow. There is more to all this than money and raw luxury, though. Standards of style and living are also rising rapidly. People dress better than they did in the past. It is no longer acceptable to wander around in cargo shorts and a singlet in Bali. Some of the clubs have strict dress codes, enforcing 'no shorts' and 'no sandals' rules. Young beauties flock to the restaurants of Seminyak, and they come dressed to impress.

Anyone who makes the mistake of coming to Bali without fashionable frocks in their bags can now find cutting-edge apparel in Bali's boutiques, much of it made locally. Seminyak's main road, from Jalan Double Six to Jalan Laksmana, is the best stretch to explore, with new shops opening all the time, offering the collections of Indonesian, Australian and European designers. Elegant gold and gemstone jewellery are nearly as easy to find now as cheap beads and baubles were before; and boutiques and dealers in south Bali and Ubud offer artisanal statement pieces and ancient excavated treasures to well-heeled clientele. Art and antiques shopping in Bali has moved up several notches as well. Now, billionaire collectors compete with noted international art dealers and interior designers to snap up the best works of tribal art in the back roads of Kerobokan.

THIS PAGE: *The talented designers and architects of COMO Shambhala Estate at Begawan Giri created a luxurious resort in harmony with nature.*

OPPOSITE (FROM TOP): *An exquisite pendant from Treasures; a guestroom in one of the residences of COMO Shambhala Estate at Begawan Giri seamlessly blends Eastern and Western aesthetic traditions.*

The laid-back lifestyle of the past is being replaced by global luxury lifestyles, especially in the far south of the island. Lavishly appointed villas are popping up everywhere. Yacht leasing, air charter and personal concierge services are available to assist affluent customers. The island now has a fine riding stable, a complete country club and even Harley Davidson Martini tours. The latter is offered by the people who brought us Bali's ultimate lifestyle bible, *The Yak*, a glossy magazine found throughout the island. Read it to catch the buzz of the emerging haut monde of Bali.

loving this island can lead to living on it

Bali is experiencing a real estate boom. Thousands of Baliphiles from all over the globe have decided that an annual holiday on the island is not enough and have chosen to move here instead, or at least to own a holiday home, rather than renting. There is lots of variety in the market. At the affordable end are simple but sometimes

poorly constructed mini-homes on as little as 300 sq m (3,229 sq ft) of land, usually complete with a mini-pool and a patch of garden. At the high end are enormous, architect-designed luxury villas on sandy beaches or with panoramic views. Between the two extremes are scores of apartment, condominium and villa developments. Some island dwellers are starting from scratch, acquiring empty land, then building their dream homes. This seems to work best for people who have lived in Bali for a long time; the challenges are too great for newcomers unfamiliar with the island's idiosyncrasies.

Architects, contractors and home servicing companies are rapidly being established to meet the needs of Bali's new property owners. Schools of international calibre and supermarkets are growing in number. Financial,

legal, insurance and healthcare sectors are also getting up to speed to serve an increasingly sophisticated clientele. Living well has not just become possible in Bali, but relatively easy. Although laws governing property ownership and legal residency are complex, thousands have found satisfactory solutions. Some have also navigated the complexities of setting up businesses here, often with gratifying results.

Particularly in creative fields such as design, fashion and retail, Bali is proving to be an excellent base. The talents of local artisans and the wealth of fine materials available here offer tremendous opportunities for entrepreneurship. Shopping in boutiques and showrooms in south Bali, one discovers how many talented foreigners have settled in and successfully run businesses producing and selling their creations. The business services sector is booming as well, supporting enterprises in other areas. Advertising agencies, photographers, film studios, web designers, high-speed Internet providers, printers and publishers are growing in number and in quality. Many are collaborative operations, with Indonesian and foreign talents joining hands.

A handful of new property sector publications and scores of estate agents in desirable areas attest to the strength of the Bali boom. Among the most trusted are Elite Havens, Tropical Homes and Exotiq. Though worries are voiced about poor town planning and infrastructure, the arrival of serious players with a stake in residential property, notably St. Regis Residences, Outrigger, Aston International, Novotel, Alila and Banyan Tree, promises success.

THIS PAGE: *Natural materials and Zen-like simplicity bring a deep sense of peace to this villa located in a coconut grove near the sea.*
OPPOSITE (FROM TOP): *Old masks used in Javanese and Balinese dramas and dances are now avidly sought by collectors; relaxed elegance characterises the new homes being built in Bali for those who love the island so much that they decide to become permanent residents.*

around the ultimate island

Most people stay in the south of Bali or around Ubud, and with good reason. Only these two areas offer the comforts and luxuries everyone craves, plus fantastic food, nightlife and complete spa therapies—or intensive retail therapy for those so inclined. This does not mean one is isolated from the 'real Bali'. This is a small island and it is not at all difficult to explore some of its hidden corners without giving up the luxe life at one's favourite resort in the south or near Ubud.

Day trips from these areas can take one deep into non-touristy parts of Bali in almost no time. The roads shown on better maps are almost all paved and in at least fair to moderate condition, often better. A car and driver-cum-guide for the day can be obtained at a moment's notice from almost any hotel, and the cost is reasonable. Rental cars are also easy to get and cheap, but one should opt for a driver to avoid communication problems. A pre-arranged itinerary is fine, but following one's nose is much better in Bali. Getting totally lost is also highly recommended. It is never very hard to find your way back on this friendly, safe and conveniently small island.

Arranging some provisions in advance is not a bad idea as most of the food out there in the villages may be disappointing. Many hotels can prepare superb picnic hampers for guests, as can catering companies such as the Bali Catering Company in Seminyak. All the makings of a self-catered portable feast can also be found at supermarkets such as Bali Deli, Bintang and Carrefour, and some hotels will lend guests a portable cooler to keep the bubbly chilled.

There is no excuse to miss the magic of inner Bali—it is easy, it is safe and it is impossible to know when setting out in the morning what enchanting surprises lie in store. Just keep an open mind, and keep those eyes open too.

the mountains

The mountains in the interior of Bali offer the island's most awe-inspiring outings. It is best to bring a guide, picnic hamper, ice box and an empty memory card for the digital camera. One need not be terribly intrepid either. Most of the roads are in quite good shape, mobile phone coverage is almost complete, and local communities have small shops and fairly solid basic services, which means day trips are possible and should definitely be made by anyone spending more than a few days in Bali.

The highlands of Bali enjoy a refreshing climate that can be a relief from the heat of the beach; but mist and rain can arrive at any time, so unobscured views and dry socks are not guaranteed. The moist and cool environment at high elevations supports a different kind of farming from the south: plantations of cloves, coffee, cacao, mixed vegetables, organic greens, oranges, starfruits and flowers give scenic insights into the bounty found in Bali's markets and on the tables of its fine-dining restaurants. Walking or cycling through the fields makes for a pleasant outing to whet one's appetite for all the good stuff produced.

Bali's mountain peaks, with summits topping 3,000 m (9,843 ft), provide some of the island's best scenery. Smoking volcanos tower over lakes in an almost alpine atmosphere. Waterfalls plunge from forested hilltops into chilly cauldrons below. Lava fields of bare boulders and scree look more like a moonscape than a tropical island. Sightseeing can involve little more than lounging in a comfortable car and stopping to

THIS PAGE: *Clear rivers and streams thread their way down the steep slopes of Bali to the sea, watering the fields and forests as they go.*

OPPOSITE: *Mount Agung serves as a dramatic backdrop to rice fields, where white flags flap in the breeze to ward off thieving birds.*

snap the best shots. At the other extreme, challenging treks can lead to remote summits and hidden mountain temples. Guides can be arranged by most hotels and are essential in such rugged terrain.

Best out west are the highlands of West Bali National Park for its forests and wildlife. The landscape around Pupuan Village is an eco-trekker's dream and the mountain temple of Batu Karu offers mystical moments early in the day or late in the afternoon, when monkeys, exotic birds and other critters are bold enough to drop in. A mist-shrouded shrine sits in the middle of a sacred lake here, with a semi-submerged rope ferry to reach it. The climb to the summit of Mount Batu Karu is arduous, with great rewards for bird-lovers, though there is not much of a view from the forested summit.

Further east is Bedugul, with a chain of scenic lakes and a big, beautiful botanical garden. Both are popular with domestic tourists, but are magical in the late afternoon after the crowds have left. The footpaths and side road attractions nearby are more intriguing and less trampled. A ridge road beyond Bedugul leads to the mountain town of Munduk, Bali's answer to a Himalayan hill station. Some savvy expatriates craving seclusion have built their own modest cabins here, and it's no wonder with the kind of scenery that surrounds Munduk. Walks to waterfalls and farming valleys lead through steep coffee plantations to isolated villages with no road access. Between Bedugul and the slopes of Mount Batur are a network of peaks, ridges and deep gorges hiding all manner of marvels. Those who know the hidden treasures here generally will not tell, so take a willing driver, the *Bali Street Atlas*, and go exploring or intentionally just get lost. Don't worry, as a general rule, heading 'downhill' in Bali leads straight to civilisation.

THIS PAGE: *Lake Bratan, surrounded by dense forests, is home to a small community of mountain-dwellers.*

OPPOSITE (FROM TOP): *Hot mineral springs feed a peaceful bathing pool near Singaraja in north Bali.*

Batur has a fantastic crater lake and the volcano can be climbed, though it is somewhat active. The touts around here can be ruthless to the point that one hardly dares venture from the car without a local guide to fend them off. A quick peek at the awe-inspiring scenery from the Penelokan ridge is a must, but steer clear of the big tourist restaurants and bring earplugs because the road up from the crater is filled with roaring trucks hauling volcanic rock and sand to build villas in Bali's boom towns. Grinding gears and revving engines shatter the silence. Further along the ridge is the temple Pura Luhur Ulun Danu, a Bali classic. Heading down the road, passing pine forests, one arrives at Pura Pucak Penulisan, a temple on a towering peak, with profoundly beautiful statuary from an 11th-century kingdom standing guard inside.

Beyond Batur, to the east, a ridge road towards the temple of Besakih passes Mount Abang, which offers a pleasant trek to the summit, but a guide is absolutely necessary. Acrophobics take note: in some areas, the ridge-top trail is like a tightrope with no safety net. The winding way from here to Besakih is one of Bali's most scenic roads and it is refreshingly cool no matter what the season or hour of day. Besakih, Bali's much-lauded 'mother temple', is regarded as a destination for Balinese worshippers only—its tourism potential having been ruined by its own attractiveness. It is better to try some of the minor roads climbing just as high or higher up the slopes of Mount Agung. Each one leads to stunning surprises, highland villages, almost forgotten temples, and fields of marigolds grown for use in offerings. Be warned that some of these roads have been abused by trucks hauling black stone for the construction of temples; an all-wheel drive vehicle might be welcome in places.

The most scenic and best road going up is the one from Selat to Pura Pasar Agung, Besakih's auxiliary *pucak*, or summit temple. It can be driven with ease, even with an engine under two litres in size. The road is smooth but has some treacherous switchbacks. The temple itself is one of the most mysterious and scenic in Bali.

east bali

While Ubud and its surroundings are famous for culture and scenery, east Bali offers plenty of the same, but with less development and few foreign travellers. Reaching the east has never been easier, with a new highway connecting the Sanur area to the royal city of Klungkung, and to Kusamba on the coast beyond. Now, areas that once required an arduous journey from Ubud or the south can be enjoyed in day trips.

Bali's easternmost tip is surmounted by Mount Lempuyang, a perfectly formed volcano seldom visited by tourists. High on its slopes stands a grand temple of white limestone with breathtaking views of Mount Agung and beyond. From here, a steep path leads to a small summit temple of entrancing, otherworldly beauty, with views all the way to Lombok. A scenic road now circles Mount Lempuyang via Seraya, passing remarkably diverse terrain. Coastal cliffs, goat-nibbled hillsides and isolated villages mark the southern and eastern stretches, giving way in the north to fishing towns and bays with crystal-clear waters for snorkelling and diving. Turning south, the road climbs through dramatic rice terraces and forests between two steep mountain slopes.

Candidasa was once a tourist enclave of some popularity, but beach erosion lessened its appeal. More alluring are attractions to the east: Tirtagangga, a fantastic royal bathing complex set in tropical gardens; and Taman Ujung, a fairytale pleasure palace built in 1919 on a lake near the sea. Taman Ujung collapsed when Mount Agung erupted in 1963. It was abandoned but has recently been restored as a historic monument and is also available for functions, including weddings.

East of Candidasa, in Manggis, lie beautiful beaches beside two luxury resorts, Alila Manggis and Amankila. Both are the only options for real cuisine in east Bali.

Nearby, the village of Tenganan is famous for its distinctive culture and crafts. Populated by the Bali Aga, or 'original' people of Bali, it maintains age-old traditions existing nowhere else in the world. The village's double *ikat* weavings, called *geringsing*, fine basketry and intricately etched *lontar* leaf texts are sought by avid collectors.

The Unda river valley, from Satria up to Selat, is among the most scenic areas of Bali, with stunning views of rice terraces, mixed farming, charming villages, hilltop temples, mountains and more. The town of Sidemen, halfway up, is famous for *ikat* and *songket* weaving. Klungkung, the largest town in east Bali, has a marvellous market for textiles and ritual apparatus, the remains of a palace that once ruled all of Bali, and an utterly traditional people's market slightly south of the town's centre. Just beyond that lies the famous town of Kamasan, a centre of traditional Balinese *wayang*-style painting for centuries.

THIS PAGE: *The black-sand beach at Kusamba in east Bali is home to a community of fishermen and salt-makers.*

OPPOSITE (FROM TOP): *The top of a meru shrine at Pura Besakih, juxtaposed with a red hibiscus, known as pucuk bang in Bali; the weavers of Klungkung and Sidemen in east Bali produce fine textiles in silk, cotton and silver or gold thread.*

west bali

West Bali begins where the action of Seminyak starts to taper off. Encompassing trendy residential areas around Canggu, it extends to the end of Bali and becomes more wild and unexplored the further one goes. Coastal areas as far as Tanah Lot are becoming more developed, but beyond that, facilities for upmarket travellers are few. Other than a few eco-retreats, beach bungalow resorts and the homes of reclusive or bold foreigners, the flavour is entirely local.

This does not mean that west Bali is lacking in beauty or interesting attractions. In fact, it offers unique opportunities for adventure and leisurely exploration in places still unaffected by tourism. Staying in a villa west of Seminyak allows one to enjoy every comfort and luxury, while putting the 'wild west' within striking distance for day trips or overnight outings. Forests, wildlife, rugged shorelines and the famous buffalo races and big bamboo *gamelan* of Negara are just some of the attractions of the region.

Sadly, many visitors go no further west than Tanah Lot, a temple set on a rock jutting out towards the open sea. It is wildly popular with tourists, especially at sunset, but some generally give it a miss. There are plenty of scenic temples in Bali providing more peaceful visits. Immediately beside Tanah Lot, the greens of Nirwana Bali Golf Club roll along the rocky sea coast. This Greg Norman-designed course is a visual and sporting masterpiece. The 7th hole is especially challenging, requiring the golfer to hit with a middle iron from a clifftop, across a chasm of thundering ocean surf, to a scenic and well-guarded green. The bar of Le Méridien Nirwana Golf & Spa Resort, beside the course, has superb sunset views over Tanah Lot, far from the madding crowds.

The beaches of west Bali have been known to surfers for decades. Most have sparkling black sand, but few are protected enough for safe swimming, although Candikusuma Bay has intriguing possibilities. There is already one attractive hotel here, with villas of dark, polished wood, a traditional schooner for sailing, and a power boat for serious sea fishing.

Inland, west Bali is a wonderland waiting to be discovered. Much of it is mountainous, covered in wild forests and dotted with villages reached by rambling roads. The Balinese Catholic town of Palasari is charming, with a scenic church, lake and a luxury eco-retreat nearby, reached by buggy. Many surprises await those who take the time to explore Bali's west. One long-time Bali resident says, 'Go there. Get lost. But don't throw away the map in your glove box.'

north bali

While Bali's south side catches the rain of the wet season, the north stays far drier and so the landscape is less luxuriant, as are its options for sightseeing and recreation. The coast is famed instead for its rich coral reefs and marine life, with dive outfitters concentrated around Amed, Tulamben, Lovina and Pemuteran. A diving hot spot is

THIS PAGE: *The hands of a musician playing the* gender, *a metallophone which is used in traditional orchestras, and as the musical accompaniment to shadow puppet plays.*
OPPOSITE: *Bull racing is one of the many unusual features of the culture of west Bali.*

Menjangan Island, a marine reserve with healthy reefs, rare marine life of all sizes, and plenty of scope for snorkelling over shallow coral shelfs swarming with colourful fish.

Out of the water, there is not a lot to do in the north except unwind, explore and get away from it all. Still, there is more here than silence, seas and scrubland. The area does have a rich history and culture, however, with distinct local styles of architecture, music, dance, drama and weaving. In contrast to such cultural attractions in Ubud, here they are largely unpackaged and unexposed. This is typical of north Bali; it is not touristy or glamorous, it simply operates on its own terms.

Take the timeless town of Singaraja (the capital city of the north, although not a particularly busy one), long before tourism brought prosperity to the south, it was already a lively commercial town with the best harbour in Bali. Its distinctive Arab, Chinese, Bugis and Indian quarters attest to a long history in sea trade. Evidence of colonial history is prominent, too, with many Dutch-style buildings from the 19th and early 20th centuries in various states of disrepair.

At higher elevations, north Bali's forested slopes hide waterfalls and picturesque villages amid coffee and clove plantations. Steep slopes rise to ridges with views stretching all the way down to the sea. Filling the narrow valleys are sculpted rice terraces that glow with an otherworldly green in the early morning or afternoon light. Sadly, with all this scenery, there are no facilities of quality for travellers to north Bali. Most of them are concentrated in the remote west and east.

Pemuteran is a gem of a place with a handful of delightful boutique hotels on the black-sand shore of a scenic bay. Lovina was a booming bungalow town in the 1980s, full of *Lonely Planet*-toting youth, but its prosperity was fleeting, leaving little behind but a smattering of cottages and some rundown cafés with funky names. A revival may be underway now, heralded by a European restaurateur who has opened a nice café that is undoubtedly the best place to eat along this stretch of coast. In the east, Tulamben, Amed and Bunutan are sprouting small hotels and bamboo bungalows, with an atmosphere that harks back to the early days of tourism in Kuta.

THIS PAGE: *Barracudas lurk in the crevice of a coral reef off north Bali.*
OPPOSITE: *A vortex of schooling jacks surround a diver at Tulamben, the site of a well-known shipwreck.*

...plenty of scope for snorkelling over shallow coral shelfs swarming with colourful fish.

dining in bali

Bali is known as 'the island of a thousand temples'. Now, it has at least as many restaurants, and their standards are rising as rapidly as their numbers. With so much to choose from, there is no excuse to settle for a mediocre meal in Bali.

Bali has seen a surge in unusual eating experiences. **The Yak** (Jalan Kayu Jati 9Y) organises Martini motorbike picnics on Harley Davidsons. **Air Bali** (Jalan Bypass Ngurah Rai 100X), a charter company, has a menu of exotic picnic excursions by helicopter. **Esprite Nomade** (Jalan Resi Markandya) organises luxury safari-tent repasts with all the extras, including a flower foot massage at sunset. Many resorts can arrange gourmet picnics, but independent travellers can order their own baskets from the **Bali Catering Company** (Jalan Petitenget 45) in Seminyak or the **Bali Good Food Group** (No. 29A Jalan Sekuta) in Sanur.

Dining is becoming more about the experience, since good food is almost a given in Bali. There is a trend towards more social meals—making new friends and hosting dinner parties in villas or exotic locations. Most Balinese staff at luxury villas love nothing more than orchestrating a great party. Alternatively, professional party caterers, such as **Mozaic** (Jalan Raya Sanggingan) or **Bali Experience** (Jalan Raya Semer), artfully manage everything from mixed nuts to dessert. The latter even provides glamourous 'rent-a-guests' if a crowd is required.

Making a meal with friends is a convivial option. Cooking schools with attractive dining areas encourage guests to bond through shared learning, then partake of their creations at the table. **Mozaic's** school is top notch; the **Four Seasons Resort Bali at Jimbaran Bay** (Jimbaran) has one with a charming Indonesian village atmosphere; and **Casa Luna Cooking School** (Jalan Bisma) in Ubud is a favourite.

To dine, see and be seen, hurry to **Hu'u** (Gang Gagak 1, Jalan Petitenget) and **KU DE TA** (No. 9 Jalan Laksmana), or to **Warung Made Seminyak** (Jalan Raya Seminyak), with its Bali-bohemian atmosphere, where creative types table-hop and feast on *nasi campur*.

For relaxed meals with reliably good food, regulars count on **Terazo** (Jalan Suweta), and **Batan Waru** (Jalan Dewi Sita) in Ubud and **Tuban** (Jalan Kartika Plaza). Indulge in Indonesian cuisine at **Warung Batavia** (Jalan Kunti Gang 33) in an old Javanese house in Kerobokan, or **Warung Enak** (Pengosekan Road), a funky upscale café in Ubud. Popular beach breakfast spots include **KU DE TA** and **La Lucciola** (Jalan Laksmana) in Seminyak, which has the best croissants in Bali.

Outside the main tourist zones of the south and Ubud, however, there are slim pickings for gourmands. It would be smart to bring along a gourmet picnic hamper, unless one of the following restaurants is on the day's route. In northwest Bali, **Puri Ganesha Villas** (Pantai Pemuteran) has excellent food, wine and atmosphere, but do call ahead. In Lovina, **Kwizien** (Jalan Raya Singaraja) has a great international menu and a nice garden and gallery setting—it is the second successful restaurant by Belgian Rudy Kerremans of **Café des Artistes** (Jalan Bisma 9X) in Ubud. Above Kwizien, in the hills, is **Damai** (Jalan Damai, Kayuputih), a retreat resort with gourmet organic Asian and European dining overlooking forests and the sea far below.

In the northeast, eating well means eating at **Dancing Dragon Cottages** (Amed Beach), where Southeast Asian cuisine is served by the sea in Amed, one of Bali's best snorkelling and diving destinations. In the east, **Seasalt** at Alila Manggis in Karangasem (Buitan), is a casual yet elegant option, with excellent food and produce picked fresh from their organic gardens.

Finally, a food phenomenon is happening along Jalan Laksmana in Seminyak, known locally as '**Eat Street**'. It is lined on both sides with restaurants that seem to open, close and reinvent themselves constantly. The current favourites are **Ultimo** (Jalan Laksmana 1004X) for Italian and **Bali Café** (Jalan Laksmana Sebelah Khaima) for good European cooking plus superb dim sum entrées in a romantic neo-colonial atmosphere.

THIS PAGE (FROM TOP): *Seasalt restaurant at Alila Manggis is a prime dining stop during outings to the east; Bali Catering Company boasts a menu that will satisfy the most discerning gourmand.*
OPPOSITE: *Outdoor dining and lounging areas make KU DE TA a favourite at any time of the day.*

night fever

Many people come to Bali for a good time on the town, but navigating the range of bars, clubs and events can be tricky. Fortunately, there is *The Beat*, a magazine covering every aspect of the nightlife and entertainment scenes. It is the party-goer's guide to Bali and is available at popular restaurants and supermarkets. The action is still centred in Kuta, Legian and Seminyak, each with its own highs and lows.

The Wave (No. 1 Jalan Pantai Kuta) and the **Hard Rock Café** (Jalan Pantai Kuta) on the beach in Kuta please the young and wild crowd, and **Double Six Club** (Jalan Arjuna) in Seminyak continues to be popular with just about everyone. Its annexe, a more elite lounge once called Paparazzi, has been relaunched as **Syndicate**, and a short shuffle down the strand brings revellers to a new club by the same promoter, **Bacio** (Jalan Arjuna). Do not even think of arriving at all three clubs until after midnight, and be prepared for anything. A dress code is enforced at Bacio.

Since the bombing in Kuta in 2002, the nightlife scene has fanned out. While some central Kuta clubs still reverberate until the wee hours, notably **MbarGo** (Jalan Legian 998), the once riotous Jalan Dhyana Pura in Legian is hardly the circus it once was. **Q Bar** (Jalan Dhyana Pura), however, continues to attract the same colourful, alternative crowd.

Party people get more chic the further north one goes, with Seminyak as the epicentre for upmarket evenings. **KU DE TA** (No. 9 Jalan Laksmana) commands pole position on the beach and holds the best parties, but is prone to over-crowding at sunset during high season. Others welcome the sunset just up the beach at **The Legian** (Jalan Laksmana) and **The Breeze** (Jalan Laksmana) at The Samaya Bali, with sexy sofas by the sea on a huge, green lawn. Nearby, Sentosa Private Villas and Spa's **Blossom Restaurant & Lounge Bar** (Jalan Pura Telaga Waja) is gaining ground, and its neighbours, **The Living Room** (Jalan Petitenget) and **Hu'u** (Gang Gagak 1, Jalan Petitenget), reliably fill up with smooth party types, pumping music from the hip end of the spectrum until late.

For some travellers, the shape of nightlife is shifting. There has been a move towards private partying and mingling at cultural events. Crowds in some clubs are getting rougher and Indonesia's social underbelly has begun to show in others, with the ladies looking shadier and the activities more dubious. This, and concerns about security, have fed the trend for private nightlife and members' clubs may be the next development. In-villa parties are easy to organise, with excellent caterers, DJs and professional event managers such as **Bali Experience** (Jalan Raya Kerobokan 8X) and **Elite Events** (Jalan Rayar Semer 883).

Cultural events such as gallery openings, film nights and benefits are increasingly popular, and special interest gatherings such as **Bali Fashion Week**, the **Ubud Readers and Writers Festival**, wine dinners and tango nights at **Warung Made** (Jalan Raya Seminyak) now figure prominently on the social calendars of the cognoscenti.

THIS PAGE (CLOCKWISE FROM TOP): *Blossom Bar at Sentosa Private Villas and Spa; wines of the world and tropical cocktails tempt the tastebuds; Hu'u epitomises the move upmarket in Seminyak nightlife.*
OPPOSITE: *Funky colours spell 'fun' at The Wave.*

being beautiful in bali

The quality and availability of its spas and salons is one of the best benefits of being in Bali. The Balinese are natural nurturers; it is ingrained in their culture. Being of service to others and grooming them are not considered demeaning. Instead, the Balinese view it as a great honour and a pleasure. Local beauty secrets and natural herbal treatments are also treasured in Balinese tradition. The island is therefore the ideal place to visit for excellent spa and beauty services.

From destination spa resorts with multi-faceted, multi-day treatment regimes, to pop-in neighbourhood salons and spas, Bali has perhaps the most extensive selection of body and beauty treatments to be found anywhere. Almost every hotel and resort offers a range of spa services, and most private villas have therapists and beauticians on their staff or on-call. Stand-alone spas and salons are found in every popular area of Bali at various price ranges, with environments ranging from spartan to outrageously luxurious.

The most dramatic spa on the island is **Kirana Spa** (Desa Kedewatan) in Ubud, a vast wonderland adjacent to Pita Maha Resort and Spa. Created by Shiseido, Kirana is popular with Japanese guests and with anyone who appreciates uncompromising luxury combined with ingenious architecture and breathtaking views. Also near Ubud, **Bali Botanica Day Spa** (Jalan Sanggingan) was just listed among Bali's top ten spas. **Ubud Bodyworks Healing Centre** (Jalan Hanoman 25) continues to deliver expert Balinese healing massages, but in an environment that is unassuming. They will send therapists to one's villa, if requested. All of Ubud's luxury hotels have excellent spas, but **COMO Shambhala Estate at Begawan Giri** (Desa Melinggih Payangan) has the most comprehensive multi-day holistic wellness programmes, with day spa options as well.

Down in Seminyak, **Espace Spa** (Jalan Raya Basangkasa 3B) is a favourite among aching expatriates, with expertly trained therapists, especially the male masseurs. Espace began as a massage institute, training staff for luxury resorts. Nearby, **Jari Menari** (Jalan Raya Basangkasa 47) gets a thumbs up from Bali residents and in-the-know visitors, especially for their four-handed massage, the focus on male massage talents, and weekly massage classes.

For reflexology, folks flock to **Chill Reflexology** (Jalan Kunti 118X) in Seminyak for its Zen-like minimalist chic, and to **Cozy** (Jalan Sunset 3 Blok A), which is less showy but also popular. **Luxe Lounge Spa** (Jalan Pura Telaga Waja) at Sentosa Private Villas and Spa, near Petitenget beach, offers gorgeous surroundings and unusual therapies such as a chocolate fondue treatment. It may be the only spa with its own 'champagne escape bar' and a big cocktail list—deliciously decadent.

To get gorgeous, go to emerging salons of international calibre near Seminyak. **Rituals** (Jalan Legian 476) is rich in talent and Kerastase hair products. **Spoiled Hairdressers** (Jalan Umalas II) brings European expertise to a neighbourhood nearby, and everybody still loves **Ubud Bodyworks Healing Centre**, which offers cheap and cheerful, clean and reliable salon services covering all bases, from manicures and pedicures to expert waxing.

Bali now boasts several clinics for cosmetic medical procedures too, notably the **Anti-Ageing Rejuvenation Clinic** (Jalan Bypass Ngurah Rai 1) and **Bali International Medical Centre** (Jalan Bypass Ngurah Rai 100X).

THIS PAGE (FROM TOP): *Skilled therapists soothe away stress; the serenity of a pavilion at Sentosa Private Villas and Spa; a spa villa at Four Seasons Resort Bali at Sayan.*

OPPOSITE (FROM TOP): *Sea breezes and the sound of the waves deepen relaxation at Bali's beach side spas; a Balinese body treatment enjoyed al fresco.*

the art of life

Of course, Bali is famous for art. But not all of it is fine art, unfortunately. What's called a gallery in Bali is sometimes little more than a gift shop or handicraft stand. What's called a museum is often just a showroom for one person's random collection of paintings, or a sales strategy. For those who want to see the real thing or acquire something of value and significance, there is a fairly short shortlist.

Beginning a search for art in Bali at the museums is smart. In Ubud, **Museum Puri Lukisan** (Jalan Raya Ubud) houses a chronologically organised collection of outstanding works by acknowledged masters of painting and sculpture in Bali. It provides an excellent overview and is maintained by a Dutch non-profit foundation and the royal family of Ubud. The occasional big exhibitions here are marvellous affairs and the opening parties are usually attended by VIPs of art and culture.

On the south side of Ubud, the **Agung Rai Museum of Art** (ARMA; Jalan Pengosekan) also gives a decent overview of the art and sculpture scene which blossomed in Bali during the 20th century. While there are perhaps fewer great masterpieces here, ARMA's wing showing recent works by European and living Indonesian artists is notable. The complex is a multi-arts centre, with many activities from conferences to kids' *gamelan* and dance programmes. **Neka Art Museum** (Jalan Raya Campuhan) is perhaps the most elegant of Ubud's museums, and its founder amassed a fine collection of iconic paintings by both Indonesian and European artists working in Ubud. Conveniently, the infamous Naughty Nuri's Warung & Grill sits right across the street, pouring killer Martinis for exhausted art lovers and local characters.

The **Bali Museum** (Jalan Mayor Wisnu 1) in Denpasar and the **Archaeology Museum** (Desa Bedulu Jalan Tampaksiring) in Pejeng is only worth the time for experts enthralled by excavated oddities. The **Gunarsa Museum of Classical & Modern Art** (Jalan Raya Banda 1) in Klungkung is worth a stop during a drive out in that direction, simply to ogle an eccentric collection of genuine antiquities and classical *wayang*-style paintings beside the owner-painter's studio, where he sells his decorative and internationally popular modern artworks.

Among the hottest galleries in Bali are: **Gaya Art Space** (Jalan Raya Sayan) near Ubud, with groundbreaking shows and a multimedia, multidimensional web of events and enterprises; **Biasa Artspace** (Jalan Raya Seminyak 34), owned by a talented Italian clothing designer and patron of emerging artists; **Ganesha Gallery** (Jimbaran) at the Four Seasons Resort at Jimbaran Bay; **Seniwati Gallery of Art by Women** (Jalan Sriwedari 2B) and **Komaneka Gallery** (Jalan Monkey Forest) in Ubud, especially when they put on a focused show; and finally, the gallery at **Jenggala Keramik** (Jalan Uluwatu II) in Jimbaran, which organises exhibitions of work by local and visiting artists in various media. All of the galleries mentioned here hold wonderful preview parties, which are one of the best ways to meet and mingle with Bali's artistic and intellectual elite.

THIS PAGE (CLOCKWISE FROM TOP): At Gaya Fusion, the gallery space itself is a work of art; Gaya often exhibits cutting-edge conceptual work by local and international talents; sculptures set on a staircase at Komaneka Gallery.
OPPOSITE: Komaneka regularly showcases the talents of Bali's avant garde.

theartoflife 45

island shopping

In response to the demands of an increasingly sophisticated clientele and the effects of globalisation, shopping in Bali has headed upmarket, as have the prices. Imported goods which were once rare in Indonesia are now widely available and shoppers' expectations have risen accordingly. While bargains are still aplenty, don't expect to walk off with something really special for a song.

The less interesting side of the move upmarket are the large modern shopping malls, department stores and mega-marts. On the other hand, globalisation and an influx of cosmopolitan foreign talent has also brought many benefits. Collaboration between locals and cultivated foreign partners has brought about an increase in creativity in the fashion, jewellery, furniture and homeware industries, and in the retail landscape. Shops are looking better by the day, with stylish façades and sleek interiors, creating a more enjoyable experience. Nevertheless, foraging through dark, dusty shops and *gudangs* still turns up treasures.

fashion

The style quotient of clothes on the racks in Seminyak is better than ever, with the most interesting street being Jalan Raya, starting just south of Bintang Supermarket (the general store for villa dwellers), then heading north. Fashion landmark **Biasa** (Jalan Raya Seminyak 36) shows fine cotton and silk separates in original cuts and colours that go from beach to ballroom without missing a beat. The well-stocked men's department is upstairs. Across the street is **Paul Ropp's** (Jalan Raya Seminyak 39) first shop (today there are dozens), blazing the fashion trail with intense colours in wild combinations and an urban Indian flair. Nearby, **Ika Ika** (Jalan Raya Seminyak 29X) offers designs by Indonesian celebrity couturier Ika Butoni; **Kerry Grima** (Jalan Raya Seminyak 26) does alluring, buttery leather so soft it drapes like silk; and **Michel Harcourt** (Jalan Raya Basangkasa 1200A), a veteran of Europe's top fashion houses, raises the bar with upscale apparel which is meticulously made.

In Kuta, make a pilgrimage to the **OKANÉ** (Jalan Legian Kelod 329) boutique by Oka DiPutra, the darling designer of Bali who dresses Hollywood stars and does runway shows at Asian fashion weeks. The Warung Made Shopping Arcade houses **Milo's** (Jalan Sarinande 1A), for distinctive patterned silks, and beside it, **Bin House** (Jalan Raya Seminyak), with one-of-a-kind creations of batik on silk that are masterpieces of textile art. Wrap Bin's translucent shawls over bikinis from **Blue Glue** (Jalan Raya Seminyak and Jalan Double Six), the shining star of local swimwear stores.

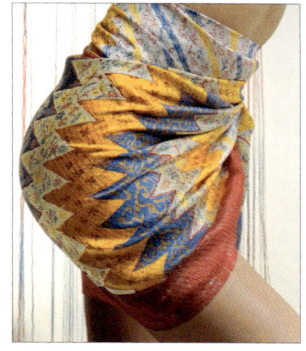

THIS PAGE (CLOCKWISE FROM TOP): Chic tie-dye tops from the SimpleKonsepStore; a dazzling turquoise creation from Treasures; Ika Butoni's stylish menswear; silk batik becomes art at Bin House.
OPPOSITE: An Ika Butoni gown of sophisticated femininity.

island shopping

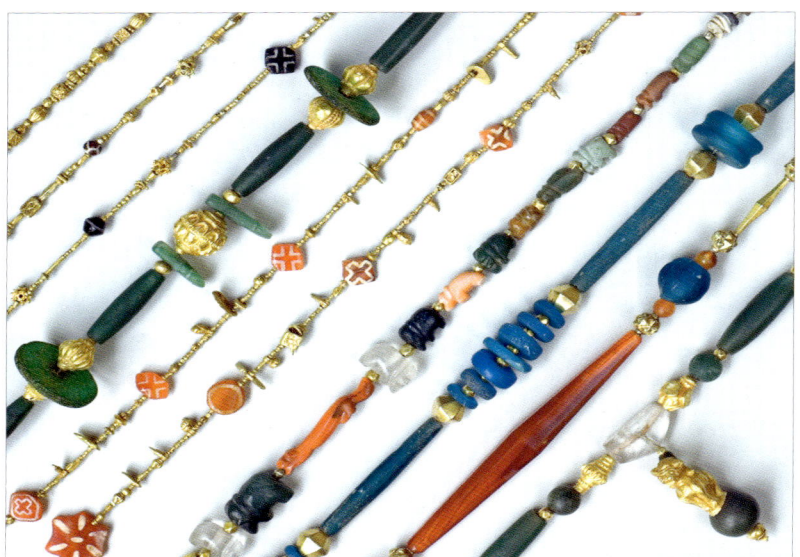

Trawl all of Jalan Raya from Kuta to Jalan Laksmana to witness a rainbow of clothes, accessories and fashion jewellery. Check the side streets towards the beach for more. Jalan Laksmana is bursting with new boutiques, the standouts being **SimpleKonsepStore** (Jalan Laksmana 40) for minimalism with an edge; **Maru** (Jalan Laksmana 7A), a small 'body-art-space' that is a window to a world of high design and hand-work; **Quarzia** (Jalan Laksmana 3A) for modern batik gone chic; and **Nilou** (Jalan Raya Kerobokan), with the best sexy footwear made in Bali.

jewellery

Bali is loaded with every level of bijouterie. Cheap bead and shell accessories line the streets of Kuta—good for the beach, but they will not last the week. Silver sparkles everywhere at tempting prices, but for the best in silver, head to **John Hardy** (Banjar Baturning Mambal), a household name in fashion circles, who only shows in Bali at his workshop near Ubud, and strictly by appointment only. For good work and diverse contemporary designs, **LED Studio** (Jalan Bisma 9X) in Legian is the spot. Their workshop nearby caters to wholesale buyers and will produce any design one can draw. Local designer **Suarti** (Jalan Raya Celuk 100X) has become the top name for Bali-style silver. Suarti is headquartered in Celuk with showrooms throughout the island.

The best of fine jewellery is found at **Treasures** (Jalan Raya Ubud) in Ubud, with artistic pieces in high-carat gold by Bali's best designers. Nearby is the deliciously lavish boutique of designer **Jean-François Fichot** (Jalan Suweta 6). Finally, for the best authentic ancient jewellery, Bruno Piazza of **Sriwijaya Jewels** (Jalan Laksmana 17) sells excavated gold treasures to serious connoisseurs by appointment in Seminyak. He also showcases his work in the galleries of the Amandari and Amanusa hotels.

antiques and artefacts

Bali is like a trade mart and design centre for all of Indonesia. Furniture, antiques and artefacts from the whole archipelago are found here. Interior designers, retailers and tribal art dealers from around the world make regular stops in Bali to buy their inventory. The warehouses and showrooms they visit are open to the public, if you can find them. Some are on the high streets, others scattered in the bumpy back lanes of Kerobokan.

Warisan Gallery (No. 68 Jalan Raya Kerobokan) and its furniture factory showroom are good starting points. For top-notch antiquities and artefacts, try the elite galleries of Ubud and Seminyak—**Macan Tidur** (No. 10 Monkey Forest Road), **Toko Antique** (Jalan Raya Ubud), **Shalimar** (corner of Jalan Raya and Jalan Hanoman), **Pourquoi Pas** (Jalan Basangkasa 23) and **The Bali Antique Shop** (Jalan Raya Basangkasa 34X). In Sanur, avid collectors visit Bruce Carpenter at **Island Arts** (Jalan Duyung Gang 1/3X) by appointment. Travellers with time to kill and who speak fluent Indonesian can try trawling through the less salubrious showrooms found everywhere in the south. Remember that fakes abound and prices are arbitrary. It is best to stick with the more discriminating dealers mentioned above to avoid buyer's remorse. **Macan Tidur** and **Island Arts** both offer curatorial, advisory and sourcing services as well.

THIS PAGE (FROM TOP): *An ancient gold mamuli from Sumba island; The Bali Antique Shop.*
OPPOSITE (FROM TOP): *Excavated gold, stone, and glass beads by Sriwijaya Jewels; Jean-François Fichot incorporates antique elements in his one-of-a-kind creations.*

island**shopping** 49

island shopping

furniture and homeware

The abundance of furniture and homeware in Bali is overwhelming. Professionalism and quality are not always a given, so go with the best, otherwise it's caveat emptor. **Warisan Gallery** (No. 68 Jalan Raya Kerobokan) is the first name on everyone's lips for furniture. Their lighting line is good, too. **Evata Eastern Furniture & Accessories** (Jalan Raya Kerobokan 100ZZ) is a reliable furniture shop with many satisfied customers overseas. For the best synthetic rattan, head to **Hishem** (Jalan Gunung Athena 10). Modern lines surfaced with unusual materials feature at **Carlo** (No. 22 Jalan Danau Poso) and **Etienne d'Souza** (Jalan Raya Seminyak), an eccentric and charming furniture artist.

For soft furnishings, **Disini** (Jalan Raya Seminyak 6–8) definitely delivers, with fresh styles constantly evolving in their boutique and wholesale–retail showroom. **Haveli** (Nos. 15 and 38 Jalan Basangkasa) does the same and more, but with an exotic flavour.

Baskets are best from **Mekar Sari** (Jalan Raya Kedewatan 22) in Sayan and the extraordinary **Acuh Tak Acuh** (Jalan Raya Seminyak), which offers fine traditional baskets with surprising graphic patterns adorning the surfaces. Small accessories big on quality and finishing come from **Tropis Equator** (Jalan Goa Gong), which has the best modern wood wastebaskets and bathroom counter-top amenities in town. Indulge in Italian-Indian high design at **SimpleKonsepStore** (Jalan Laksmana 40), where shopping is an experience in itself. The shop is the Bali equivalent of Milan's Corso Como 10.

For ceramic arts and all manner of fabulous homeware, linens and tiles, run to **One World Gallery** (Jalan Raya Basangkasa 1200B), the showroom for Pesamuan collections, by renowned artisan and artist team Philip Lakeman and Graham Oldroyd, whose workshop is in Sanur. Also originating in the Sanur matrix is **Jenggala Keramik** (Jalan Uluwatu II), the most influential ceramics workshop in Indonesia, now with a vast showroom and art gallery in Jimbaran. The same level of importance in glass can be attributed to Seiki Torige, whose showroom **Galeri Esok Lusa** (Jalan Raya Basangkasa 47) offers glassware to use and glass artworks to amaze.

Bali has also been booming in lighting, with the most brilliant designs coming from **Piment Rouge** (Jalan Raya Seminyak 60X), **Radiant** (Jalan Raya Seminyak 4A) and **deLighting** (Jalan Gatot Subroto Barat 99), all with showrooms in the Seminyak area.

If it's all too much, which is understandable, smart shoppers turn to the professionals—Bali's sourcing agents, each with their own specialities. **Sourcing Bali** (Jalan Gunung Salak 31A) is the biggest and most mainstream, and is great with production goods, furniture, handicrafts, stone and more. **Linda Garland** (Jalan Nyuh Gading) shops for and with elite interior designers and moneyed home owners for stylish and eco-minded antiques and accessories. **Macan Tidur** (No. 10 Monkey Forest Road) scouts out exclusive tribal art, artefacts, antiques and ethnic accessories, for designers and private clients, and produces custom furniture from reclaimed teak timbers.

THIS PAGE (FROM TOP): *These pieces from Warisan will make welcome additions to any living room; a Nyepi bed from Warisan.*

OPPOSITE: *Warisan Gallery is a definite 'must-visit' for those shopping for high-quality furniture.*

the best views of bali

While some tropical islands offer little more than shots of white-sand beaches beside turquoise waters, Bali has a wide spectrum of images to snap. From landscapes to lively festivals and warm, open faces, this island is a photographer's dream destination. And there is no need to be a professional either. Casual snaps taken in Bali can surprise with their remarkable beauty. It is a very photogenic island.

scenery + sunsets

Sunsets inspire the trigger-happy masses. At hotspots such as **KU DE TA**, when 6 pm rolls around more flashes are ignited than on Oscar night in Hollywood. But a flash can never catch a sunset, as amateur photographers soon discover. It can light up a friend at close range, silhouetted against the sky, but it will not get that classic postcard shot, so shut it off in this instance. **Jimbaran Bay** and the clifftops nearby are prime sunset sites. **Kuta**, **Legian** and **Seminyak** are excellent, too.

Scenery more unique to the island is found in the heartland and mountains. Rice fields, of course, are a beloved subject. Upper **Tabanan**, **Jatiluwih** and the hills above **Ubud** have the best sculpted terraces.

For mountain landscapes with smoking volcanos, the crater of **Mount Batur** is a good start, but aggressive touts and poor facilities demand that the stop be brief. The road from Batur past Mount Abang to Besakih has superb vantage points to shoot from. Still, no mountain scenery beats the clear views of **Mount Agung** from the top of **Mount Lempuyang** in the far east. The trek to Lempuyang's summit is aided by paved stairs leading to a lovely temple at the top.

temples + ceremonies

Fortunately, there are no strict taboos about photographing temples or ceremonies in Bali. Whether empty and mystical or in full festival swing, temples are rich with 'Kodak moments'. Often, details can tell more than ordinary architectural shots. Polite visitors may be permitted to take close-ups of priests conducting rites, offerings on display and people praying, but discretion and respect is absolutely advised. A long lens and tripod can be helpful, too.

people + portraits

The faces of Bali are fantastic and its people are normally not shy, nor do they demand compensation for photographs taken of them. Cool youths, old farmers and wizened priests sometimes take pride in posing. Do show one's subject the result on screen immediately, or send a print to them by email or post.

the unexpected

Bali abounds with unexpected beauty and dramatic contrasts. Urban environments, markets and even traffic jams present excellent photo opportunities for the creative eye. Natural scenery and village life are best shot after dawn or just before sundown—the tropical glare is too harsh at midday. Keep a camera at hand for unexpected moments: rapid changes in weather, sunlight through incense smoke and colourful processions occurring without warning.

THIS PAGE (CLOCKWISE FROM TOP): Rice paddies are best photographed at dawn and dusk; the crater of Mount Agung; a sunset silhouette; full-on festivities are excellent photo opportunities.
OPPOSITE: This photographer took a novel approach to a classical tropical subject.

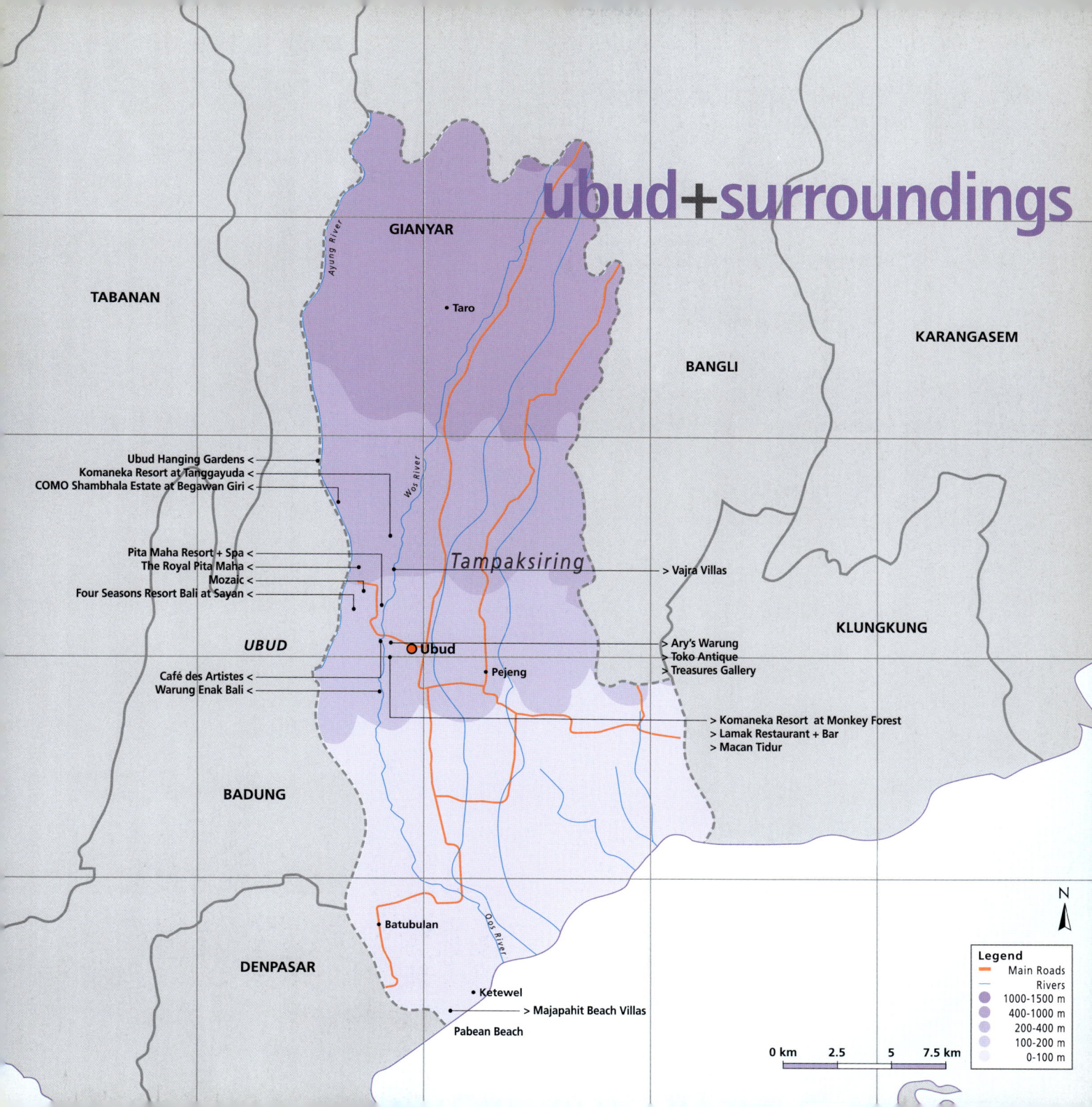

a marvellous middle ground between the mountains and the sea

The southern slopes of Bali are the most fertile and are considered the heart of the island. This terrain is covered with lush rice terraces and the most exotic forest foliage. And it is fertile not only in terms of its land, but in terms of culture as well. Its ridges and river valleys were the cradle of classical Balinese culture as we know it.

The almost ideal climate helped to foster a rich cultural life that has thrived for more than two millennia, supported by food in relative abundance and a pleasant environment for work and leisure. The mountains above this fertile land catch more rainfall and feed the complex irrigation systems that make its rice terraces so scenic. But mountain weather is damp and chilly, and the terrain at higher elevations is often too rugged to comfortably call home. The shores below are hotter, drier and have seen more foreign influence, thanks to their accessibility. This coastal environment proved ideal for beach tourism and urban development, but the landscape and prominence of tradition and culture are less extraordinary. It is the heartland, with Ubud at its centre, that has most shaped the world's image of and love affair with the island of Bali.

Ubud is a remarkable town which has been the island's pre-eminent centre for fine arts, dance and music for over a century. While it still retains a traditional and natural atmosphere, its downtown areas are becoming increasingly urbanised. Having first attracted artists, bohemians and spiritual seekers, it now draws more literati, glitterati, art collectors and connoisseurs, but keeps an alternative undercurrent all the same. The sheer numbers of 'Ubudophiles' who love the town enough to visit, and even move here, have helped the local community to prosper and have drawn investment from elsewhere. Now, traffic can be a bit of a headache and buildings are getting taller and more modern, but other than that, the charm of the place is as magnetic as ever.

PAGE 54: *A rainbow palette of ceremonial umbrellas backlit by the bright Bali sun.*

THIS PAGE: *Ubud is renowned for its spiritual side, and many visitors come to deepen their knowledge or learn a new philosophy. Here, a woman meditates at sunrise beside a lotus pond at the Four Seasons Resort Bali at Sayan.*

OPPOSITE: *Ubud is surrounded by dramatic landscapes such as these terraced rice fields.*

a bumper crop of culture built this boom town

Anyone who knows Bali knows that the dance performances, museums, galleries and art studios of Ubud are a big draw, and with good reason. The quality and quantity of both continue to increase. Notable newcomers on the performance scene include the marvellous Gong CW, who perform above a dreamy lotus pond in front of the Saraswati temple in central Ubud. The open-air performances at the main Ubud palace never fail to enchant either, except when it rains and they have to be moved across the road to the *wantilan* (community hall). They just look much better at the palace, with oil lamps illuminating the carved palace gate which is their backdrop.

The special nature of Ubud is largely a result of its tight local community, which is defiantly Balinese and adamantly traditional. One of its traditions is to welcome curious and well-meaning guests from afar. Since the 1920s, talented foreign painters, musicians, choreographers, writers and anthropologists have been welcomed to Ubud, and many called it home for extended periods of time. With the encouragement of the royal family, they helped shape the society of this extraordinary little hill town, which was already culturally rich before the foreigners arrived. Old Ubudians still grow misty-eyed recalling their friendships with 'Tuan Blanco', 'Tuan Spies' and other long-time residents of Ubud. Antonio Blanco was a Spanish painter of great panache, personally and in paint. His extravagant house near the centre of Ubud is now home to a museum of his work. Walter Spies was a Russia-born German primitivist painter of great talent, whose haunting landscapes were inhabited by mysterious beings, often with mystical undertones. He co-created the film *The Island of the Demons* in 1936, which greatly influenced the way the world looked at Balinese art and culture. It introduced a deeper and darker side of this so-called paradise to foreigners.

Both of these masters, and many other creative figures, were endorsed enthusiastically by the Ubud royal palace and their presence was encouraged in the town. The royal family continues now, as it did then, to cultivate talent, intelligence and style. They are also the custodians of Ubud's strong spiritual side. The palace co-ordinates and sponsors many of the grandest ceremonies seen on the island of Bali. A simple annual temple anniversary in Ubud has all the drama and grandeur of high opera: even a gala performance at La Scala cannot top the costumes, sets and the sheer number of participants in palace-sponsored ceremony in Ubud. But here, it is never put on for show—the motivation is religious belief and a commitment to the powers of tradition, both seen and unseen. Many elaborate ceremonies take place without a single foreign witness.

The presence of foreigners in Ubud's ceremonial life is generally most welcome. This is one of the great attractions for visitors. To the Balinese, guests at a wedding or cremation are doing the host an honour. The more the merrier, and the more in attendance, the higher the status and efficacy attributed to the ceremony. Guests from further away seem to score extra points for the ceremony's host, and foreigners are sometimes urged, or

THIS PAGE: *Religious ceremonies in Ubud are full of pageantry and colourful processions which involve the whole community.*

OPPOSITE: *An afternoon rehearsal at the open-air stage of Taman Saraswati temple in central Ubud. Evening performances here present an enchanting tableau, with the dances reflected in vast lotus ponds.*

THIS PAGE: *The royal family plays an important role in Ubud society and is honoured and respected. At royal cremations, the extended family and the entire community join together in grand processions to honour the deceased.*
OPPOSITE: *The silhouettes of legong dancers practising with their teacher. Some of the most talented dancers and performers in Bali hail from the Ubud area.*

nearly dragged into the activities. For their part, foreign guests need only show earnest respect and learn the correct behaviour in order to fit in without causing offence. This is not so difficult. Almost any Balinese acquaintance or hotel employee in the heartlands of Bali will happily advise guests, explaining the proceedings and how to be involved without making a faux pas. Most resorts even have Balinese temple clothes in the latest styles available to rent, and staff will assist guests in donning them properly.

a mixed palette paints a pleasant community picture

Foreigners and locals mix more easily in Ubud and the communities surrounding it than anywhere else on the island. Here, people from all walks of life and from all corners of the globe work together, relax together and dream together. The local Balinese are also a diverse population who tend to mix with ease among themselves as well. They range from rice farmers inhabiting dirt-floored houses, to urban sophisticates who speak several languages and have interests in global business, fashion and politics. One also discovers quickly how rich the local population is in quirky characters, mystics, musicians, healers, dreamers and even potentially hazardous heartbreakers.

Ubud has a large expatriate community which is equally diverse, with ascetics, the global bon ton and widely recognised intellectuals, painters, photographers and writers. Some are here because life is easy, still relatively cheap, and there is a large and easily impressed audience. Others are here to further serious work in their respective fields or to contribute something of their knowledge to the future of the community. Still others stay for the long term to pursue business opportunities, such as exporting Balinese arts and crafts. Many foreigners are also in the island's heartland because they married a Balinese. Whatever brought them all here, they contribute to the dynamic life in and around Ubud.

Travellers to this area have always had a somewhat more educated profile, or at least more curiosity about the 'real Bali' than the crowd down south. This is still true and is likely to remain so. The area is known for its abundance of classes, seminars, festivals

One also discovers quickly how rich the local population is in quirky characters...

and workshops. One can learn how to carve wood, cook local dishes, make temple offerings, wear Balinese attire, dance the *legong*, paint batik and more. The diversity of programmes at any given time reflects the diversity of people living in and visiting Ubud. There are sessions with world-class yoga masters, alternative health authorities, meditation teachers and other experts in many fields. The unrivalled highlight of the local calendar for the learned and learners is the Ubud Readers and Writers Festival, usually held in September, when renowned authors, publishers and inspirational speakers descend on the town to share their work and enjoy each other's company.

success with a sensitive spirit

The most upscale and up-and-coming area around Ubud is the ridge overlooking the Ayung River. About 10 minutes north-northeast of downtown Ubud, this district has the greatest concentration of luxury resorts and villas with expensive views. The natural scenery is stunning and access by road is easy, explaining its success. Once, this elegant enclave comprised a small luxurious cluster around the Amandari, stretching a mile or so along the ridge in either direction. Now, the area is expanding and moving further up the ridge and up the ladder of sophisticated living. Chic retailers dot the main road and some of the most superb destination resorts in Asia sit above glorious views in the higher elevations of the Ayung ridge. Miraculously, the natural scenery, environmental integrity and traditional communities have not been degraded. One feels that a new and more enlightened vision of development could be dawning along the Ayung ridge, from Semana, north to Payangan and beyond.

A noted trailblazer is John Hardy, a successful jewellery maker who began creating handcrafted works in silver in the hippy days of the 1970s. With his feet firmly planted on Ubud soil, he eventually found himself with nearly 1,000 employees, having unwittingly built a small empire. But this is an empire like no other; it is an environmental and humanitarian empire as much as a commercial one. Despite his high profile in the world's elite style and design media, John is a humble character who dashes around

in an old but elegant batik sarong and bare feet most of the time. His factory has an open-air canteen serving organic meals to his healthy team and his friends. The food is cooked in mud ovens and stored in a walk-in mud refrigerator housed in a huge bamboo kitchen pavilion. Some of the ingredients come from John's own organic fields. Cooking fuel is of recycled material, which is pelleted. His grand showroom is a soaring, cathedral-like space built of bamboo, a renewable resource, and he is currently constructing the world's first production factory built totally of bamboo. A bamboo school with an enlightened international curriculum is soon to follow.

This kind of enterprise, full of heart and full of art, typifies the success stories that frequently get written in Ubud. There are many of these successes, both large and small, all offering something unique to the visitor and the world.

Somehow, the Ubud area manages to move forward without losing its soul. Its personality is too strong to be destroyed. The town still draws people who want to give something to the community; people who are actively involved in art, nature, social projects, the environment, music, dance, architecture, alternative philosophies and many other areas.

THIS PAGE: *Modern luxury is juxtaposed with lush greenery at Ubud Hanging Gardens, a luxury resort.*
OPPOSITE (FROM TOP): *Ubud is renowned as a centre for physical and spiritual well-being. Here, a yoga teacher practices advanced asanas beside the Ayung River at the Royal Pita Maha resort and spa; artichoke earrings from Treasures.*

start in the heart of Bali

Ubud's central location makes it easy to get away from it all. Exploring mountains, forests and rarely visited areas of Bali's far north and east will not entail giving up comfort at the end of the day. Round trips to almost anywhere on the island can be made from here without totally exhausting the driver. Arguably the best area to use as one's base in Bali, the heartland affords easy access to resources and attractions. The many things that bring people to Bali are found nearby in abundance—sculpted rice terraces, small villages, colourful ceremonies, arts and crafts communities, ancient temples, palaces, and the comforts of unique luxury hotels. Learning, healing, dancing, creating and discovering new ways to see the world are daily activities in the Ubud area. The scope for shopping here has broadened dramatically, while fine dining and even a little nightlife complete the indulgent side of the Ubud experience.

In the unlikely event that all of this fails to please a jaded globetrotter, the scene in Seminyak and the sands of Bali's southern beaches are only an hour's drive away. Many travellers who plan to split their holiday between the Ubud area and the south find no reason to move downhill and simply stay put. Setting off in any direction from a base in Bali's heartland leads to something special. Uphill, the volcanos offer stunning scenery and challenging hikes. The road journey upwards usually takes longer than planned, however, with delightful villages to stop in, lush surroundings for trekking and biking, and even elephants to ride at Taro's Elephant Safari Park, just north of Ubud.

East of Ubud, the Pejeng and Tampaksiring districts have the highest concentration of ancient sites in Bali. Mysterious meditation temples built a millennium ago stand beside sacred rivers, and holy springs pour forth healing waters for the devout. The best way to learn and understand is to explore by vehicle and on foot, with a guide from one of the area's resorts, or independently with a copy of A. J. Bernet Kempers's *Monumental Bali* in the rucksack, and a sarong and sash for entering sacred sites without disturbing their sanctity.

Nature beckons the moment one leaves the grounds of any luxury hotel in the area. Most hotels offer guided tours to get things started, and intrepid ramblers can really stretch their legs once they have procured a good walking map from their hotel or one of Ubud's many bookshops. Mountain biking is a popular way to take in the scenery while keeping fit, and for the lazy, downhill rides are arranged by high-end hotels or through Sobek Bali Utama, which also organises enjoyable river-rafting trips near Ubud. For a different experience of nature, the Bali Bird Park near Batubulan is alive with splendid plumage, equally splendid gardens and a special 'Breakfast with the Birds' for avid lovers of avifauna. Birdwatching in the wild is very rewarding in Bali's heartland, too. Guided tours by Bali Bird Walks delight newcomers and seasoned experts alike. Their guides were trained by Bali's number one bird buff and prominent peripatetic personality, Victor Mason, who wrote the bible of Bali's birds, *Birds of Bali*—a concise and entertaining little volume.

shopping safaris from the sublime to the ridiculous

The burgeoning retail heart of Ubud supplies discriminating shoppers with almost everything they might desire these days, from daily necessities such as S. Pellegrino and mobile phones, to museum-quality antiques and masterpieces of art. Most of the

THIS PAGE: *The hills, villages, valleys and country roads around Ubud provide excellent terrain for explorations by mountain bike.*
OPPOSITE: *An elephant vanishes into the mist at the Elephant Safari Park in the village of Taro, near Ubud.*

THIS PAGE (FROM TOP): *The skilled hands of Ubud's many artists and artisans bring tradition to life. Here, a mask maker puts the finishing touches on a topeng dalem dance mask; a kokokan, or white heron, wades gracefully through a flooded rice field.*

OPPOSITE: *In the early morning, Ubud's traditional market is a blur of activity as local women bargain for the best prices on fruit, flowers and fresh palm leaves for temple offerings.*

finer clothing and jewellery boutiques offer something a bit different, showcasing the products of local artisans and Bali's expatriate entrepreneurs. Visitors and residents alike can find all the treasures they need or simply cannot resist, alongside unique creations they never dreamed of. The most fruitful shopping areas are the upper stretch of Monkey Forest Road, Jalan Raya in the centre of town, and Jalan Hanoman. These three streets contain more than enough to delight and even overload the senses. It is no longer necessary to stay down south if shopping is high on one's must-do list.

Ubud's traditional market for locals has moved aside and gone underground, literally. It is down a slippery ramp, hidden amid dark concrete arcades, and is still 'real' but not particularly pleasant. The main market area has been given over almost totally to tourist merchandise. Some are decent trinkets, while others take kitsch to new highs and lows. The selection of traditional Balinese sarongs and other temple gear is acceptable here, but there are better selections in small boutiques on the main street and beyond. To prance into a palace-sponsored ceremony in a sarong from a market or a cheap polyester *kebaya* is unacceptable to elegant native Ubudians. Only when viewed as an inexpensive option for future fancy dress parties back home do the sarongs and sartorial trappings of the Ubud market make sense.

Ubud's 'handicraft highway' is a 10-km (6-mile) stretch of road running from Andong at the eastern edge of Ubud, north up the mountainside to the lovely town of Pujung. Between the two is a bewildering array of handicraft and homeware shops that defy description. Everything from gilt giraffes and armchairs in the shape of human hands, to mirror-mosaic mannequins is displayed to attract the passing public. Buyers for retailers and mail-order catalogues from all over the globe come here to purchase container-loads of products. Travellers who love to bring home souvenirs with humour will find something strange enough to shock the folks at home. Many knick-knacks come with wire loops attached, making them marvellous ornaments for the Christmas tree. The baskets and ceramics are worth a look, and everyone is bound to find some treasure or other at a bargain price if they wander down this remarkable road.

The burgeoning retail heart of Ubud supplies discriminating shoppers with almost everything they might desire...

como shambhala estate at begawan giri

...reinvented as a forward-thinking healing resort...

THIS PAGE: *The hills of Ubud are spread out for the appreciation of nature lovers by the pool.*
OPPOSITE (FROM TOP): *Relax within view of the courtyard; the bedrooms are designed specifically to soothe and relax; the spa treatments are aimed at rejuvenating body and spirit.*

In the 1990s, an entrepreneurial couple with exquisite taste came to Bali and built the ultimate villa hotel, Begawan Giri. Located on a remote ridge above a river valley with stunning views, it quickly became a legend for its uncompromising luxury, superb setting and influential architecture. The number of design books and magazines it has been featured in is almost impossible to count, as are the famous names who have enjoyed Begawan Giri and raved about it, from Mick Jagger and Barbra Streisand to heads of state. Begawan Giri was described as gorgeous and elite. It seemed impossible to improve on it.

But someone has. Under the umbrella of Christina Ong's COMO Shambhala luxury brand, the estate has been reinvented as a forward-thinking healing resort, which is being hailed

as a new paradigm in residential health retreats. Villas have been added to the estate in various categories, and the original five residences have been re-configured, allowing them to be booked by the room, rather than by the villa only. Re-configuration was done with both privacy and conviviality taken into consideration, and without compromising the original beauty of the residences.

Also new are a large and lavish spa building with a 25-m (82-ft) pool, and extensive facilities to support the spa's offerings, including a large, open yoga space. Tennis courts and an activities centre with fitness and consultation rooms complete the wellness programmes. The main restaurant has followed suit, changing its focus to healthy but delicious cuisine, and its name to Glow. The reincarnated Begawan Giri is devoted to the well-being of its guests by maximising holistic health.

Programmes are custom-designed for guests on arrival or before, in consultation with a wellness specialist. Three- to seven-day packages include detox, Ayurvedic, anti-ageing and stress management options. Therapies, activities and diet are combined to enable guests to achieve their goals during their stay, whether they be healing, or simply taking a step back from the hectic pace of life to rediscover an inner peace within themselves.

These bespoke programmes draw expertise from among the estate's professionals, who are skilled in areas such as massage, body and mind therapies, naturopathy, iridology, yoga, pilates, martial arts and outdoor sports. Whatever treatment guests have in mind, it can be provided. An Ayurvedic doctor from India and a psychologist are also available to assist with integrative wellness for body, mind and spirit.

ROOMS
5 Residences (21 suites) • 5 Villas (11 rooms) • 5 Retreat Villas (one-bedroom and two-bedroom)

FOOD
Kudus House: Indonesian • Glow: gourmet organic, healthy and raw cuisine

DRINK
Glow • in-room service • Kudus House

FEATURES
Ayurvedic doctor • activities centre • acupuncture • chiropractor • diverse spa therapies • helicopter transfers • hikes and cycling • martial arts • nutritionist • pilates • pools • reflexology • saunas • steam rooms • tennis • yoga

NEARBY
Ubud city centre • art galleries and studios • cultural events • museums • mountains • restaurants • shopping • temples • villages

CONTACT
PO Box 54, Ubud, Gianyar 80571 • telephone: +62.361.978 888 • facsimile: +62.361.978 889 • email: es@cse.comoshambhala.bz • website: www.cse.comoshambhala.bz

four seasons resort bali at sayan

Camouflaged amid lush foliage and steep terrain...

Four Seasons Resort Bali at Sayan is undoubtedly one of the most complete luxury resorts in the Ubud area. Set dramatically against the Ayung River, it comprises a site that stretches from the top of the river gorge down to rice fields by the river. Camouflaged amid lush foliage and steep terrain is an astonishingly beautiful boutique hotel with just 42 villas and 18 suites.

The Royal Villa is a palatial three-bedroom residence entered through its rooftop. From a distance, it appears to be a lily pond and private meditation area on a raised circular platform, but descending the stairs from the roof one finds, beneath a soaring ceiling, three bedroom suites, a dining room, three sitting rooms, a full-sized pool and outdoor areas for relaxation or entertaining. The awe-inspiring views, the lavish yet understated elegance of the interior and the extraordinary construction of this villa all serve to make a stay here truly spectacular.

Perched at the resort's highest point, the Sayan Villas offer breathtaking views of the valley below. Honeymooners prefer these for their added seclusion, four-poster canopy beds, flowing water features, and dining room for candlelit dinners. No less pleasant are the resort's one-bedroom villas, which have wooden decks, plunge pools and equally splendid views, while two-bedroom villas along the river benefit from the calming sounds of rushing water, extra large terraces, living and dining rooms, and outdoor soaking tubs and showers.

The spa at the resort combines simplicity with sophistication. Three treatment villas, all built using Balinese architectural styles and natural furnishings such as teak wood cabinets and flooring, Sulawesi silk furniture coverings and terrazzo massage tables, offer perfect privacy and comfort. Tandem treatments for couples are popular, as are individual escapes into solitude. Treatments range from a 30-minute hand and foot massage to four-day rejuvenation regimens for individuals and couples. Offerings include mud wraps, body scrubs, a red ginger body polish and a 'Sole to Soul' day package.

The Ayung Terrace restaurant is superb, as its popularity with non-hotel guests proves. The Asian-flavoured menu covers extensive terrain across a world of fine cuisine—a menu guests will never tire of, even during a long stay.

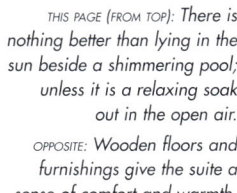

THIS PAGE (FROM TOP): *There is nothing better than lying in the sun beside a shimmering pool; unless it is a relaxing soak out in the open air.*
OPPOSITE: *Wooden floors and furnishings give the suite a sense of comfort and warmth.*

ROOMS
37 one-bedroom villas • 18 suites • 2 Sayan Villas • 2 two-bedroom villas • 1 Royal Villa

FOOD
Ayung Terrace: Asian • Riverside Café: casual dining • picnic hampers

DRINK
Jati Bar • Riverside Café

FEATURES
24-hour concierge • 24-hour dining • gym • cycling • satellite TV • car rental • DVD and CD players • high-speed Internet access • pool • spa • trekking

BUSINESS
24-hour business centre • AV equipment • conference facilities • meeting room

NEARBY
Ubud city centre • art studios • museums • galleries • shopping • river rafting • temples • villages

CONTACT
Sayan, Ubud, Gianyar 80571 • telephone: +62.361.977 577 • facsimile: +62.361.977 588 • website: www.fourseasons.com/sayan

komaneka resort at monkey forest

...an oasis of peace amid the bustle of Ubud.

THIS PAGE: *With a lush forest just outside the rooms, guests enjoy a comforting and restful stay, close to nature.*
OPPOSITE: *The inviting jacuzzi in the spa welcomes guests.*

Being in the centre of Ubud has great advantages, but most hotels within walking distance of the main market lack the luxury and style that sophisticated travellers expect. Komaneka Resort at Monkey Forest is an exception. A boutique-size resort with just six pool villas, two suites and 12 deluxe rooms, it is ideally located in the middle of Ubud, right on Monkey Forest Road.

Being equidistant from the road and the Ubud market means that Komaneka guests need not rely on motorised transport, but can enjoy Ubud at a more relaxed pace on foot, with greater flexibility and without facing any of the hassles of traffic and parking. Ubud is fast becoming urbanised and the streets are becoming crowded, so this ease of movement matters. Also within walking distance are Ubud's best shops, restaurants, cafés and nightlife, and traditional Balinese entertainment is within reach too. Nightly cultural performances are available at Ubud Palace, Pura Taman Saraswati and Pura Dalem. Being in such a central location, however, does not mean Komaneka Resort at Monkey Forest is noisy or cramped. Accommodation is set far back from the street in extensive gardens that slope down to a tree-lined stream and bordered by rice fields on two sides. It is a welcome change from the active street scene outside—an oasis of peace amid the bustle of Ubud.

The resort comprises 12 rooms, six villas and two one-bedroom suites, all furnished with comfort in mind. Like the deluxe rooms and the suites, the pool villas come with sunken marble bathtubs for a touch of luxury. All offer calming views of the tropical landscape of Bali. Throughout, amenities such as air-conditioning, satellite TV and CD players also allow guests to enjoy their stay in comfort.

There is something indulgent about knowing that one is staying in a tranquil resort set in the centre of a busy city, and the exclusive spa treatments offered here only accentuate that feeling. Among the offerings at Komaneka Spa are massages that use soothing blends of oils with intriguing names such as Ubud Spice (ginger, cloves and nutmeg) and Bali Sunny (mint, cajuput, patcholi and citrus). Guests may also try a herbal body scrub, a royal Javanese treatment called *lulur* that uses rice and spices to cleanse

THIS PAGE: *The lobby's décor expresses the Bali style too, with wooden furniture beneath a traditional ceiling.*
OPPOSITE: *Sitting beside the pool, surrounded by overhanging trees branches and sheltered by sunshades, one can appreciate the difference between bustling Ubud just outside the resort and the serenity within.*

the body and soften the skin. Facials, manicures and pedicures are all available at the spa as well. There is also an aromatic herbal bath that uses more than 20 types of herbs and spices, leaving one's skin with a lingering fragrance. It smells exotic and enticing—it may even sharpen one's appetite for dinner.

Meals at Komaneka Resort at Monkey Forest are available at the Garden Terrace Restaurant, which is the main restaurant here. It provides international and Indonesian cuisines, while the Pool Bar serves lighter fare and drinks. The Pool Bar's location makes it a popular place to go for a refreshing drink or a snack while one relaxes by the water.

The resort also has other surprises. It is owned by a Balinese couple, Koman and Mansri, the son and daughter-in-law of Pande Wayan Suteja Neka, a revered figure in Bali's art world. Koman inherited his father's love of art. When Komaneka Resort was created, he launched Komaneka Fine Art Gallery, recognised as one of the leading contemporary art galleries in Bali. It periodically presents groundbreaking exhibitions that draw patronage from as far as Jakarta and Singapore.

Koman's wife, Mansri, is also a connoisseur of art and a collector of rare and old traditional textiles from around Indonesia. Her collection of fine batiks and *geringsing* double *ikat* (a fabric where both weft and warp threads are dyed before they are woven) from Tenganan village in east Bali is exceptional. This love of textiles is apparent throughout Komaneka Resort, where prominence is given to hand-spun and handwoven cloth made on local looms. Koman and Mansri were also among the pioneers of a new style in art and interior design— 'primitive-modern', where objects such as weathered wooden furniture and twisted branches are deliberately left in their natural state, cracks and all, to create a back-to-basics aesthetic.

This approach to beauty, which is akin to Japanese aesthetic traditions, has become wildly popular throughout the world. Komaneka Resort was among the first in Indonesia to incorporate this style in its décor and guests will appreciate the various ways it is presented in the resort. Simple and natural materials from local sources are used, with an emphasis on soothing, unaffected serenity. The decorators look after guests the Balinese way too. For example, the resort's rooms are swathed in unbleached, natural white cotton and Balinese *poleng*, a traditional black-and-white chequered fabric that is believed to have magical powers of protection for the user. This combination of Balinese folk tradition and the primitive-modern aesthetic is certain to make guests feel welcome and cared for.

The effect is meditative and supremely relaxing too—just what one needs after the sensory overload of Ubud's arts and culture offerings. There are so many activities to pursue within walking distance of the resort that an extended stay is recommended in order to enjoy them. Guests can try their hand at woodcarving, try on Balinese dress, observe ceremonies, visit museums and seminars or socialise with Ubud's intellectuals.

Spa and yoga options at Komaneka Resort at Monkey Forest can also deepen the process of relaxation, leaving one fresh to begin exploring Ubud again the next day. Those looking for a secluded stay may like to try Komaneka Resort at Tanggayuda, a sister resort further in the hills, set on the edge of a scenic river gorge, which offers the best of Bali's nature.

ROOMS
12 deluxe rooms • 6 one-bedroom pool villas • 2 one-bedroom suites

FOOD
Garden Terrace Restaurant: contemporary Indonesian and international • Pool Bar: casual lunch

DRINK
Pool Bar

FEATURES
CD and DVD players • Komaneka Fine Art Gallery • woodcarving, dance, Balinese dress and cooking classes • library • satellite TV • privileges at Komaneka Tanggayuda • pool • spa • yoga

BUSINESS
business services on request • high-speed wi-fi Internet access

NEARBY
Monkey Forest • Padang Tegal • Pura Taman Saraswati • Pura Dalem • Ubud market • Ubud Palace • art studios, galleries and museums • cultural performances • nightlife • rice fields • shopping • restaurants

CONTACT
Jalan Monkey Forest, Ubud, Gianyar 80571 • telephone: +62.361.976 090 • facsimile: +62.361.977 140 • email: sales@komaneka.com • website: www.komaneka.com

komaneka resort at tanggayuda

...an ideal place to retreat, relax and recover from the stresses of life.

Art and natural scenery are two good reasons to choose the Ubud area as a base in Bali. Komaneka Resort at Tanggayuda combines the two in a unique way. The owners, a married couple, are both connoisseurs of fine art. Koman, the son of the founder of Neka Art Museum, owns a contemporary art gallery in the city centre of Ubud. Guests enjoy privileged access to events at his gallery as well as entry to his father's museum. A selection of paintings, which are available for purchase, is also exhibited in the lobby of the resort. His wife Mansri is a collector of Indonesian antiques and traditional textiles. Pieces from her substantial collection provide decorative accents throughout the property, and the antiques, textiles and crafts displayed in the boutique were chosen by her personally.

The couple enjoyed great success with their first hotel, Komaneka Resort at Monkey Forest, located behind Koman's gallery, where their artistic spirit and taste in design were applied in abundance. Its success was also partly due to the superb location on Monkey Forest Road, within walking distance of the town's most popular cultural, culinary and shopping hot spots. But Koman and Mansri longed to share the natural beauty of Ubud with their guests as well, so they created the resort, Komaneka Resort at Tanggayuda, on the edge of a scenic river gorge, 20 minutes outside of town. Dividing one's stay between the two is a delightful way to experience both sides of Ubud: the cultural side and the natural one.

With just 16 pool villas and four suites, Komaneka Resort at Tanggayuda is a quiet boutique-size hotel. The villas come with private garden areas and sundecks with plunge pools. It is cooler here, being at a higher elevation than Ubud's city centre, so a dip in the pool is refreshing and bound to revive the senses after a day of trekking. But on chilly evenings, guests can opt for a warm soak. The villas' bathrooms have remarkable bathtubs: each originated as a massive volcanic boulder, and the tub has been hewn directly into

it and polished smooth on the inside. Add to this lashings of hot water and fragrant natural bath products from the spa, and a soothing experience is assured, one that is enhanced by the glow of candlelit lanterns in the bathroom and the closeness of nature just outside.

All villas and suites open to forest, garden or valley views, so guests can fully appreciate the surroundings. The rooms are decorated in an understated manner with local, natural materials, tastefully used but not overly ornamental. The effect is peaceful, creating an ideal place to retreat, relax and recover from the stresses of life.

The spa offers excellent treatments, including Balinese massages, body scrubs and traditional facials. A light and airy enclosure houses the fitness centre, with excellent views that motivate one to keep to an exercise regime. But with so much scenery surrounding Komaneka

THIS PAGE: *Peaceful surroundings by the pool provide an ideal spot to relax during the day and to enjoy a romantic poolside dinner in the evening.*
OPPOSITE: *By night, lanterns hung high up in the trees gently illuminate the resort.*

THIS PAGE: *The valley pool villa is decorated with comfort in mind and offers guests views of the greenery outside.*

OPPOSITE (FROM LEFT): *Nestled among coconut trees and the tropical forest, guests here can learn what it is like to live in the Balinese countryside; fine dining in the restaurant comes with warm service.*

Resort at Tanggayuda, most guests get their workout walking in the hills, or trekking through rice fields and traditional villages. A guided two-hour walk is a good introduction to the surrounding landscape. And what a landscape it is: the resort is located on the brink of a dramatic drop to the sacred Oos River, which cuts a deep gorge through grass-covered hills and tropical forests as it rushes south towards Ubud. For the adventurous traveller, the trekking potential of this river valley is tremendous. Nature lovers can spend a whole day here just watching the native birds and even spotting the occasional monkey.

For the lazy, there is absolutely no need to work up a sweat at all to fully enjoy the scenery. The resort's swimming pool is built directly on the lip of the valley, and provides a perfect perspective of the landscape from its edge.

The pool is also the setting of one of the most romantic dining experiences in Bali. Every evening, the hotel's nimble kitchen crew sets up candlelit poolside dinners for guests. The food at these feasts is a Balinese smorgasbord, served the traditional way and accompanied by the haunting melodies of *gender wayang*, an intimate *gamelan* ensemble. Another dining option is Warung Kudus, the hotel's restaurant, which serves excellent Indonesian and international cuisines in a setting that recalls a traditional village, but one accented with authentic antiques.

Guests may also enjoy meals served in their villa for an intimate dining experience, or anywhere that tickles their fancy on the grounds. The Komaneka team is creative and flexible, and they seem to delight in unusual requests—a refreshing change from hotels with regimented, rule-bound attitudes and staff. The whole Komaneka approach is characterised by personal attention, flexibility and creativity. This means that guests can put together a customised escape based on a wide range of à la carte options.

For a calming, healing retreat, the spa offers peace and privacy. The spa team can schedule a programme of cleansing and rejuvenating treatments, while complimentary yoga classes take place twice a week, and at other times by appointment. But if the purpose of visiting Bali is to delve deeply into its unique culture, there are interesting ways to do so. One can explore the villages nearby with a guide and gain a perspective on the traditional Balinese way of life. Complimentary classes on Balinese carving and dance are also offered at the resort.

For a truly memorable souvenir, the resort also offers guests the chance to be photographed in traditional dance attire. For men there is the *baris* warrior dance dress, complete with spear and sword, and for women the lovely *legong* costume, with its accessories and headdress.

ROOMS
12 one-bedroom valley pool villas •
4 one-bedroom courtyard pool villas •
4 suites

FOOD
Warung Kudus: contemporary Indonesian and international cuisines • Terrace Café: light lunches and drinks • 'Red Lantern' dinners by the pool

DRINK
Terrace Café

FEATURES
classes on carving and dance • guided excursions • DVD and CD players • gift and antiques shop • gym • library with books • games • pool • satellite TV • spa • steam room • shuttle bus to Ubud • whirlpool • yoga

BUSINESS
business services on request • high-speed Internet access • meeting room

NEARBY
Ubud • cultural performances • river rafting • shopping • temples • traditional villages

CONTACT
Banjar Tanggayuda, Kedewatan Ubud, Gianyar 80571 •
telephone: +62.361.978 123 •
facsimile: +62.361.973 084 •
email: sales@komaneka.com •
website: www.komaneka.com

majapahit beach villas

...the living and dining spaces are arranged around the pool...

While there are a number of beautiful beachfront villas in Bali, Majapahit Beach Villas, on the southern end of Gianyar, is a particularly delightful surprise. Fabulously luxurious, it comprises four villas, two beachfront villas and two villas with beach access and views.

Located right on Pabean Beach near the traditional village of Ketewel, Majapahit Beach Villas are just up the coast from Sanur and surrounded by terraced rice fields, tobacco plantations, and papaya and banana groves. From the resort, it is easy for guests to visit Ubud, eastern Bali or the mountains on day trips. And it is even quicker to get to the towns of Sanur, Kuta and Seminyak, where shopping, cultural entertainment and excellent restaurants await.

Staying in is much more tempting, though. There is really no need to go anywhere at all, given the size, style and spaciousness of these villas, and the services and facilities available. Each villa sits in its own private enclosure with a 14-m (15-yd) pool, a big, breezy *bale* for lounging and a spa treatment pavilion. In fact, the living and dining spaces are arranged around the pool, allowing guests to enjoy the comfort of the outdoors and soak up the garden atmosphere that comes with living in a tropical villa. The dining area in each villa, for example, overlooks a lotus pond.

The most striking feature of the two beachfront villas, Villa Maya and Villa Samudra, is the garden which has wooden steps leading down to a 14-m long (15-yd) beach. The two garden villas, Villa Nataraja and Villa Raj, share timber decks and access to the beach, entered via a walled pathway from each villa's garden. From the beach, one can see the cliffs of the nearby Nusa Penida.

The villas all have grand proportions. In each villa, a huge master suite monopolises the second floor, with soaring ceilings and a wide viewing terrace, allowing cool, gentle breezes to enter and

THIS PAGE (FROM TOP): A curved floating staircase made of wood can be seen just outside the brightly furnished bedroom; the objets d'art are genuine but never overpowering.
OPPOSITE (FROM TOP): The living room and pool of Villa Samudra face the sea; stone lions stand guard outside a traditional Balinese entrance.

circulate. Below the master suite are two other bedrooms with spa-style luxury bathrooms in grey terrazzo and stone. Silk, suede and hand-rubbed teak furnishings, as well as the natural tones of white limestone, warm wood and off-white terrazzo, also enhance the richness of the décor. Particularly noteworthy is a curved floating staircase, made of dark wood, that adds a sense of drama to the living room, while Balinese art and artefacts, charmingly displayed, allow guests to appreciate local culture.

But that is not all. Privacy is assured here by staff quarters and laundry areas set apart from the villas, as are the kitchens, which are discreetly screened from living spaces by a row of wide stone pillars. When needed or anticipated, the staff appear—with a chef, five cooks, butlers, waiters, gardeners, chauffeurs and an on-site property manager, nothing will be overlooked. Guests may punctuate long, peaceful days here by holding an elegant party, with preparations made effortless by the friendly staff.

ROOMS
2 three-bedroom beachfront pool villas • 2 three-bedroom ocean-view pool villas

FOOD
24-hour dining • chef and 5 cooks provide Western, Japanese, Thai, Chinese and Indonesian

DRINK
service anywhere on the premises

FEATURES
DVD and CD players • butlers • boutique • car and chauffeur • on-site villa manager • pools • spa treatments on request • satellite TV • wi-fi Internet access

NEARBY
Bali Bird Park • Celuk silversmiths • Denpasar • Kuta • Pura Segara • Sanur • Sukawati market • bamboo and rattan workshops • shadow puppet and mask makers • stone carvers • surf breaks

CONTACT
Jalan Ida Bagus Mantra, Banjar Pabean, Desa Ketewel, Sukawati, Gianyar 80571 •
telephone: +62.361.730 668 •
facsimile: +62.361.736 391 •
email: info@balihomes.com • website: www.majapahitbeachvillas.com

pita maha resort + spa

...evoking the lavish pavilions of Ubud's main palace.

THIS PAGE: *The grand-looking décor of the Pool Garden Villa makes one feel like royalty.*

OPPOSITE (FROM TOP): *Flowers used in the Balinese style bathroom; a spa treatment pavilion overlooking lush gardens; when lazing on a lounge chair by the pool, the sky and hills seem to be within arm's reach.*

The magic of Ubud is guarded by its royal palaces. The royal families of Ubud are still respected, even revered, in local society. Two of Ubud's royal princes are successful hoteliers as well, and it was they who created Pita Maha Resort in 1994. This boutique-sized hotel consists of 24 villas on the slopes of the Wos River in the Tjampuhan Valley, just outside Ubud.

The style here is completely Balinese and absolutely regal. The entire resort was designed by Tjokorda Gde Oka Sukawati, a descendant of the last king of Ubud, in partnership with his brother Tjokorda Gde Putra Sukawati, the reigning prince of the dynasty. Villas are decorated with royal touches, evoking the lavish pavilions of Ubud's main palace. Finely carved traditional Balinese doors mark the entry to each villa. Doorposts and architectural accents in local stone

are also ornately carved. All of the work was carried out by the same artisans who worked on many of the temples and palace pavilions in the area, including Ubud Palace. Each villa is enclosed in a private walled garden: the garden villas have open terraces as well, while the pool villas have private swimming pools and sundecks.

Interiors feature deluxe Balinese bathrooms, traditional paintings, cool marble floors as well as soaring ceilings of golden thatch. Views throughout the property are splendid, taking in a deep river valley, steep green hillsides, and terraced rice fields on the opposite side of the gorge. When the air is clear early in the morning, Bali's volcanos are visible on the horizon.

The Pita Maha spa takes advantage of the resort's natural surroundings to provide a relaxing experience. Overlooking the Tjampuhan Valley, it was created especially for couples, who can enjoy massages, body scrubs and other beauty treatments together.

Pita Maha Resort was named after an artists' association created in the 1930s by the raja of Ubud, with Walter Spies and Rudolf Bonnet, both talented painters working under the patronage of the royal family. Since then, family members have continued to serve as patrons of the arts and as voluntary cultural liaisons for foreign visitors. Artists, musicians and experts under royal patronage visit the hotel regularly to give classes in painting, carving, *gamelan*, dance and traditional healing, and guests are welcome to participate.

ROOMS
10 one-bedroom Pool Garden Villas •
10 one-bedroom Pool Villas •
4 two-bedroom Pool Villas

FOOD
Terrace Restaurant: Asian and Western

DRINK
pool bar

FEATURES
art and cultural classes • access to Ubud Palace and temple ceremonies

NEARBY
Ubud city centre • Ubud Palace • artists' studios • cultural performances • museums • galleries • lounge-bars • nightlife • restaurants • shopping

CONTACT
PO Box 198, Jalan Sanggingan, Ubud, Gianyar 80571 •
telephone: +62.361.974 330 •
facsimile: +62.361.974 329 •
email: sales@pitamaharesorts-bali.com •
website: www.pitamaha-bali.com

the royal pita maha

...this captivating property truly celebrates the Balinese heritage of art, culture and tradition.

THIS PAGE: *The Royal House comes with an infinity-edged pool that seems to flow out into the tropical richness of Bali.*

OPPOSITE (FROM TOP): *Yoga lessons are more peaceful by the river; the bedrooms are dressed with royal flair and a lavish touch; the Terrace Bali Restaurant (ground level) and the Ayung Valley Restaurant (first level) allow guests to enjoy both food and scenery at the same time.*

The royal princes of Ubud have created numerous hotels and resorts over the years. They began in the 1930s, taking visiting dignitaries into pavilions in their palaces as guests. They also hosted the famous painter Walter Spies in a house on palace-owned land near Ubud, and that house has since become Hotel Tjampuhan. In the 1990s, Ubud's princes created Pita Maha. Both Hotel Tjampuhan and Pita Maha have been successful and many guests have returned, particularly those who enjoy the stories of Ubud culture, as well as the privileged access—reserved for hotel guests—to temple ceremonies sponsored by the royal family. This is a family with more than nobility in their blood: there is a natural talent for hospitality as well.

The royal family has now created The Royal Pita Maha. A scenic 55-minute drive from the Ngurah Rai International Airport, this resort has been blessed with one of the best parcels of land that the island of Bali has to offer. Nestled deep within the serene rural village of Kedewatan on the outskirts of Ubud, this captivating property truly celebrates the Balinese heritage of art, culture and tradition. Built with rare sensitivity towards the environment, the

entire resort, comprising 52 villas staggered over 16-hectares (40 acres) of prime valley land, descends to where the Ayung River has etched a meandering pathway towards the south. The setting is breathtaking, with a ridge that slopes dramatically down to a bend in the river, offering stunning views in three directions. Along the river, the land is covered with meadows, spring-fed lagoons and traditional organic farms, bursting with vegetables, herbs, grains and fruits. Closest to the river are the newest villas of The Royal Pita Maha, the Healing Villas, which have large terraces and open onto lagoon pools fed by the waters of a holy spring.

The other villas are arranged on the slopes above. There are 40 one-bedroom Pool Villas, while at the top end are the Royal Villa, which is a three-level residence, and the Royal House, which boasts a charming and intimate wedding chapel and reception spaces. All villas are decorated in authentic Balinese style, and each has a spa-like bathroom with an enormous sunken tub, private terrace and swimming pool—and of course sweeping views

A magnificent three-storeyed building houses the Terrace Bali Restaurant and the Ayung Valley Restaurant, as well as the Dewata Lounge on the third level, all offering stunning vistas of the valley. Those seeking an impressive location for business conventions or conferences can make use of the Royal Convention House, which is in a separate wing. Set within a traditional courtyard, with an open-air stage for performances, it houses a multi-purpose hall for up to 200 participants, a smaller committee room, two pavilions and two further meeting rooms. All of these are lavishly appointed in true royal style.

Relaxation and exercise at the The Royal Pita Maha are offered with royal pomp too. The Resort's Royal Wellness and Healing Yoga Programmes are conducted by a full-time staff of certified yoga instructors. Held in a grassy *bale* by the river valley of Kedewatan, the timeless spirituality of this setting penetrates the senses to nurture the body, mind and soul.

ROOMS
40 Pool Villas • 10 Healing Villas • 1 Royal Villa • 1 Royal House

FOOD
Terrace Bali Restaurant: Balinese • Ayung Valley Restaurant: international • Ayung River: healthy organic cuisine

DRINK
Dewata Lounge • Palace Bar

FEATURES
satellite TV • DVDs • private pool • private terrace • yoga centre • organic farm • river rafting

BUSINESS
Royal Convention House

NEARBY
Ubud city centre • temples • palaces

CONTACT
Desa Kedewatan, Ubud, Gianyar 80571 •
telephone +62.361.980 022 •
facsimile: +62.361.980 011 •
email: sales@pitamaharesorts-bali.com •
website: www.royalpitamaha-bali.com

ubud hanging gardens

Brilliant feats of engineering allow the whole resort to literally hang over the edge...

THIS PAGE: The infinity-edged pools in the middle of the resort are among the main attractions.
OPPOSITE (FROM TOP): A private pool just outside reflects the warm interior of the villa; Balinese-inspired furnishings create a distinctive look; each villa has its own pool and sundeck overlooking the valley.

Ubud Hanging Gardens probably has one of the most unusual locations of any hotel in Bali. On the hotel's shuttle bus that starts its journey in Ubud, one moves steadily uphill for about 20 minutes along a winding country road that disappears into a rainforest. The bus emerges at the other end, enters a river gorge, crosses a scenic bridge and snakes up the steep hillside opposite. After passing through the centre of a small, traditional village, the bus finally arrives at Ubud Hanging Gardens, a luxury resort close to nature, right in the heart of Bali.

The location is incredible. Every structure stands on stilts anchored on the side of a steep river gorge covered in tropical greenery. Brilliant feats of engineering allow the whole resort to literally hang over the edge, right above one of Bali's most gorgeous rivers, the Ayung River. The dramatic views and the way they are achieved are one of the top attractions of the resort. Every part of Ubud Hanging Gardens, including its infinity-edged pools, scores of timber terraces and its spa, opens directly onto, or cantilevers, over the valley.

Just getting to one's room is a thrilling experience. The entire resort is connected, vertically, by two funicular lifts that look like thatched cottages and which whisk guests from the reception hall at the top of the river gorge to the level of their suite or villa. Built in contemporary Balinese style, each villa uses local furnishings and sports ylang-ylang roofs. While each villa and suite has its own infinity-edged pool, which can be heated, there are two larger pools for the use of all guests, both set into the hillside with one cascading into the other.

A superb spa sits just above the river at the resort's lowest level. It is luxuriously appointed, yet in keeping with the tone of the resort, it is also very close to nature. The three treatment pavilions are all open to the rushing river just below, and a complete range of treatments for men, women and even children can be enjoyed here.

Two restaurants offer delicious food to accompany the gorgeous views. Chef Renaud Le Rasle at Beduur Restaurant creates fine French-Asian dishes while Diatas Pohon Café offers treetop views and serves light and healthy food, including a 'Back from the Spa' menu.

As part of the Orient-Express group, Ubud Hanging Gardens offers excursions that let guests learn more about Bali and its countryside. Guests can also join the hugely popular temple tour to Pura Besakih, also known as the 'mother temple' of Hinduism.

ROOMS
30 one-bedroom pool villas •
2 one-bedroom pool suites •
6 two-bedroom pool villas

FOOD
Beduur Restaurant: Asian-French •
Diatas Pohon Café: lunch, snacks and juices • picnics

DRINK
Bukit Becik Bar

FEATURES
boutique • children's activities • cooking and painting classes • cycling • excursions • shuttle bus to Ubud • spa • yoga

BUSINESS
business services on request • corporate retreats • high-speed Internet access

NEARBY
Bali Bird Park • Pura Besakih • Ubud art market • golf • river rafting • traditional villages

CONTACT
Desa Buahan, Payangan, Ubud, Gianyar 80571 •
telephone: +62.361.982 700 •
facsimile: +62.361.982 800 •
email: reservations@ubudhanginggardens.com • website: www.ubudhanginggardens.com

vajra villas

...a luxurious hideaway in a dream-like world...

The deep interior of Bali is where the magic is. Nowhere is this more evident than in the villages and river valleys above Ubud. The landscapes here are lush, the views are stupendous and the traditions of village life still flourish. Things have changed little here since Walter Spies found paradise near Ubud in the 1930s and immortalised it on canvas.

The village of Keliki is just a few kilometres uphill from Ubud as the crow flies, but reaching it involves a memorable journey along a winding, paved road. Leaving Ubud, one passes first through the traditional village of Payogan, where farmers sit in the gateways of their houses in the afternoons, comparing fighting cocks. Leaving the village, the road passes in front of Pura Pucak Payogan, a temple founded in the 8th century by Rsi Markandeya, a wandering Buddhist mystic from Java who arrived on pilgrimage with his followers to found a Buddhist community in the highlands of Bali, and later established Besakih temple. Whenever he happened upon a beautiful or auspicious spot, he stopped to meditate. The people of Bali declared those places sacred and built temples on them, many which still stand to this day.

The road then plummets into a deep gorge, crossing a river where men cut *paras* stone from the cliffs and women carry the stones up precipitous paths, balanced on their heads. A winding ascent on the opposite side leads to a plateau of emerald-green rice terraces between

THIS PAGE (FROM TOP): *Villa Sati is perfectly sized for a couple; the wooden deck extends dramatically into the forest.*
OPPOSITE (FROM TOP): *A Buddha statue stands over the pond; bold, dramatic prints add colour to the décor in Villa Sati.*

two river valleys. Turning left along the ridge, passing a few village painters' studios and farmers' huts, one arrives in Keliki and finds Vajra Villas, a luxurious hideaway in a dream-like world.

At first glance, Vajra Villas presents a modest face to the world: low, thatched roofs, wood-mullioned windows and an earth-plastered wall. It blends smoothly into its natural surroundings. Beyond the modest Balinese gate, however, lies a grand surprise: Villa Vajra, a luxurious modern residence sitting on the edge of a river gorge, and Villa Sati, a smaller, one-bedroom villa, both with views in three directions taking in tropical forests, grass-covered hills, rice fields and a fast-running river.

The capacious compound of Villa Vajra is built on four terraces, descending from the entry level, into the river valley. It encompasses 800 sq m (8,611 sq ft) of living space, with three lavishly appointed bedroom suites, a living room with a high ceiling, an intimate library which can be used as a fourth bedroom, big timber terraces, and pools and ponds spreading out between them all.

Pavilions are connected by white stone slabs that seem to float on the surface of the lotus ponds, watched by statues of a standing Buddha. The upper ponds feed a cascading sheet of water which drops down beside the swimming pool, and veils another stone Buddha figure seated in meditation behind it. A sense of peace prevails throughout the place. The ambience is soothing, with natural materials, neutral colours and warm-hued woodwork. Outside, the

THIS PAGE: *The villa's pools are illuminated for those who prefer to take a dip in the evening.*
OPPOSITE (CLOCKWISE FROM TOP): *The intimate dining room; a charmingly prepared bath; the décor integrates island bohemian and contemporary styles to put guests at ease.*

property is intimately connected to the landscape. The terraces cantilever over the forested gorge, providing splendid views of the valley. For those who love to explore at their leisure, an orchid garden and aviary bring nature that much closer. At the property's lowest level, a 'moon garden' of white flowers spreads out near a relaxation *bale* overlooking the river.

There is an otherworldly feel to all of this, yet the 'real world' of sophisticated living is never far away. The library in Villa Vajra has satellite TV, a DVD player, Internet access and a sound system that extends throughout the house. The kitchen is built with minimalist European design in mind, using grey stone and wood tones. Fitness club users appreciate the fully equipped gym and heated jacuzzi, while massages and other spa treatments are available on request.

The massage deck is complemented by a dedicated yoga and meditation space. Yoga and pilates coaches can also be called in, allowing guests to devise their own health retreat programmes. Villa Sati, though smaller, provides similar amenities and comforts as well.

The location of Vajra Villas provides entertainment all by itself. Possibilities for exploring the most untouched and enchanting parts of Bali are many—on foot, by bicycle or by car. Driving or cycling uphill from Vajra Villas reveals a world of ancient villages, river views, rice fields, forests and moss-covered temples. It is as though the place is lost in time. While the paved road to Keliki is a circuitous one, a footpath along an open grassy ridge connects it directly to Ubud. The path first leads down to another temple founded by Rsi Markandeya, Pura Gunung Lebah. It is cared for by the Ubud royal family and sits at a river confluence, shaded by enormous banyan trees, and is worth a visit.

Just up the stone steps from the temple is Ubud's main road. The walk from Vajra Villas to Ubud takes just 30 minutes: long enough for a light workout, short enough for a quick shopping trip. Or if guests prefer, they can make a day trip by car to the city centre in Ubud to enjoy its excellent restaurants, lounge-bars and cultural performances.

ROOMS
Villa Vajra: 3 bedrooms (library may be converted into a fourth bedroom) • Villa Sati: 1 bedroom

FOOD
full-time chef • event catering • shopping service

DRINK
service by staff • self-catered

FEATURES
aviary • bicycling • chauffeur • DVDs • gym • gourmet kitchen • jacuzzi • library • pool • orchid garden • satellite TV

BUSINESS
translation and secretarial services upon request

NEARBY
Elephant Safari Park • Pura Pucak Payogan • Pura Gunung Lebah • Ubud city centre • rice fields • traditional villages • river rafting

CONTACT
Banjar Sebali, Desa Keliki, Tegalalang, Ubud, Gianyar 80571 •
telephone: +62.361.730 668 •
facsimile: +62.361.736 391 •
email: info@balihomes.com •
website: www.villavajra.com

ary's warung

...reminiscent of similarly refined spots in cosmopolitan cities around the world.

It is easy to find one's way to Ary's Warung since it occupies one of the most central and lively spots along the main road. Many come to dine on the cool terrace of Ubud's renowned restaurant, enjoy the tantalising food and take obligatory snapshots at the nearby temples.

Indeed, there is nothing at all average about an evening at this restaurant. Considering the many Balinese dining options available around the island, Ary's Warung is not for the feeble or undiscerning. It very strongly establishes its position as a leading restaurant with an uncompromising dedication to providing a truly memorable dining experience marked by quality and style. This is immediately obvious in the lower level, which is occupied by a lavish lounge that is reminiscent of similarly refined spots in cosmopolitan cities around the world. Wine and cigars are the order of the day in this retreat. The lounge is perfect for occasional luncheons and cocktail receptions, and its chic interior hints at the type of guest who will feel right at home here. The broad dining area on the upper floor includes an open verandah which benefits from the breeze that wafts by regularly.

Since its inception in 1986, Ary's Warung has been consistently drawing the crowds with its evolving and innovative menu. In fact, guests will find decision-making quite a challenge as the bold range of options calls for a little bit of everything. For this very reason,

THIS PAGE (FROM TOP): *The Zen minimalism of the décor at the bar is punctuated by its row of fur-lined bar stools; from the terrace-level dining room, guests can get a clear view of people at the bar.*
OPPOSITE (FROM TOP): *Tropical martinis tempt the palate; the dining environment achieves a fine balance of comfort and refinement.*

both the lunch and dinner menus comprise a four- and six-course tasting menu respectively, served in modest portions so that diners are free to enjoy a more varied encounter with the restaurant's signature tastes and flavours, though single dishes may be requested if any are particularly preferred.

A typical dining experience could include the full-bodied Chilled Seasonal Vegetable Soup, served with black rice bread croutons, followed by a dish of succulent Lobster Wontons or Coconut King Prawns served with sweet corn, black beans and avocado. Then, guests can expect a pleasant change of taste and tempo as a plate of classic Seared Sea Scallops, accompanied by juicy asparagus and green beans, is presented, or as a delightful serving of Steamed Zucchini Flowers with seafood and a pomelo salad arrives at the table.

The kitchen unfailingly lives up to its promise of only serving catch while it is still firm and fresh, and employs condiments largely to enhance the original flavour instead of overpowering it. Ary's Warung prides itself on the use of fresh, organic ingredients and choice meats, combined with inspired yet unpretentious preparation.

One of many popular dishes here is the Pork Belly 'Babi Guling' in spices, served with young coconut and banana flower

THIS PAGE: Cocktail time at the lounge-bar is one of the best ways to savour well-poured spirits while reviewing the day's adventures in Ubud.
OPPOSITE (CLOCKWISE FROM TOP): Some specialities of Ary's Warung; express service is a given; diners can enjoy the haute cuisine without having to be dressed up in haute couture.

lawar. A spiced baked apple rounds off this succulent dish. Another favourite is the Lamb Rack served with a clever combination of chilli mint sauce and sautéed *bok choy*. Also high on the list are the Roasted Veal Cutlets that come drizzled with just a touch of tangy wasabi butter and Lombok water spinach. The Grilled Salmon is served with spinach gnocchi and a kaffir lime leaf broth and the Slow Roasted Duck 'Betutu' is served with fern tips: both are as mouth-watering as they are joltingly creative.

For those who have a sweet tooth, Ary's Warung has a dessert menu that will leave them dizzy with joy. For guests with an experimental palate, the best of this selection is the Durian Brûlée, which has warmed the heart of a jaded food critic or two. The accompanying sesame seed wafers provide a refreshing contrast to the aromatic and strong flavour of the durian. In a similar manner, the rich Chocolate Ginger Kahlua Cream Tart, which comes with a mango

sauce, at once delights the chocoholic with its intense chocolate flavour and teases with a hint of ginger and a Kahlua rush. There are also concoctions such as Ary's Coconut Custard Pie and Fresh Mixed Berries with Champagne Jellies. These delicious, imaginative creations will please one's palate and leave one wondering about the geniuses at Ary's Warung who came up with these combinations.

As might be expected, the wine list does not disappoint either, and serves to complement the menu as far as possible. Ary's Warung has a wine cellar carrying about 160 noteworthy labels from around the world for guests to choose from, with an emphasis on

SEATS
140

FOOD
contemporary Balinese-Asian

DRINK
bar • wine cellar

FEATURES
innovative tasting menu • cigar lounge

NEARBY
Ubud city centre and market • Ubud's water garden

CONTACT
Jalan Raya Ubud, Gianyar 80571 •
telephone: +62.361.975 053 •
facsimile: +62.361.978 359 •
email: aryswarung@dekco.com •
website: www.dekco.com/aryswarung

French and Australian wines. There is also a selection of cocktails and Balinese beverages that promises to add a little kick to one's dining experience.

This restaurant has a positively upmarket vibe and no matter when guests choose to turn up, there is bound to be an exciting mix of people, either enjoying a romantic dinner, catching up with friends and family or simply having a couple of drinks before venturing out into Ubud's buzzing nightlife. In short, this is a centre for sophisticated wining and dining, and it is also quite clearly a leading light in Ubud's dining scene. Indeed, nothing less should be expected of Ary's Warung.

café des artistes

...an oasis of modern sophistication...

THIS PAGE: *Evenings at Café des Artistes are unexpectedly congenial, with art previews and good company.*
OPPOSITE (FROM TOP): *The salad is artistically presented, as befits the name of the café; paintings on the wall make good subjects of conversation.*

Ubud is becoming busy and noisy these days. Its main roads were once pleasant places to linger, perhaps to sip a cool drink or coffee while seated by the side of the street in a café or *warung*. An entire afternoon could be spent in this fashion, reading a newspaper, chatting with a companion or simply people watching. Now, one has to search for that sidewalk café experience. In Jalan Bisma, one's search will be rewarded at Café des Artistes.

The location is ideal: the café is on a quiet lane, yet remains close to the Ubud market and a host of other attractions. Comfortable wicker chairs and umbrella-shaded tables on the terrace provide exactly the vantage point a frequenter of sidewalk cafés demands. There is enough life on the street to amuse, but not enough to annoy. Most of the passing traffic is of the pedestrian variety, with an occasional bicycle or car, and they represent a fine cross-section of Ubud life: expatriates, artists, farmers and women ferrying offerings to the temples.

Whether one chooses to be seated at the sidewalk, inside, or be surrounded by fish ponds and fountains in the corner lounge, Café des Artistes is an excellent hangout in which to relax and sip a drink. But it is not easy to choose just a drink here: there is a good selection of wines from Australia, France, Italy and elsewhere, and in the evenings, a wide variety of cocktails, aperitifs and after-dinner drinks made using both local and international spirits are available.

Whatever one chooses, the attractions of Café des Artistes are unforgettable. Many travellers who have discovered it return again and again, and so do Ubud residents. It is busy every night and like any good European bistro-bar, many locals and expatriates have come to consider it their second home. A place that has regulars is an excellent choice to visit when one hopes to soak up the local atmosphere.

The idea that a sidewalk café would be rustic or shabby is totally wrong here. Café des Artistes is an oasis of modern sophistication, but one that has not abandoned the spirit of Bali. The atmosphere is relaxed and welcoming, like Bali itself. As its name implies, this is also a cultured café. The walls are hung with art by local and foreign artists, providing a convenient and constant change of décor. Should a work of art or a painting prove to be particularly appealing, one can even choose to bring it home—the works are all for sale. The public is also invited to art previews, which are congenial gatherings and a good way to meet Ubud residents and artists in temporary residence.

Café des Artistes was created by a Belgian, Rudy Kerremans, who came to Bali in 2001 and set up exactly the kind of place he himself would enjoy. The menu contains Indonesian

SEATS
indoor: 40 • outdoor: 20

FOOD
international, Indonesian and Belgian

DRINK
bar

FEATURES
Belgian beers • cigars • art exhibitions

NEARBY
Monkey Forest • Museum Puri Lukisan • Pura Gunung Lebar • Ubud city centre • cafés • galleries • hotels

CONTACT
Jalan Bisma 9X, Ubud, Gianyar 80571 •
telephone: +62.361.972 706 •
email: café_desartistes@hotmail.com •
website: www.cafedesartistesbali.com

and international food, and star dishes on this menu include perfectly grilled tenderloin steaks, the Grilled Prawns Salad and the Wok-Fried Crab. Dishes such as the Fetuccini Carbonara are excellent, with the pasta made daily in the kitchen. There is also an array of unusual but delicious Belgian dishes, a nod to Rudy's origins, that is sure to surprise and delight guests. Among them are the Carbonades a la Flamande (beef braised in brown beer) and a superb pear and blue cheese salad. The food helps to create a congenial atmosphere that reminds one of Belgium. And what would Belgian food be without real Belgian beer? Several varieties are served here.

lamak restaurant + bar

...a twist is put on everything, often with delightful results.

Lamak, which look like aprons of colourful leaves woven into graphic patterns, are temple hangings essential for decorating ritual offerings in Bali. They are rarely made these days, as most women prefer to buy them ready-made, woven from plastic straps or silkscreened on cheap polyester: a development that presents a strange twist on tradition, blurring the borders between art and kitsch, conservation and innovation.

Lamak Restaurant & Bar probably chose its name to reflect this poignant collision of tradition and modernism. The cuisine and the décor revere tradition, but a twist is put on everything, often with delightful results. The interiors, rich with visual puns, were concocted by the talented team led by Made Wijaya, Bali's beloved architect and master of tropical outré in-jokes. Made called on Indonesia's most celebrated steel sculptor, Pintor Sirait, to put heavy weight behind the light touches, in the form of punched-out steel panels and doors, repeating small *lamak* motifs on a gigantic scale. His steel bathroom doors, for example, look like industrial freezers, heavy as a house; but they swing effortlessly on hidden pivots, with red and green lights on the outside to indicate occupied and available cubicles. Made's haute kitsch touches are evident elsewhere too. Lavatory sink spouts drop from the ceiling, and nearby walls are adorned with numerous photographs of celebrities wearing Balinese ceremonial dress, such as one of Francis Ford Coppola, framed in baroque gilt plastic.

In décor and cuisine, Lamak is funky but very fashionable, and a bit tongue-in-cheek, like its sister restaurant Warung Enak on Pengosekan Road, also in Ubud, but more dressed-up and swanky. Above all, it is an artistic restaurant. Creative and literary types like to gather in the Lamak bar around sundown for chilli martinis or jumbo margaritas for two. Lamak sponsors the Ubud Readers' and Writers' Festival, and the writers and artists are faithful to their patrons, not only during the festival, when events are held here, but throughout the year. Teetotalling intellectuals shun the innovative cocktail menu and vast wine list, sipping Lamak's Ginger Lemongrass Lemonade instead.

THIS PAGE: *Behind the distinctive doors is an informal, friendly place for a good meal.*
OPPOSITE (FROM TOP): *The Cured Ocean Trout prepares the palate for more good food; the bar has the warm feel of a private club for close friends; the lamb comes highly recommended at Lamak.*

The cuisine here could never be upstaged by the dramatic décor or clientele, though. Female chef Ni Luh Sutini is a rare talent: she won four silver medallions and was the Best Chef in the ICA Culinary Challenge at the Sanur Village Festival 2007. She masters tradition, yet in keeping with the overall style of Lamak, puts a twist on it. Her Chicken Kiev stays firmly in Kiev, even while wrapped in wonton skins. Her crème brûlée is still brûlée but artfully touched with orange and ginger. The Balinese Bouillabaisse offers barbecued seafood in a starfruit, turmeric and lemongrass broth with chilli-sambal mayonnaise. With her expertise, Chef Ni Luh can and does take license to show off: her Ceviche of Opaka, fish marinated in coconut cream, lime juice, turmeric and capsicum, is a daring dish. Classics such as Carpaccio Beef (a dish of raw beef slices) reach the upper echelons of taste here; it is enhanced with a complex Gorgonzola cheese and hazelnut sauce. Simpler fare is excellent at Lamak too: the sandwiches, noodle dishes and soups are clever without abandoning that element of comfort one appreciates.

Four-course set menus showcase Chef Ni Luh's flair, and à la carte selections are individual essays of innovation. With the range of flavours and the relaxed Balinese atmosphere, it is hard not to dine 'family style' here, with all members of a dining party dipping into each other's choices. In fact, it is encouraged. Extra plates are enthusiastically provided.

SEATS
outdoor: 78 • air-conditioned lounge: 22 • courtyard: 16 • lobby lounge: 16

FOOD
innovative Asian and international light fusion

DRINK
bar

FEATURES
air-conditioned lounge • courtyard seating • extensive wine cellar • party and wedding services

NEARBY
Ubud city centre • Ubud market • Monkey Forest • cultural performances • shopping

CONTACT
Monkey Forest Road, Ubud, Gianyar 80571 •
telephone: +62.361.974 668 •
facsimile: +62.361.973 482 •
email: info@lamakbali.com •
website: www.lamakbali.com

mozaic

...be prepared for delightful surprises at the table.

Mozaic is a place of pilgrimage for serious connoisseurs of fine food, and for some, it is the main reason they came to Bali in the first place. Rave reviews have poured in from around the world, and Mozaic was recently granted membership in the prestigious French culinary fraternity, Les Grandes Tables du Monde.

The very idea was slightly mad: to establish an ambitious restaurant gastronomique outside an artsy hill town on the Island of Bali. The mind behind this folly was Chris Salans, Mozaic's chef-owner, who is certainly a bit mad himself: mad about food, impassioned about flavours and fanatic about quality—and it shows in every dish. Chef Chris rarely leaves his kitchen, except to accept accolades from diners who beg his presence at their table. He is dedicated, in the time-honoured tradition of the world's greatest chefs.

Also in that tradition, he loves to share his love of food. In 2007, Chef Chris opened the Miele-sponsored Mozaic Workshop, a culinary school that is more than a teaching kitchen: it is an inspiring upscale environment for learning, exchanging ideas with visiting chefs and for dining. That passion for fine food contines further still with Mozaic's exclusive catering department. The dedicated Mozaic events team provides conceptualising, décor and menu planning services, and of course, delectable cuisine, beautifully presented and served.

Describing the style of Mozaic's menu presents a quandary. On a Cordon Bleu-pedigree of classic French, modern French and fusion haute cuisine, add a wealth of unusual Indonesian ingredients, a splash of eccentricity, then garnish it with audacious showmanship: that is the Mozaic style. To dine here is not a meal but an experience. Book well in advance, allocate at least two hours, and be prepared for delightful surprises at the table.

Diners may choose from three-course set menus or six-course tasting menus, both with a dazzling array of ingredients that requires self-restraint and pacing during the meal. A three-course menu on any given day could include rare ingredients such as Wagyu beef, ginger flower, rock lobster, *kluwek*, foie gras, Mangu Mountain blackcurrant and milk-fed baby lamb.

But Mozaic is not for serious foodies only; novices to fine dining are welcome too. The pricing here reflects the fact that this is Bali, and those accustomed to dining at exclusive restaurants in the world's capitals will be stunned by how small their bill is. At the same time, the service and atmosphere here are completely without pretensions. There is no dress code, and tables are set simply in a classic Balinese garden. Those who have never experienced haute cuisine can comfortably enjoy their first taste of serious gastronomic artistry here.

THIS PAGE: *Foie gras with cherry sauce is a favourite among guests at Mozaic.*
OPPOSITE (CLOCKWISE FROM TOP): *One of the signature appetisers; Chef Chris hard at work; dining in the garden combines fine cuisine with the green, tropical richness of Bali.*

SEATS
indoor: 60 • outdoor: 60 • private dining: 14 indoor, 14 outdoor • cooking classes for up to 24

FOOD
French, international and Balinese haute gastronomie

DRINK
lounge

FEATURES
cooking classes • catering services

NEARBY
Neka Art Museum • Ubud city centre • Sayan ridge

CONTACT
Jalan Raya Sanggingan, Ubud, Gianyar 80571 •
telephone/facsimile: +62.361.975 768 •
email: info@mozaic-bali.com •
website: www.mozaic-bali.com

warung enak bali

...a range of subtle, strong, tangy and always interesting flavours...

THIS PAGE: *Large groups can be accommodated easily here.*
OPPOSITE (FROM TOP): *Cool down with a frozen margarita; the bar has a comfortable, inviting atmosphere; a popular main course.*

It used to be that only brave travellers could sample the authentic regional cooking of Indonesia. The best 'real' local food was found only in roadside food stalls called *warung*. To try these specialities meant venturing into places where plates get washed in a bucket and restrooms rarely exist. Now there is Warung Enak Bali, where signature dishes of the archipelago can be enjoyed in a restful, comfortable setting. The place is run by the people behind Ubud's celebrated Lamak Restaurant & Bar, with its artistic direction overseen by the maestro of retro-tropical funky style, Made Wijaya.

The ambience of the place is entertaining and amusing at the same time. It is impossible not to smile the minute one enters Warung Enak Bali. This place may call itself a *warung*, but it is really a cutting-edge restaurant-cum-bistro and bar, created by international food and design experts. The décor is both witty and comfortable, with bold colours colliding in a gleeful mix. It is all done with brilliant balance though, and meticulously maintained throughout. The bar, fashioned of stainless steel, frames vintage Indonesian advertising posters that add a quirky touch. Wrought iron lamps in Dutch colonial style in the dining area, painted white with coloured glass shades, complete the retro look. This is postmodern tropical style with Balinese touches. It makes a perfect backdrop for a private celebration and has a zany edge that never fails to surprise and delight.

Diners can take a gastronomic voyage through the Indonesian archipelago without leaving their electric-blue enamelled rattan chairs. The development of the menu involved travel to some of the most exotic corners of the country to bring back the best recipes. As a result, Chef Rai Adnyani offers specialities that are not easily found elsewhere in Bali. Alongside classic rice and noodle dishes are culinary rarities from Sumatra, Manado,

Kalimantan, and even West Papua. Dishes that hail from these travels include *Woku Blanga Cakal Putri* from Manado, which is a fish dish of poached trevally in a spiced herbal broth of lemon grass, ginger, chilli, *pandan* and Kaffir lime leaf; and *Pangek Sapi* from Sumatra, a spicy beef stew with sweet basil leaves, served with steamed rice and wing beans. Desserts such as *Kue Pepe* from Betawi (layered tapioca cake) and *Kue Lumpur* from Kalimantan (sultana and young coconut pancake) complete the culinary adventure.

Curious epicures might also try the Balinese *Sate Sakul*, a dish of marinated snails with sweet soya sauce, ginger, chilli, Kaffir lime leaf and rice cakes. Larger gatherings might seek the Rijsttafel ('rice table' in Dutch), an elaborate meal of Indonesian dishes, served with steamed rice, that includes curried meat, fish, vegetables and side dishes—as many as 40 dishes might be served. To prepare all the dishes in Warung Enak Bali, Chef Rai uses over 60 herbs and spices, as well as by an array of lesser known nuts and regional legumes, to achieve a range of subtle, strong, tangy and always interesting flavours.

Dining spaces are spread over several levels, gardens and terraces, promising a variety of experiences and encouraging first-timers to revisit. Couples will enjoy the courtyard, while families might prefer the upper floor, which overlooks the rice fields. And the bar is just the place to order a locally produced *arak* (palm wine), infused with cinnamon and star anise.

SEATS
ground level indoor: 26 • courtyard: 16 • bar: 8 • upper level indoor: 16 • terrace *bale*: 26 • open terrace: 12

FOOD
authentic regional Indonesian

DRINK
bar

FEATURES
cooking classes • courtyard dining • rice field views

NEARBY
Monkey Forest • Ubud city centre • dance performances • shopping

CONTACT
Pengosekan Road,
Ubud, Gianyar 80571 •
telephone: +62.361.972 911 •
facsimile: +62.361.972 922 •
email: info@warungenakbali.com •
website: www.warungenakbali.com

gaya fusion

...a fusion of East and West, modern and ancient, art and technology.

Near Ubud, on the main road through Sayan, drivers slow down to gape at a striking building in the form of an upended ship, poised on a ziggurat-like base of stone and glass. This is the home of Gaya Fusion, an establishment that is more than the sum of its parts.

Gaya is indeed a fusion of artistic endeavours that combines traditional and modern trends while crossing disparate cultural milieux. Within its dynamic field are an art gallery, restaurant, ceramics studio, cluster of villas, web developer, network of creative people, and live manifestations of art in many forms. Gaya is a multidimensional art-and-life concept and, with all of its diverse elements and spin-offs, it is not easy to describe with only a few words.

The Gaya concept was born when an innovative engineer of ultra-sophisticated engines came to Ubud from Italy. Stefano Grandi came across a Balinese entrepreneur, Nyoman Birit, and together they envisioned the creation of an enterprise that would be a fusion of East and West, modern and ancient, art and technology. Eventually, they went on to build Gaya as a catalyst of creativity and contemporary culture that is as international as Bali itself.

Gaya's flagship building in Bali holds a vast and dramatic exhibition space, with a stylish restaurant and bar upstairs. This building is set in a modern garden landscape, which often becomes an exhibition space itself. Gaya Art Space, the gallery and formal exhibition area,

THIS PAGE: *The attention-grabbing landmark that is Gaya Fusion.*

OPPOSITE (FROM TOP): *Gaya Restaurant's offerings are at once delicious and original; the villa's interior has a traditional Indonesian thatched roof, marble floors as in many Italian homes, and a pool in true Balinese villa style.*

is recognised as the leading contemporary art venue in Indonesia. It has hosted groundbreaking exhibitions, art installations, multimedia events and exciting opening parties, which never fail to draw Bali's most interesting and prominent residents together in one place. Artists such as Made Wianta, Krisna Murti, Heri Dono and Dadang Christanto—all of whom have represented Indonesia at the Venice Biennale—have exhibited here. In fact, many artists started here, holding shows that later drew widespread attention, allowing them to break into the international art market. News of the latest art shows and offerings are available in *Gaya Art News*. It covers Gaya's exhibitions

and lists openings at other places around Bali, as well as overseas exhibitions of work by Gaya artists. Events and film schedules are included, along with intelligent critiques of art works and exhibitions and creative writing. *Gaya Art News* is also available on Gaya's website.

Gaya Art Space also hosts weekly art film nights, showcasing some of the best and most challenging cinematic creations of the past century. But younger ones are catered for as well. Sundays are set aside for children's art programmes, with top local artists leading the children in the exploration of art using paint, paper and clay. Parents invariably have brunch at the Gaya Restaurant upstairs while their progeny express their creativity freely below.

Dining at Gaya Restaurant is an artistic experience as well. The menu showcases a large number of original dishes, all prepared by the Italy-trained chef who fuses Mediterranean cuisine with Asian ones creatively, using flavours in the same way an artist would use colours

THIS PAGE: The shared swimming pool is set in a restful garden that invites guests to sink into artistic contemplation.

OPPOSITE (CLOCKWISE FROM TOP): The sunken bathtub in the first villa; a large art installation fires the imagination of observers; the 35-m-long (38-yd-long) bamboo zeppelin is just one of the many ways in which Gaya Art Space surprises.

on his palette. Freshly picked herbs accent the dishes, and favourites include the freshly caught local fish and grass-fed Australian beef, flown in daily. The delicious homemade Italian breads, pastas and desserts are also certain to please both adults and children. Overall, the food is light and tasty: a good approach for a tropical climate, where heavy-handed sauces seem burdensome and their flavours a little too dominant.

Behind the main building is a group of villas, initially built for visiting artists but they now offer respite for all kinds of travellers, thinkers, creators and friends of Gaya Fusion. An option for people who want more than sightseeing on a visit to Ubud, the three villas merge art, life and nature in subtle ways. All have large glass doors that face the gardens to provide guests with views of greenery, and all offer the essentials of luxurious villa living, such as air-conditioning, resort-style service and designer bathrooms. The architecture is also an expression of Gaya's 'fusion' concept, bringing together high-end Italian design and Balinese traditions in surprising unity. One of the most obvious examples of this fusion is the combination of polished marble floors below and thatched *alang-alang* roofs above.

The first villa opens towards the shared swimming pool and its bathroom has a sunken stone bathtub overlooking a tropical garden. The second one enjoys a semi-private garden and its bedroom has a mezzanine with a bed for the kids, or a third guest staying over, perhaps a friend who has celebrated heartily at one of Gaya's widely anticipated openings. The third

villa is the most romantic, set at the far end of the property in a forest with a creek running past and a Japanese-style bedroom and stone shower chamber. Its distance from the other two villas provides more than enough privacy for guests. But there is no fear of boredom or isolation.

Down the road from the main building is Gaya Ceramic, a studio creating ceramic tableware and accessories for home use, and organic surfaces for interiors. Ceramic and stoneware sculptures are on display as well. Slightly further along is the interior showroom, where Gaya designers display a variety of materials and objects for the home, fusing art and function in innovative ways. Textiles and woven pieces are the highlights here, alongside the ceramics. There are off-the-shelf creations, but custom work for resorts, design houses and private clients is a forte as well. In fact, Gaya counts big names such as Armani Casa and Bulgari Resorts among their clients.

Spin-offs from the Gaya Fusion concept include interior design, graphic design and web development. These are areas where Gaya Fusion's role as an incubator of artists has been invaluable. As supporters of Balinese and Indonesian art, all proceeds from Gaya are reinvested into its art enterprise and its artists. Lovers of contemporary Indonesian art will find much to appreciate here.

PRODUCTS
fine art • dining • ceramics • design • accommodation

FEATURES
Gaya Art Space: art exhibitions and cultural events •
Gaya Ceramic and Design: ceramic decorations, homeware, sculptures and design consultancy •
Gaya Villas: 3 one-bedroom villas •
Gaya Art News • Ubud shuttle • web development • wireless Internet access

FOOD
Gaya Restaurant: Mediterranean-Asian fusion

DRINK
bar in Gaya Restaurant

NEARBY
Ayung River • Ubud city centre • cafés • restaurants • shopping

CONTACT
Jalan Raya Sayan,
Ubud, Gianyar 80571 •
telephone: +62.361.979 252 •
facsimile: +62.361.975 895 •
email: gaya@gayafusion.com •
website: www.gayafusion.com

macan tidur

...there is nothing sleepy about this multifaceted enterprise.

Macan Tidur means 'sleeping tiger' in Indonesian. The name must be a misnomer because there is nothing sleepy about this multifaceted enterprise. Macan Tidur is best known for its Ubud gallery on Monkey Forest Road. In 1996, when it opened, it was only the second antique shop in Ubud, and it has been delighting a discerning clientele ever since. It occupies two adjacent spaces, the larger inside a remarkable three-storey building that looks like a Bali-style haunted house. This is the main gallery, showing fine tribal and antique textiles, weaponry, jewellery and ethnographica. Interior designers have been known to squeal with delight upon seeing the quality of the collections displayed here, and they never walk out without a cartload of objets d'art and textile pieces.

It takes a keen eye to select works of art such as these and to display them with such sensitivity and panache. The secret is that this 'tiger' has three 'eyes'; Macan Tidur is a collaboration between an American art historian, an Italian Renaissance man and a Balinese prince who is also an architect. The diversity of talents behind this enterprise is its strength. The main gallery is only the beginning. Beside it is a smaller shop with a different approach. If one

THIS PAGE (FROM TOP): *An antique copper dye vat juxtaposed with rice barn panels from the Torajan highlands of Sulawesi; a Dayak guardian figure stands out against the minimalist backdrop of a bark collage.*

OPPOSITE (FROM LEFT): *The array of objects and textiles shown in Macan Tidur's Ubud gallery creates a changing visual feast; this 19th-century Balinese guardian figure is among the many artefacts on display.*

sees the main gallery as a 'museum', as some people do, then this is its 'museum shop'. Inside are changing collections of indigenous art, including quality crafts and contemporary textiles that are easy on the pocket and small enough to fit in a suitcase. Although new, the objects displayed have an authentic connection to Indonesian culture as the owners are devoted supporters and scholars of indigenous traditions.

Macan Tidur currently also sells fine artefacts and ancient jewellery in the boutiques of the three Amanresorts hotels in Bali, but it has more to offer. Its third retail space, in Seminyak, opens in May 2008, and it will be a place where collectors and connoisseurs can consider Macan Tidur's substantial collection in comfort. Minimalist and metropolitan, it aims to be a contrast to the quirkiness of the Ubud venues. The gallery will be divided into two distinct spaces around a central sculpture garden, with a rotating collection of artefacts in front. At the back, there will be special, themed exhibitions that challenge the eye and engage the mind.

Beyond the sculpture garden is the main office of Macan Tidur and its international sourcing agency, Sumaru Sourcing. For over a decade, the Sumaru team has been assisting clients and interior designers to select and acquire works of art, antiques, custom architectural elements, furniture and accessories in Southeast Asia. Their clients' homes regularly appear in *Architectural Digest* and other leading design magazines.

PRODUCTS
ancient jewellery • antique textiles • ceramics • ethnographica • indigenous art • tribal art • weapons

FEATURES
Sumaru Sourcing • custom furniture

NEARBY
Ubud city centre • Ubud Palace • Ubud market • Seminyak beach (Seminyak gallery) • boutiques • cafés • restaurants

CONTACT
No. 10 Monkey Forest Road, Ubud, Gianyar 80571 •
telephone: +62.361.977 121 •
Jalan Lesmana 17, Seminyak Beach, Seminyak, Badung 80361 •
telephone: +62.361.733 875 •
email: toko@macantidur.com •
website: www.macantidurbali.com

toko antique

...shoppers with a discerning and sophisticated eye recognise Ubud as a collector's hub...

THIS PAGE: Antiques and artefacts from many cultures and periods that will catch the eye of admirers and buyers.

OPPOSITE (CLOCKWISE FROM TOP): A mask portraying a Balinese man in a headdress; small sculptures, such as these antique kris handles, are a unique buy; the gallery is a cornucopia of Balinese artwork.

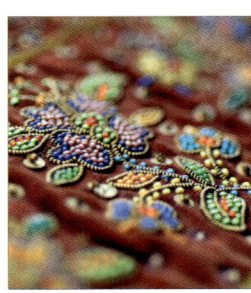

The loose conglomeration of museums, artist studios and art galleries in the Ubud area have earned this destination a lively reputation with culture-seekers and those that appreciate Balinese art. Even the more modestly entrepreneurial art collectors are known to routinely fund their Bali sojourn by picking up a few local pieces (paintings, carvings, sculptures or batik) here at a bargain and selling them for a significant profit when they return home.

Antique shoppers with a discerning and sophisticated eye recognise Ubud as a collector's hub too. It is a haven where must-have indigenous arts and crafts can be found hawked along the streets and at sidewalk stalls. For the avid collector visiting Bali for the first time though, negotiating a path through the sheer range of potential acquisitions can prove overwhelming. This is where a gallery like Toko Antique, located along Ubud's main street, comes into play.

Launched in August 2003, this member of the arts scene—run by the same group behind Treasures and Toko East—is an informative and spacious gallery housing a wide collection of artwork from Indonesia's various regions and historical eras. Indeed, shoppers dropping by the gallery will find that the general quality of available pieces remains impressive, and the array of stone, wood and terracotta statues, Chinese Indonesian ceramics, textiles, antique puppets, teak products, architectural remnants, lacquerware and many other items make for an afternoon of thoroughly engrossing and educational browsing. The artworks for sale are often tagged with helpful notes on their background (regional origins, material and age/period) along with other useful information. To further assist buyers, whether they be

millionaires, collectors new to the Indonesian arts scene, shoppers looking for something to dress up their homes, or tourists simply souvenir hunting, Toko Antique provides a selection of choices that will fit every need and budget. The staff are always approachable and ready to listen and suggest something suitable.

Of particular interest are the intricately woven fabrics and textiles from around the Indonesian archipelago, which would make perfect wall features, and the traditional masks and puppets that will surely add colour to a living room. Other highlights include ceremonial objects such as holy water containers with repoussé designs featuring local motifs, tools and objects from life in ancient Indonesia, such as bronze and stone oil lamps, carved axes, rice plow handles, and jewellery such as gold hair combs, hair pins and belt buckles.

Unlike some of the less established bargain outposts in the area, Toko Antique handles air and land deliveries with reassuring professionalism. This is indeed a point of convenience holiday-makers will whole-heartedly appreciate. Shoppers are safe in the knowledge that their painstakingly chosen purchases will soon take a place of honour in their homes.

PRODUCTS
antiques • artworks and artefacts • textiles • jewellery • lacquerware • masks • puppets • sculpture • stoneware • woodwork

FEATURES
overseas delivery

NEARBY
Ubud city centre • lounge-bars • cafés • restaurants • shops

CONTACT
Jalan Raya Ubud,
Ubud, Gianyar 80571 •
telephone: +62.361.975 979 •
facsimile: +62.361.978 359 •
email: tokoantique@dekco.com •
website: www.dekco.com

treasures

...tastefully balanced with delicate metalwork and intricate designs.

THIS PAGE: **Step into a world where old and new jewellery designs are harmoniously combined together.**
OPPOSITE: **Fine filigree and chain-making are some of the techniques used to create these objects of unsurpassed beauty.**

Treasures specialises in exquisite handmade jewellery, all of which feature intricate designs, expertly created from 18–22K gold, which is rich in cultural significance. What makes this store stand out from the rest is its marriage of traditional Balinese goldsmith techniques with the artistic visions and talents of a select group of enterprising designers.

This dynamic collaboration of traditional techniques and innovative designers works well since the old practices of crafting jewellery tended to place a heavy emphasis on breaking new ground as well, through inventive techniques, the materials used, the objects represented and the moods or subject matter addressed. The result is a wide range of original and one-of-a-kind jewellery that is as much a work of fine art as it is an exclusive accessory.

The collection at Treasures, though unique in style and personality, finds common ground in influences such as nature, mythology, the animal kingdom, tribal symbolism and ancient cultures. These modes of inspiration eventually materialise in the shape of wearable and distinct jewellery made with raw gold or fine silver and set with precious or semi-precious stones, treading a fine balance between creativity and tradition. A wide variety of gems are used and many retain natural characteristics that are best described as captivatingly brazen and earthy. They are tastefully balanced with delicate metalwork and intricate designs.

Carolyn Tyler, one of Treasures' in-house designers, enjoys using antiquated goldsmith techniques such as granulation, filigree and repoussé to give her creations a look which is evocative of eras long gone. Unlike other jewellers, she prefers using 'offbeat' gems rather than flawless stones as she believes that gems, like people, gain their character or 'spirit' through their imperfections. Fellow in-house designer Penny Berton has dedicated herself to work on creations that celebrate femininity. Her fascination with the representation of pagan goddesses in history inspired the 'Gifts of the Goddess' collection. This stunning range of jewellery brings together ancient Chinese, Balinese and Western mythologies and have found expression in a number of innovative styles.

A third designer, Jean Francois, breathes new life into the ancient practice of body adornment with his unique collection of tribal-inspired jewellery. He artfully combines unusual and often asymmetrical elements of diverse origin to create unique pieces. Other than these three, two new designers at Treasures to check out are Tricia Kim and Lyn Fenwick. Tricia's designs are a blend of Eastern and Western styles, while Lyn focuses on classic designs that use tourmalines and Indonesian pearls to create memorable pieces of wearable art.

PRODUCTS
innovative handmade designer jewellery using precious and semi-precious stones

FEATURES
certified products • international delivery • in-house designers • varied collections

NEARBY
Ubud city centre • cafés • restaurants • shops

CONTACT
Jalan Raya Ubud, Ubud, Gianyar 80571 •
telephone: +62.361.976 697 •
facsimile: +62.361.978 359 •
email: treasures@dekco.com •
website: www.dekco.com/treasures/home.asp

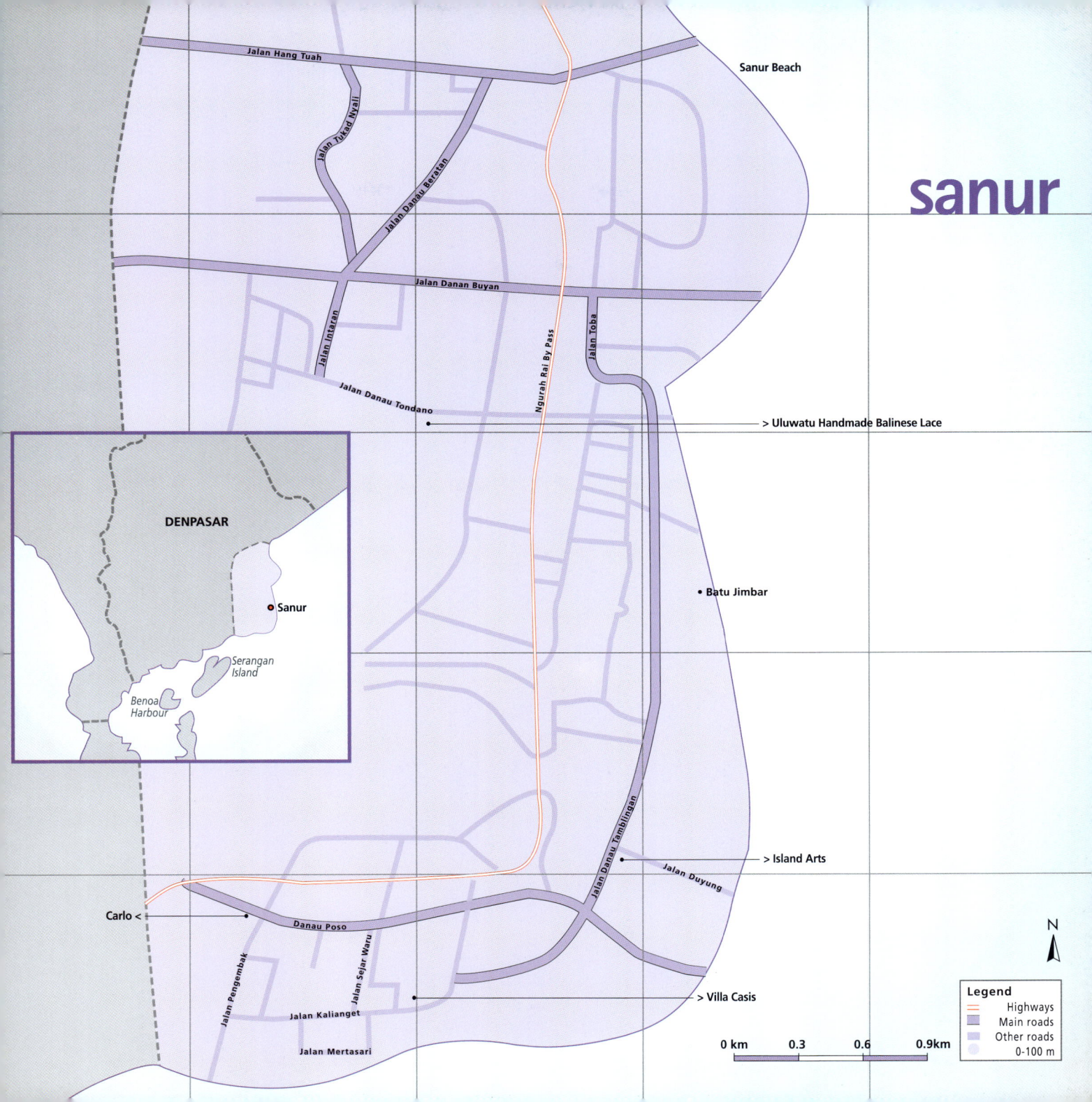

the dignified side of the south

Bali wags refer to Sanur pejoratively as 'Snore'. Yes, it is a bit sleepy, but in the best possible way. From a Sanur point of view, Kuta, Legian and Seminyak are overdone—there is some rivalry here. While the Bukit Peninsula enjoys its real estate boom and the Kuta coast resounds to the booming bass of its nightlife, Sanur stays slightly smug, and for good reasons. It is a liveable, genteel alternative to Bali's more revved-up hot spots.

Sanur has its history to thank for that. For at least a millennium it has been an enclave of the *brahmana*, Bali's priestly caste. Their homes, called *geria*, are bastions of tradition, centres of learning and spiritual power-generating plants. During the 20th century, as Sanur became a magnet for Western eccentrics and elites, and a tourism hub, it somehow managed to retain its gentility, intelligence and tradition. Perhaps the *brahmana* dynasties have been at work behind the scenes, and so have a vast array of foreign artists, intellectuals and glamourous beings who chose Sanur as their base on the island of Bali.

a sleepy beach town for elite dreamers

Sanur was one of Bali's first tourist areas. By the 1930s it had already become a private paradise for a handful of expatriates and artists living in simple beach bungalows. Belgian Impressionist painter Adrien le Mayeur de Merprès arrived in 1932 and built an elegant Balinese-style house, which still stands just north of the Grand Bali Beach hotel. Le Mayeur immersed himself in the local culture and married a famous Balinese dancer in 1935. Most foreign figures in Sanur at this time were culturally and intellectually focused, setting the tone of the town. Among them were skilled photographer Dr Jack Mershon and his anthropologist wife Katherine, who wrote *Seven Plus Seven*, a detailed account of Balinese rituals. Katherine also helped painter Walter Spies choreograph the *kecak* dance, which is now a favourite spectacle for tourists. Other early Baliphiles in Sanur were writer Vicki Baum, author of *A Tale of Bali*, anthropologist Jane Belo, who wrote *Trance in Bali*, and seminal art

PAGE 114: *Sanur beach is sheltered by an offshore reef, which makes it safe, tranquil and charming, and a popular choice for families with small children.*

THIS PAGE: *Young women take part in a procession to welcome their gods during a temple festival, wearing golden perada cloth and cempaka flowers of beaten gold in their hair.*

OPPOSITE: *Fishing nets have been a common sight in Sanur for centuries. Now they are joined by volleyball nets set up in front of the town's beach resorts.*

connoisseurs Hans and Rolf Neuhaus, who opened an art shop in Sanur in 1935 to sell Balinese art and antiques to moneyed travellers.

These early Baliphiles hosted a steady stream of celebrity visitors during the 1930s, including Charlie Chaplin, Barbara Hutton, Doris Duke and British diplomat and writer Sir Harold Nicholson. Their travel tales, photographs and souvenirs spread the word about Bali to the cultural and social elite of Europe and America. Thus, Sanur was seminal in shaping the world's understanding of the island.

the 1960s, sanur style

During World War II, some diehard expatriates stayed on Sanur's shores and waited for the unsettled years that followed to pass. In 1963, Indonesia's first president, who was half Balinese, used Japanese war reparation funds to build the Grand Bali Beach hotel in Sanur. It is still Bali's tallest building, but not among its most attractive. Nevertheless, it signalled a new era of development for Sanur and heralded Bali's future as a global tourism destination.

In the 1960s, a new generation of travellers discovered Sanur. Among them was Australian painter Donald Friend. This larger-than-life character arrived in 1966 and settled in Sanur. By then, Indonesian architect Wija Waworuntu had already established a charming cottage hotel on the beach, called Tandjung Sari, which became a base for Donald and for the beautiful people who started flocking to Sanur's social scene.

Wija's bungalow homestay was jam-packed with Indonesian antiques and artefacts: old furniture, carvings, terracotta products, bronzes, textiles and Balinese paintings. When Donald met Wija and fell head over heels for his beautiful Indonesian antiques and bric-a-brac, the now famous 'Bali style' of eclectically cluttered interior decoration was the inevitable outcome. Again, Sanur played a seminal role. Donald, Wija and others who shared their distinctive aesthetic expanded the empire of elegance around Tandjung Sari. Donald built a remarkable Bali-style house and studio, Wija added important elements to the hotel, and both enlarged their social circle. Tandjung Sari still stands today as a testament to their understanding of and sensitivity to local aesthetics, conditions and culture. The charms of Tandjung Sari are indelible and any visit to Sanur should include a stop here for a drink, or a week of drinking, on this fabled patch of beachfront land.

batu jimbar, sanur's epicentre of elegance

By 1970, Bali had an international airport, with Pan Am Clippers delivering travellers in increasing numbers. Sanur continued to attract the most well-heeled among them. Professionals, intellectuals and bons vivants from America, Europe, Australia and Singapore made a beeline for Sanur. Social life for this set revolved around the bars of Tandjung Sari and La Taverna Hotel (still operating today). As favoured party pads, Donald and Wija's houses enchanted their cultured guests. Soon, they all wanted their own bits of beachfront on which to build. As Sanur pundit Made Wijaya puts it, 'The tenor of Sanur was still low-key and discreet...but the foreigner enclave along the beach was quickly becoming an island within an island...'

With this urgent impetus spurring them on, Donald, Wija and Sri Lanka-born architect Geoffrey Bawa embarked on a historic, and sometimes strained, collaboration

THIS PAGE: *The 'Bali style' of architecture and interior design was born on the shores of Sanur at Tandjung Sari, which is rich in antiques and traditional materials.*

OPPOSITE (FROM TOP): *Mature gardens invite exploration and exude a dignified calm that is distinctly Balinese; man-made creations and nature blend effortlessly here.*

that firmly established Sanur as an epicentre of elegance and taste. Together they created Batu Jimbar Estate, a residential community of 15 plots, each fronting the beach. The complex included a private museum, a visitors' centre and an open-air theatre for performances by its resident Balinese troupe of dancers and musicians. It was like a 'bohemian grove' for the creative and crazy characters of Sanur to gather in. It still is, but Batu Jimbar's lofty social spires cannot be scaled by outsiders, and the place is adamantly private. Don't even think of showing up to gawk. One is better off perusing the plethora of coffee-table books on Balinese architecture and garden design, which are filled with photos of Batu Jimbar properties. Travellers can get a taste of this at Tandjung Sari and La Taverna Hotel too, and in any number of Sanur's excellent villas and resorts.

The charming style established at Batu Jimbar is recognisably Balinese, with local materials and indigenous architectural elements. Separate living pavilions are arranged within extravagant but meticulously designed gardens surrounding a central pool. Buildings and landscapes are generously spiced-up with whimsical local artefacts and antiques. This idiom, stated eloquently by Donald, Wija and Geoffrey, has influenced tropical home design for half a century, and still does. Australian architects Peter Muller and Kerry Hill, and design doyennes Linda Garland and Made Wijaya, spread the style throughout Bali and beyond, even to the Mustique home of David Bowie. Singapore, Shanghai, Hawaii, Belize, Costa Rica and other far-flung places now boast Bali-style mansions and resorts. Yet, few champions of the craze know of its humble roots in Batu Jimbar.

a private paradise for the beautiful people

One man who definitely knows the significance of Batu Jimbar is Sanur's sardonic scribe, the aforementioned landscape architect Made Wijaya. An Australian who has been residing in Bali for almost 35 years, Made has documented the Sanur social scene with pithy remarks in his newspaper and magazine columns, and still does. His

infamous column appears now in the free magazine Hello Bali!, which is available throughout the island, and has been immortalised in his book and website, both called Stranger in Paradise. Made's privileged position as the darling designer to Bali's social stars has put him at the centre of all the action for decades. Through the 1980s and 1990s, Made recorded the zeitgeist as the Sanur social scene boomed. Rich and famous figures flocked to Sanur for the August season, while the cultured core, including Made, stayed all year, slaving away in their ateliers. Many were artists, artisans, designers and writers who built arts-based businesses over the years. They welcomed celebrities in style, and still do. Over the past two decades, the guest books of Sanur's private homes have been signed by the likes of David Bowie, the Duke of Bedford, the Duchess of York, Elizabeth Taylor, Sean Lennon, John Galliano, Julia Roberts and the Agnellis—Italian jet-setting heirs to the Fiat fortune.

THIS PAGE: *A lush, tropical garden designed by Made Wijaya reflects his flamboyant and charming character.*

OPPOSITE (FROM TOP): *Batu Jimbar Estate, an elegant private home, blends Balinese architecture with Western standards of comfort; a painting of Batu Jimbar Estate seen from the beach, by Donald Friend, an early foreign settler in Sanur and seminal influence on its development.*

THIS PAGE: *The style of new properties popping up in Sanur proves that the town can be completely up-to-date without sacrificing its dignity and exclusivity, as seen here at Villa Cassis.*

OPPOSITE: *Local men enjoy tranquil moments angling on the reefs, especially at sunrise and sunset, when the air is cool and the winds are calm.*

sanur today savours yesterday's flavour

Sanur has certainly developed tremendously since the first foreigners settled here in the 1930s. It has developed, yes, but with a spirit and sensitivity often lacking elsewhere on the island. Property analysts call it 'mature' and refer to it as 'the Belgravia of Bali', and as in Belgravia, there is not a lot to see on the street.

Sanur is very private, with personal paradises and consular residences hidden behind high stone walls. In recent years there has been an increase in construction activity. Though much of what has cropped up is modern and urban in feeling, the underlying dignity of Sanur, for now at least, remains unaffected.

The main street of Sanur is broad and shady, with local traffic passing at a sedate pace. The roads are in good condition and the town's sidewalks do not have the gaping holes encountered elsewhere in Bali. Chic boutiques and some fine restaurants are appearing in the more built-up areas, but somehow everything maintains a deeply Balinese flavour. Big hotels, such as the Bali Hyatt, are set far back from the street and surrounded by acres of lush greenery. The Grand Bali Beach hotel, too, is hardly noticeable, despite its height, and its golf course has an unpretentious, provincial feel, making it a good place for a relaxed round without too much pressure from designer-clad handicap snobs.

Parts of Sanur started out as small fishing villages and retain a funky feeling, with brightly painted outriggers lined up on the sand and sun-scorched men in bamboo dome-shaped hats wading out onto the reef to cast a line. Its sheltering reef makes Sanur's beach safe and shallow. It is protected from the big surf, but at low tide there is hardly enough water to reach one's knees. The beachfront footpath is ideal for a leisurely evening stroll, with views to the mountains of east Bali and the island of Nusa Penida. Facing east, the beach is also a popular spot at which to watch the sun rise. Though tourists on family holidays sunning themselves on the warm golden sand with newspapers spread over their faces are a common sight, that all-encompassing quiet of Sanur never leaves.

...that all-encompassing quiet of Sanur never leaves.

villa casis

...the look of the villa changes with the time of day...

Here is a villa that is not only sleek and stylish, but also very intelligent. So is its website, which looks stylish enough to be linked to *Wallpaper* magazine. The site includes sophisticated features such as direct booking, a link to satellite views of the property and, not often seen on the websites of holiday resorts, actual architectural plans and perspective drawings of the house. Needless to say, these drawings are priceless tools to have while planning a holiday with friends or family. It is beneficial to know in advance how the spaces of a holiday villa are configured to avoid surprises on arrival or jealousy over who gets which room. Not many places are able to offer this level of information to their prospective guests.

Villa Casis is hidden along a shady lane, a short stroll from Sanur beach. It has become a landmark in this sedate seaside town, thanks to the startling look of its façade—a fine example of high-end, tropical minimalist design. This villa is dressed to impress and it certainly looks as though it was dressed by a master of minimalism such as Helmut Lang or Jill Sander.

There is a twist though, in the midst of this avant-garde design. The front door is not just a door, but the gaping mouth of a Balinese giant. The entire portico is a carved reproduction of the entrance to Goa Gajah, the 'elephant cave', an ancient landmark temple near Ubud. A huge antique gong is used instead of a doorbell, completing the mood. Such bold yet intelligent design details are characteristic of Villa Casis. While a minimalist style can look stark and unfinished, that is not the case here. Instead, the blank canvas of minimalism in this place is relieved with touches of Balinese culture, warm lighting, a sprinkling of antiques and generous splashes of hot colours such as crimson red.

THIS PAGE: *Gardens, terraces and interiors are composed of separate yet interlocking spaces so guests can mingle whenever they wish.*
OPPOSITE (FROM TOP): *The pool becomes a shimmering plane at night, visually expanding the courtyard garden; a library-cum-office offers seclusion for reading or work.*

The residence comprises four separate buildings accommodating up to 12 guests in six bedrooms. A clever division of space creates variety and privacy, and makes the compound seem even larger than it is. Togetherness is lovely, but separate spaces are also important in a villa shared with friends or family. This one is designed to provide both. All bedrooms and communal spaces are set back from the street, leaving them peaceful throughout the day. Upstairs, the bedrooms face different directions, with private sundecks providing guests with views over Sanur. The swinging hammocks on these decks invite guests to indulge in a nap, or even take some time off by themselves, during a shared holiday.

An ingenious integration of private and communal zones allows accommodation to be rented on a whole-villa basis or by the room without sacrificing the well-being of guests. The property's Balinese architect worked hard to incorporate many distinct areas in the plan so that rooms and functional spaces were secluded from each other, while remaining integral to the overall design. Spatial planning is not the whole story, though. The architect also studied feng shui and incorporated its principles into the design and decoration of the villa. Sunlight, wind, water, materials and the flow of energies are all taken into consideration. With conscious use of colour and light, the look of the villa changes with the time of day. The atmosphere changes seamlessly from afternoon into evening, washed in the glow of lights hidden in the landscaping.

The six bedrooms mix modernity with antique furniture and accents. Ground-floor rooms have open-air bathrooms with terrazzo bathtubs and gardens. First-floor rooms each benefit from a massage shower, and all rooms come with goose-down pillows, quality Egyptian cotton linens and aromatic, locally made toiletries.

The residence boasts two complete reception rooms, and a dining room large enough to seat 12. It is also fully air-conditioned, and this makes it particularly comfortable in the hot and wet seasons. Lounging in the large open-air poolside pavilion is another all-weather benefit. It features unique oval lounge beds with crisp, white cotton upholstery: each bed is big enough to fit two persons. The 70-sq m (753-sq ft) private pool is flanked by timber decks and has a soaring water-wall from which soothing sounds of water emanate, one of the de rigueur features of modern Balinese villas.

As expected, this villa has all the modern conveniences, not to mention a cosy library-retreat room over the garage, with novels in several languages, guidebooks and maps. Call it a base camp for planning expeditions, organising business affairs or cramming for exams. It is also an ideal place for a quiet chat into the night with friends.

Villa Casis is a full-service residence with 10 staff and a maid's sleeping room above the kitchen. This means that guests' needs at any time of day or night can be attended to, whether it be a bandage, a pizza or an appointment at the best beauty salon in Sanur. A kitchen team provides complete breakfasts daily and will also prepare lunch and dinner from a diverse menu or according to requests. Just about anything not already in the villa can be arranged as well:

THIS PAGE: *The multitude of terraces and open pavilions allow guests to enjoy the outdoors in comfort.*
OPPOSITE (CLOCKWISE FROM TOP): *The façade makes a striking statement from the street; the air-conditioned dining room is an excellent option during the hot and rainy seasons; bedrooms are restful and feature Indonesian accents.*

catering for parties, massage and spa treatments, tour arrangements, babysitters and dry-cleaning. The 24-hour security and maintenance staff keep things running smoothly.

Villa Casis is well-situated as a base for those who wish to explore the rest of Bali. The nightlife and chic shopping of Seminyak are accessible by express roads, as is Bali's cultural centre, Ubud. Sanur itself is pleasant and many shops, resorts and restaurants are within walking distance, or a short metred taxi ride away. Only 200 m (218 yd) from the villa is Sanur beach, with 7 km (4 miles) of boardwalk along the shore for a leisurely stroll or jog. Water sports from scuba diving to water-skiing, jet-skiing, surfing, kite-surfing and parasailing are offered. There are also plenty of beachside cafés and rental loungers for the lazy who prefer to people-watch. Outrigger fishing boats line the shore, colourfully painted according to local traditions, providing an attractive background for photographs.

Condé Nast Traveler has declared Villa Casis one of 'the best villas to rent in Bali'. With its intelligent approach to villa design and management, its ideal location and the staff's attention to detail, it should continue to live up to this reputation.

ROOMS
4 bedrooms with king-size beds •
2 twin bedrooms

FOOD
chef • delivery from restaurants

DRINK
wet bar • cocktail or dinner parties

FEATURES
cable TV • chauffeur • DVDs • library • pool • spa • two-car garage

BUSINESS
business services • high-speed Internet access

NEARBY
Sanur beach • cafés • lounge-bars • nightclubs • shopping • restaurants • jet-skiing • kite-surfing • parasailing • scuba diving • surfing • water-skiing

CONTACT
No. 3 Jalan Mertasari, Sanur, Denpasar 80238 •
telephone: +62.361.270 521 •
facsimile: +62.361.270 540 •
email: mail@villacasis.com •
website: www.villacasis.com

carlo

Every piece is meticulously crafted and surface finishes are flawless.

THIS PAGE (FROM TOP): *Stylish yet unobtrusive pieces accentuate the modern home best; neutral colours and simplicity of design enhance the style.*
OPPOSITE: *The Atauro Collection uses wood and shell finishes—this dining set could end up drawing more attention than the food on the table.*

In the 1970s, a handful of curious and artistic professionals arrived in Bali and stayed. Some of them eventually found themselves running successful businesses, blending their creativity with the abundant skills and inspiration they found in Bali. Among them are local legends such as the irrepressible pundit Made Wijaya, fashion designer Milo Migliavacca, jewellery creators Jean-François Fichot and John Hardy, and the grand dame of bamboo and interiors, Linda Garland.

Add to this list Carlo Pessina. An art director, he left Italy for Bali in 1979 to pursue a love affair. His love soon expanded to embrace all of Bali—its magical atmosphere, and the charms and skills of its people. He ventured into a totally different career as a furniture designer and found his niche as a result. What was meant to be a brief escape from the pressures of city life became the career of a lifetime for Carlo.

Carlo's success began in the 1980s when he experimented with Indonesian weaving traditions to create innovative soft furnishings to complement contemporary furniture. This led to a fortuitous collaboration with the design team hired to refurbish suites at the Grand Hyatt Singapore. Carlo found the typical materials used in tropical hotel furniture unexciting and decided that there had to be something more gorgeous than varnished wood and rattan. Challenged, he felt compelled to discover it, and he succeeded. The result was a collection of furnishings using a previously unheard-of finishing material: coconut shell. Carlo devised ways to 'clothe' furniture, accessories and architectural elements with this simple, natural material. Coconuts were crushed and reassembled, or cut in thin slices and laid out like a mosaic of fur. At the same time, he employed the natural brown and cream tones of the coconut to create

visual patterns and surface textures, and to accent the lines of modern furnishings in innnovative ways. The design world caught on quickly. Decorators, developers, designers and elite home owners quickly appeared to snap up Carlo's work. Imitators soon turned up too, but Carlo stayed several steps ahead. Breaking away from coconut shell, he experimented with other exotic natural materials: mother-of-pearl, palm fibre, tree bark, seashell, pebbles and terrazzo. At the same time, Carlo maintained a maniacal devotion to quality. Nothing has ever left his production facility in Bali without meeting the most rigorous standards of perfection.

    A visit to Carlo's showroom in Sanur confirms this. Every piece is meticulously crafted and surface finishes are flawless. Natural materials used to cover casework, seating, tables and accessories are clearly chosen only after painstaking sorting and sifting. There is no other way to reach the level of consistency in colour and texture which Carlo achieves. Constituent elements are also of top quality. Exacting standards are equally applied to hardware, handles, underlayers of wood and even the insides of drawers and cupboards.

THIS PAGE (CLOCKWISE FROM TOP LEFT): *The Morotai three-leg table makes an amusing statement against the Karimata cabinet; the Damar cabinet looks like a box bound with leather strips; the Penida two-door cabinet resembles a heavy brick column, a monolithic contrast to the curvy Nias side table.*

OPPOSITE (CLOCKWISE FROM TOP): *Both furniture and furnishings complement each other; pebbles are not the most unusual material Carlo uses; the Penida pieces have a modern, clean look.*

Until recently, the Sanur showroom was only open to the trade. International designers and hotel buyers would come by to select pieces and collaborate with Carlo in creating new designs and ways of using his signature materials and techniques. His work can be seen in the most exclusive hotels and resorts, including Amankila and Grand Hyatt Erawan. A number of Aman resorts, Ritz-Carltons, Oberois, GHM Properties, Hiltons, a Begawan Giri and Four Seasons resorts and city hotels around the world also feature Carlo's work.

Word soon got out about Carlo's showroom and soon homeowners and connoisseurs of fine design began to drop in for a look. In 2003, it was opened to the public and it is now a must-visit. With its use of unusual materials, Carlo's design philosophy suits those who value a clever and witty re-interpretation of the natural world in their interior décor. In fact, Carlo is becoming one of the most popular sources of unique, high-quality pieces. Furniture and other accessories can also be ordered at the showroom for delivery in Bali or internationally.

The range of Carlo's work is broad and expanding constantly. Core collections are named after lesser-known islands of Indonesia and each includes furniture and complementary accessories. Carlo's website shows them well and is worth a visit. In addition to his main furnishing lines, Carlo creates customised work in collaboration with individuals, design firms

PRODUCTS
modern furniture and home accessories

FEATURES
architectural elements • custom work • design collaborations

NEARBY
Sanur beach • traditional markets • Seminyak beach • Pura Petitenget • cafés • restaurants • shops

CONTACT
No. 22 Jalan Danau Poso, Sanur, Denpasar 80228 •
telephone: +62.361.285 211 •
facsimile: +62.361.281 923 •
email: info@carloshowroom.com •
website: carloshowroom.com

and architects. His design work is particularly noteworthy, and the Sanur showroom hints at his capabilities in integrating his work with architectural elements: terrazzo with glimmering brass shavings coats a free-form stair railing; wall panels appear to be woven of frozen twists of bark; and screens visually bristle with palm-fibre while remaining smooth to the touch.

The materials used in Carlo's workshops are applied to an endless range of places, forms and surfaces. An amusing example of this inventiveness is a pair of small dumbbells. Covered in coconut shell and trimmed with mother-of-pearl, they are not just exercise equipment, but can be displayed as splendid bathroom accessories or luxe paperweights. Shoppers will find that the price tag on these dumbbells, as on most of Carlo's pieces, is far from prohibitive. Aside from custom work, his furniture, accessories and gifts are reasonably priced, so shoppers can approach his showrooms without trepidation.

island arts

...an extensive collection of art and artefacts...from many different cultures...

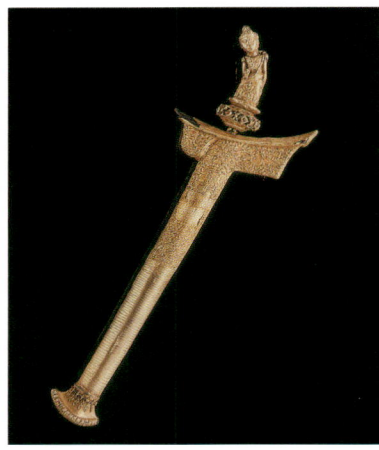

THIS PAGE (FROM TOP): A classical Hindu-Buddhist gold pectoral plate found in the Tanimbar Archipelago; an archaic gold royal kris from the courts of south Sulawesi; a Balinese temple decoration, made of old bronze coins.

OPPOSITE (FROM TOP): An exquisite north Balinese dance mask representing a princess; the showroom of Island Arts; a pair of Palace Loro Blonyo wedding figures, central Java.

For serious art lovers and collectors visiting Bali and looking for the best, Island Arts is an essential destination. Its delightful office-showroom complex is hidden away down a quiet lane in the historic village of Sanur, which has been Bali's premier centre for art and antiques since 1938, when a pair of German brothers opened an art gallery catering to early tourists. Like their illustrious predecessors, Island Arts features an extensive collection of art and artefacts in a wide variety of media from many different cultures throughout Indonesia and beyond.

That, however, is only one aspect of the business. Island Arts is not simply a private gallery; it is also a professional art consulting firm, providing a broad range of services to individual collectors, corporations, museums, scholars, art historians and interior designers. In addition to expert advice, the principals and team offer appraisals, authentication, research, restoration and museum-quality mounting for both artwork and artefacts.

They are an experienced sourcing and shipping team as well. The capable and charming Balinese managing director, Ni Luh Sukreni Asih, thrives on the challenge of seeking out work from some of the best artisans and manufacturers across Indonesia, and commissioning custom designs from them when needed. The owners and operators of numerous international five-star resorts (Four Seasons Hotels & Resorts, Amanresorts and Bulgari Hotels & Resorts) and even palaces have long relied on Island Arts for its services.

Island Arts is the brainchild of Bruce Carpenter, a passionate Indonesian art expert who has been active in the field for over two decades. A colourful figure and master storyteller, he perceives his role as that of a facilitator introducing others to the beauty and nuances of Indonesian art. However, it seems that serving as a consultant for major auction houses, museums and development projects is not enough to keep him busy. He is also a noted author, having written and co-written many books and articles on Indonesian art and culture. Among them are monographs on famous foreign artists who worked in Bali, including W. O. J. Nieuwenkamp, the first Western artist to work on the island and Willem Hofker, the paramount painter of Balinese scenes in the

1930s. Bruce's latest work is *Batak Sculpture*, a major work on the subject co-authored with a German expert on the extraordinary art of this renowned tribal group from northern Sumatra. His interest and knowledge also extend to Indonesian contemporary art, including the early Balinese Modernist School, which emerged in the 1930s.

Remarkably, with all of these activities, Bruce still manages to welcome clients to Island Arts personally, regaling them with tales of adventure, as well as the stories behind the objects he sells. And what a range it is. From tiny, precious, ancient jewellery to megaliths weighing up to eight tonnes, the ever-changing collection has many strengths. Among them are tribal sculptures, weaponry, textiles, porcelain, as well as art from the Dutch colonial era, including paintings, books, drawings, etchings and furniture. Contemporary artists are also represented by Island Arts, who often arrange commissioned works on a client's behalf. One can make a purchase with the assurance that the items here are genuine, but they are advised to call in advance; the gallery operates on a strict appointment-only policy.

PRODUCTS
accessories • furniture • Indonesian and Southeast Asian antique sculptures • paintings • statuary • jewellery • textiles • weapons • porcelain • furniture and objets d'art

FEATURES
art consulting and sales • art appraisal • restoration and mounting • sourcing and shipping • custom work

NEARBY
Sanur beach • Batu Jimbar Estate • cafés • restaurants • villas • resorts

CONTACT
Jalan Duyung Gang 1/3X, Sanur, Denpasar 80288 •
telephone: +62.361.285 713/281 690 • facsimile: +62.361.287 042 •
email: brucar@indo.net.id

uluwatu handmade balinese lace

...this boutique lace-maker uses a technique internationally known as cutwork...

THIS PAGE (FROM TOP): *Fine, ornate lacework is the speciality at this establishment; the detailing on the lace tops showcases the quality that one can expect from their products.*
OPPOSITE: *A white lace blouse is perfect for a dressy look, especially in a cool cotton fabric to ensure the wearer's comfort in tropical weather.*

Modern style, outstanding workmanship, a traditional spirit and classic comfort: these qualities are but the tip of the iceberg when contemplating the various reasons why Uluwatu Handmade Balinese Lace remains so popular with residents and visitors to the island.

A home-grown garment manufacturer with its own retail chain, this boutique lace-maker uses a technique internationally known as cutwork, or *krawang* in Bahasa Indonesia. As with most authentic Balinese crafts, Uluwatu's cutwork is still made the traditional way with foot-powered machines, which many consider relics of a bygone era.

When talented Balinese women learnt their skills in lacework back in the 1930s, they mastered techniques which were quickly disappearing around the world. The technique, used by Uluwatu, involves stretching the fabric over a bamboo hoop, placing it under the needle of a sewing machine, and then moving the hoop back and forth with expert precision. This technique allows thread to build layer upon layer to form a smooth satin finish along the edges and on pre-sketched patterns in the fabric, and the 'holes' created are then carefully cut out with sharp scissors. Lovely, delicate lace is made this way by a dedicated craftsperson who sees the entire process from beginning to end. The result is a labour of love and a work of art. Just one item can take five or more days to complete.

In comparison, lace made from an electric machine is generally less durable because the even weave produced is not as interlocked. As a result, a single, broken thread can cause a whole section to unravel. Handmade lace, however, is more lasting. Though not as even, it is also considered special simply because the buyer is aware of the time and effort put into creating such pieces.

Established in the early 1980s, Uluwatu is the brainchild of Made Jati, a 17-year-old girl from Kuta who became fascinated with the brightly coloured lacewear favoured by the era's surfer girls. The fledgling company took its name from the legendary temple Pura Luhur Uluwatu, located on a cliff above the Indian Ocean, an area that was swiftly gaining international renown as a surfer's paradise. The temple is also of personal significance because Made's family counts among the thousands that make the pilgrimage there annually to mark the temple's anniversary.

As it often happens with fashion, however, the colourful and fun surfer girl look lost its mass appeal in the mid-1980s. Uluwatu then turned its attention to creating new and contemporary designs, backed by an unwavering focus on using quality fabrics and traditional craftsmanship.

Thus prompted by circumstance, Made embraced a more mature vision for her company and boldly realigned the business to take on the boutique market. Uluwatu launched a new range of ladies' fashion and accessories, including a line of clothing (as well as nightwear), sashes, bags, bedlinen, table linen, hair

THIS PAGE: *When using a foot-powered machine, as Uluwatu does, the needle stays put while the craftsperson uses his or her hands to move the bamboo hoop back and forth.*

OPPOSITE (FROM TOP): *The lace designs remind one of the beauty and magic of Bali; bedlinens are especially popular with shoppers.*

bands, scarves and more, targeted at the sophisticated woman. The success of Uluwatu's current crop of dainty and elegant products—achieved by highlighting the intricacy of home-grown Balinese garments and reviving traditional methods of production—have allowed Made to engage with the global business landscape on her own terms.

The ancient Uluwatu site continues to inspire the whole company, however, by symbolising its dedication to upholding local heritage. Two of Made's sisters have joined her in this growing enterprise, and they continue to channel the unique talents of older Balinese craftspeople into creating lovely additions to the Uluwatu line. The company has also trained close to 300 staff who are dedicated to their craft, and painstakingly embroider, cut, wash, iron and pack the lace products for shipping at Uluwatu's informal factory in Tabanan, west of Denpasar. The price for maintaining such high levels of quality, however, is a low volume of production every year. This makes it difficult for the company to commit supplies to department stores, but also gives each item produced an almost exclusive quality. Those who put on an Uluwatu garment know that they are wearing a unique work of art.

The modest, down-to-earth luxury of an Uluwatu piece—whether a dress, blouse or pair of trousers—is immediately visible to the knowledgeable shopper. Dresses and tops are elegant and fashionable, and can be matched with accessories such as bags and scarves, also available from Uluwatu. Most items come in in three colours—black, white or cream—but to meet growing demands, Uluwatu is working on expanding the line to include other colours. The latest range also includes resort attire and casual wear perfect for use during one's stay in tropical Bali. Light fabrics such as rayon, cotton and linen ensure that the wearer remains cool and comfortable. At the same time, Uluwatu's line of table and bedlinen mean that shoppers can look forward to adorning their homes with its fine lace pieces too.

In a culture where children develop their artistic aptitude at their parents' knees and through observing the village craftspeople, musicians and artists at work every day, Uluwatu is not just helping to keep a key Balinese artform alive, but also showcasing it in the international market. The bulk of each batch produced is marked for retail outlets, while just under half heads overseas for wholesale dealers. An online catalogue is also available for armchair shoppers.

Each new wave of visitors to the island discovers that fine Uluwatu lace serves as both a unique memento that attests to Bali's rich cultural heritage, and as an intricate and impressive work of art that stands up to the stringent tests of time. This makes pieces from Uluwatu Handmade Balinese Lace so much more than just a souvenir.

PRODUCTS
lace clothing • accessories • bedlinen • table linen

FEATURES
handmade Balinese lace created using traditional methods

NEARBY
beaches • restaurants • resorts

CONTACT
No. 59 Jalan Danau Tondano, Sanur, Denpasar 80288 • telephone: +62.361. 287 638 • facsimile: +62.361.287 054 • email: info@uluwatu.co.id • website: www.uluwatu.co.id

BRANCHES
Bali Collection & Grand Hyatt Bali, Nusa Dua • Jalan Raya Legian, Kuta (two boutiques) • Jalan Pantai Kuta • Jalan Bakung Sari, Kuta • Jalan Danau Tamblingan, Sanur • Jalan Monkey Forest, Ubud • Jalan Laksmana (to open early 2008)

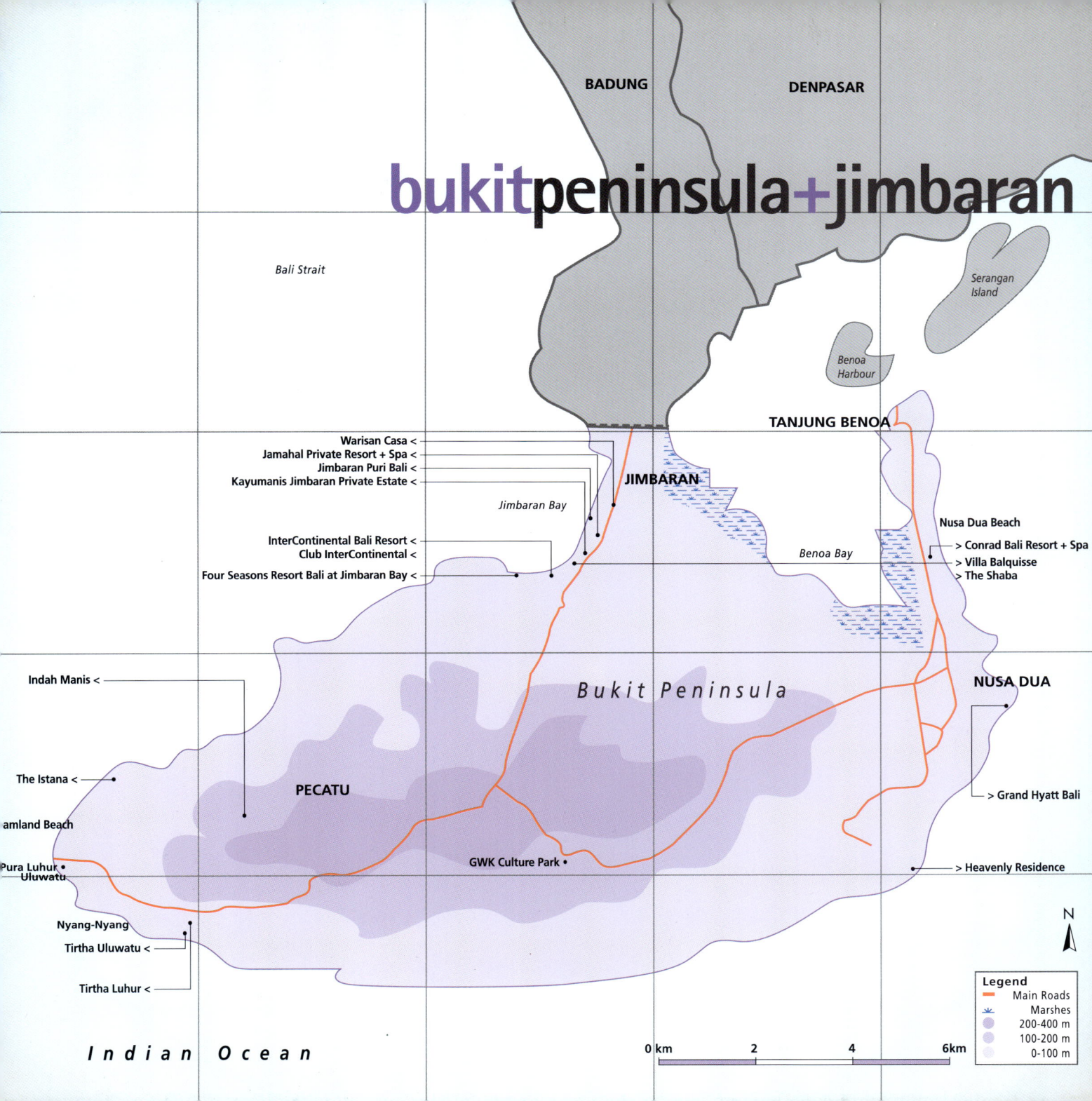

an island unto itself

At the southern tip of Bali lies the Bukit Peninsula, a doorknob-shaped piece of land with the highest concentration of luxury hotels and homes on the island. It looks a bit odd on the map, as if it were appended to Bali as an afterthought. Surprisingly, there is some truth to that. It is fair to say that the Bukit Peninsula is a part of Bali only by sheer coincidence. While the main island is volcanic, with rich soil, the Bukit Peninsula is an arid limestone plateau, like the offshore islands of Nusa Penida, Lembongan and Ceningan, to which it is geologically related. Luckily for Bukit dwellers and beach-loving tourists, this big chunk of limestone rising up to 200 m (656 ft) above sea level happens to be connected to Bali, but only by a narrow isthmus of sand and mangrove swamps.

The Bukit Peninsula is a bit sunnier than the rest of Bali, with whiter sands and clearer waters than those found elsewhere on the island. This makes it ideal for tropical beach tourism. If it weren't for tourism, the southernmost tip of Bali would have remained a bleak landscape with few inhabitants; just goats nibbling on sparse foliage on the hillside, and a few fishing settlements dotting the coast. That was the way it was until the 1980s.

As the Balinese of Kuta and Denpasar tell it, the Bukit Peninsula was, for centuries, a kind of unguarded penal colony. People who had been ostracised for one reason or another from their community were simply sent to the Bukit to eke out a living. These people were referred to as *anak buangan*, or 'thrown away people', and the area had a reputation for being full of tough characters who were best avoided. Theirs was a harsh lot because water is scarce on limestone plateaus and so is soil. Later, the tables were turned when tourism arrived, and today even a small patch of barren land on the Bukit Peninsula is worth a fortune. It is no wonder with the area's superb views, pristine beaches, dramatic cliffs and excellent surf. What was once a living hell for Balinese outcasts is now a slice of heaven for wealthy homeowners and real estate developers.

PAGE 138: A fishing net and its shadow make graphic patterns against the hull of a boat on Jimbaran Bay.

THIS PAGE: The Bukit Peninsula's offshore reefs swarm with fish. The waters here are fresh and clear, fed by currents from the Indian Ocean and the Lombok Strait.

OPPOSITE: The first tourists to discover the Bukit Peninsula were intrepid surfers, who came by motorbike or outrigger from Kuta in search of the perfect wave.

a safe harbour for some exciting activities on water

On the northeast corner of the Bukit Peninsula is a finger of land called Tanjung Benoa, which has supported a community of fishermen and sailors for centuries. It has a softer and more civilised feeling than the rocky hilltops nearby. A shady lane runs down the middle of Tanjung Benoa, with luxury beach resorts on one side and good restaurants and shops on the other. The road ends at the sleepy harbour of Benoa, a fascinating multicultural community with a Bugis traders' quarter, a scarlet-and-gold Chinese temple, and brightly painted Balinese outriggers lining the shore nearby. On the water, wooden pinisi schooners and tour boats bob alongside a few luxury yachts.

Water sports on Benoa beach are many and varied; hotels and independent operators offer banana boats, glass-bottom boats, dolphin tours, fishing, parasailing, wake-boarding, water-skiing, knee-boarding, kite-surfing and snorkelling. The latest innovation is called the 'flyfish', which is a floating bed that is dragged behind a speedboat and flies up in the air, promising more thrills and better views than a banana boat.

two little islands gave nusa dua a big name

Where the finger of Tanjung Benoa joins the Bukit Peninsula, two small bits of rocky land jut out into the sea, only barely attached to the beach by sandbars. To the Balinese they are considered islands, not peninsulas. It was these two rocky points which gave the entire Nusa Dua area its name: *nusa* means 'island' in Balinese and *dua* means 'two'. This was the locale chosen for Bali's first large-scale planned tourism development, completed in 1986 under the auspices of the national government. It was created to launch Bali with full force into the global tourism market and to provide convention facilities that could host high-level meetings and big events. Despite the ups and downs of tourism in Bali, Nusa Dua has gone from strength to strength since it first opened its gates 20 years ago.

The Nusa Dua complex is a green oasis of mature trees and well-tended gardens, filled with water features and an incredible range of facilities. Its collection of top-draw beach resorts includes a Grand Hyatt, a Hilton, a Club Med and two Starwood properties; big names which have continuously invested in expansions and improvements, despite the rollercoaster ride the tourism industry has endured in recent years. The area also has a big convention centre, a handful of nice restaurants and a recently relaunched open-air shopping centre with familiar names such as Starbucks, Surfer Girl and Sogo department store, alongside locally owned boutiques and cafés.

For people who cannot lie still on a lounge chair, the beaches of Nusa Dua are loaded with every possible water sport, and some seemingly impossible ones, such as kite-surfing. There is also a purpose-built centre for lawn bowling and lawn tennis, and even a giant tethered helium balloon for a bird's eye view of the whole area. The championship course of the Bali Golf and Country Club sits at the southern edge of the main Nusa Dua complex, flanked by several luxurious boutique hotels, including the Amanusa and a modern minimalist gem, The Balé. Also nearby is the Nikko Bali Resort & Spa, which has one of the most amazing lagoon pools in Asia.

With so many rooms, villas and shopping and sporting attractions, one might think the beaches here would be chock-a-block with sunbathers bickering over the best lounger, but this is not so. The beach is expansive and much of it is still quite peaceful. Some stretches are deserted but for Balinese seaweed farmers tending to their plants. In other places, rocky outcroppings punctuate the sandy shoreline, pounded by raging surf during storms and surmounted by picturesque stone temples.

THIS PAGE: *The beaches of Nusa Dua and Benoa offer a myriad of possibilities for the adventurous, including paragliding and kite-surfing.*
OPPOSITE: *The Bali Golf and Country Club at Nusa Dua was named one of Asia's top five courses by* Fortune *magazine.*

...a definitive statement of über-luxury on a clifftop...

trancers and toffs on the clifftops

Once past the Nikko Bali Resort & Spa, the road from Nusa Dua narrows and almost vanishes into the rugged limestone hills. Beyond this point the landscape is savannah-like and even a bit wild. The coastal scenery is dramatic, with high cliffs towering above the sea, offering unlimited views in all directions. Below them lie secluded white-sand beaches known only to a few. The whole southern shoreline and hills of the Bukit Peninsula are only sparsely developed, but that is changing quickly.

A few luxury villa complexes are already complete and open for business, or for sale as private residences. Many more are planned, including a Banyan Tree resort and residences, and numerous others, all with jaw-dropping views, envelope-pushing architecture, fabulous facilities and prices to match. Access to all of this prime real estate is by rambling roads, increasing the feeling of remoteness and exclusivity. At the end of one of these roads is the new Bulgari Resort, a definitive statement of über-luxury on a clifftop, with a funicular railway taking guests down to a splendid beach below. When it first opened, the railway had not been finished, so guests were shuttled down to the sand by helicopter. Clearly nothing is too much for the VIP guests of this resort.

A little further west is Nyang-Nyang Estate, a place that is even more spectacular, if that is possible. What makes it special has nothing to do with luxury, it has to do with legend. Nyang-Nyang was originally conceived as a private estate, with an enormous lawn and water gardens set on a cliff above the sea. Overlooking the grounds were several small villas and, at the cliff's edge, a stone swimming pool and an open-air dining and party pavilion. Below the estate lies the longest, cleanest and most inaccessible beach in Bali. A little Balinese wooden gate by the Nyang-Nyang party pavilion opens onto a treacherous, twisting stairway to the beach: ideal for those who have the thigh muscles to make it down and back up again without collapsing. Nyang-Nyang is absolutely magical. In the late 1990s, it became the open-air rave haven for an ecstatic generation of global party people. Parties there were legendary

THIS PAGE: *Villas on the Bukit Peninsula are known for their style and discreet service.*

OPPOSITE: *The new Bulgari Resort on a clifftop near Nyang-Nyang best expresses the luxury and privacy for which this area is now famous.*

and are still talked about in excited tones by those who experienced them. These parties were known for their fantastic outdoor sound systems and world-famous DJs who sent techno trance vibrations spilling across the lawns and pavilions of Nyang-Nyang Estate, over the moonlit sea and out to the cosmos. No one who was there will ever forget the harmonious mix of humanity that would come together under a full moon at Nyang-Nyang to dance with glee until the sun rose. It was a magical moment in rave history.

Another kind of craziness first put the rugged coastline of the Bukit Peninsula on the map—surfing. Moving west from Nyang-Nyang, one soon arrives at the hallowed bit of land called Uluwatu. The name itself is almost a mantra in the surfing world. There is a live webcam set up to beam the action at Uluwatu to the world and to spare surfers the trip out there if the waves are too flat or too horrifically huge on any given day. Above the legendary surf break, one of Bali's most sacred temples juts out from a cliff towards the open sky. This is Pura Luhur Uluwatu, founded by a 17th-century Hindu super priest who achieved moksha, or divine liberation of the soul, on that very spot. Without a doubt there is plenty of power at Uluwatu—wave power and spiritual power. It is a dramatic location and definitely worth seeing during a trip to Bali. But don't agitate the monkeys.

waking up in dreamland

The northwest-facing coast of the Bukit Peninsula has its own famous beaches and surf breaks. Dreamland is the best-known among them and is popular with expatriates and both domestic and international tourists. It is little more than a swathe of white sand facing a shallow, rocky reef that can make swimming rather tricky. It does have a certain vibe, though, and that is why people keep coming back. The real vibe is the surfer vibe, lending the beach a laid-back atmosphere.

All of this is about to change, however. The vast tract of empty land above Dreamland is being turned into a massive multifaceted development by Tommy Suharto,

THIS PAGE: *The beaches and reefs near Uluwatu are famous around the world for big waves and bold surfers.*
OPPOSITE (FROM LEFT): *A lone* kul-kul *pavilion at Pura Luhur Uluwatu houses a large wooden gong made from a single log. It is struck during religious ceremonies to call the community to the temple; the Uluwatu temple complex perches on a cliff high above the sea and is one of Bali's most sacred sites.*

the son of the ousted second president of Indonesia. It used to be called Pecatu Indah but has been poetically rechristened New Kuta. Phase one of the infrastructure was in place in the late 1990s, complete with wide boulevards lined with palm trees, leading to roundabouts with ornate Balinese sculptures of gargantuan proportions. When Tommy was jailed for his involvement in some dubious gunplay, the Pecatu project was put on the backburner. During the ensuing years, scavengers made off with the palm trees, the curbstones, the lighting and everything else that could be carted away. The whole Dreamland area went back to the surfers and sybaritic beach bums who loved it most.

That era is ending already, with major resort groups such as Raffles and Starwood stepping up to the Pecatu plate and a new plan by Tommy's development company. The scheme includes resorts, residences, retirement homes, apartment blocks, shopping centres, medical facilities, the biggest private nightclub in Southeast Asia and an 18-hole

golf course. Nine of the New Kuta golf holes have already opened. The dream is over for the generation of surfers and Bali-lovers who treasured Dreamland beach. It remains to be seen how the New Kuta development will pan out, but the calibre of investors becoming involved suggests optimism, or even excitement, could be in order.

The land above and around New Kuta is known as Bukit Jimbaran and was, until recently, primarily a white limestone quarry. Now, it is prime real estate for private homes. The highest hillsides have splendid views taking in almost all of Bali, from east to west, and the volcanos of Java on a clear day. Also on Bukit Jimbaran is the main campus of Udayana University, Bali's largest educational institution. Not far from the campus is an extraordinary place that is worth visiting, simply for its strangeness. It is the GWK Cultural Park, a government project intended as a cultural theme park for Bali. Partly built and partly opened, the highlight of GWK is a giant sculpture that is partly finished. This colossal work-in-progress is to be one of the largest metal statues

ABOVE: *Dreamland beach is as scenic as it is surf-worthy, especially at dawn and dusk, when the volcanos of Bali are visible in the distance from the headlands.*

OPPOSITE: *A whimsical road sign gives directions not only to local breaks, but also to famous surf spots around the world.*

in the world, standing 150 m (492 ft) tall on top of an 11-storey shopping and tourism complex. So far only the torso and head of the statue have been cast and are displayed prominently in the park as its focal point. The large amphitheatre here does host some spectacular performances, though.

a fishing village that is both local and chic

The softest side of the Bukit Peninsula is Jimbaran Bay, with its swaying coconut palms, golden-sand beaches and sophisticated resorts and restaurants. Jimbaran was once a poor fishing village, but it has slowly and steadily grown into one of the most desirable and charming towns in Bali. Here, fishermen still set out every evening in colourful *jukung*, a unique Balinese-style outrigger. The village's traditional market is an interesting place to visit simply to observe the daily activities of the locals, though the village itself is not especially scenic.

The beach at Jimbaran is pleasant, with gentle waves and soft sand. It is famous for having rows and rows of *warung bé pasisih* (open-air seafood cafés). Dozens of cafés place hundreds of tables right on the sand every evening. After a glorious Jimbaran sunset, with candles glowing on every table, the atmosphere is extraordinary. And so is the food. Diners pick their own fish and it is prepared over coconut-husk coals and brought still sizzling to the table. The ambience at these beach cafés is informal, as at a picnic, and the air sometimes gets a bit smoky with all the grills fired up. The food is very tasty, however, just like barbecue fare. When it comes to elegant surroundings and real gourmet dining, Jimbaran has plenty to offer as well. The restaurants here, both in the resorts and in town, are some of the best in Bali, with cuisine representing almost every tradition in the world—it is a diner's dream.

Jimbaran is also a shopper's dream. With the opening of the flagship showroom of Jenggala Keramik, a retail boom began in Jimbaran. Now, many popular Bali retailers, such as Paul Ropp, Haveli and deLighting can be found here, alongside an array of local boutiques and antique shops.

THIS PAGE (FROM TOP): **Umbul-umbul (Balinese banners) dance in a sea breeze on Jimbaran beach; the showroom of Jenggala Keramik is one of many upmarket shopping options in Jimbaran.**

OPPOSITE: **Luxurious beach resorts dot the shore of Jimbaran Bay, where white sands and gentle breezes paint a perfect picture of tropical tranquillity.**

The softest side of the Bukit Peninsula is Jimbaran Bay, with its swaying coconut palms, golden-sand beaches...

conrad bali resort + spa

...this beach hotel has broken the mould with flawlessly executed, innovative concepts.

THIS PAGE (FROM TOP): *Brightly lit, the pool looks enchanting by night; Spice offers excellent food in a relaxed, congenial setting.*
OPPOSITE (FROM TOP): *The pool at Jiwa Spa invites one to glide in; Infinity by moonlight has an indefinable, magical charm; all bedrooms are furnished in friendly, appealing styles.*

Many travellers have misgivings about big hotels due to their cookie-cutter image and sometimes impersonal service. At the Conrad Bali Resort and Spa, throw away those misgivings, because this beach hotel has broken the mould with flawlessly executed, innovative concepts. It is a stylish and elegant place, with minimalist-tropical architecture accented by primitive-modern artefacts and witty visual references to Indonesian traditions. The interiors and landscaping throughout the resort are presented with perfect taste; there is nothing here to offend even the most refined aesthete.

Refinement and elegance at the Conrad Bali are balanced with a casual vibe, making guests feel at ease, whether they are slouching around in their favourite shorts and baseball cap, or catwalking in couture to a champagne reception. There is plenty of relaxed conviviality around the main pool, which is so big that its size could be measured in hectares. It is, however, just the right size for people watching. For a peaceful dip, there is a meandering lagoon pool that guests can plunge directly into from ground-floor suites. Here, rooms in all categories are meticulously decorated with natural materials and in neutral colours. Since this is a Conrad, there is no need to even ask about in-room amenities, equipment and services. They are all there.

The Conrad Bali stands out with its *ne plus ultra* conference and business centre. The ballroom wing, which also houses the business facilities, has a grand drive-through entrance, completely separate from the main guest entrance, solving the problem of event attendees colliding in the lobby with people who just want to enjoy a holiday or honeymoon.

But the Conrad Bali is even more famous for its wedding facilities. At the other end from the conference centre is the hotel's showstopper: Infinity, a masterpiece of symbolic architecture. Located at the northern side of the resort, it is the Conrad's chapel for weddings, commitment ceremonies and vow renewals. The sacred space floats on a plane of reflecting water. A white marble walkway carries the bridge and groom over the sheet of shimmering water to the chapel, in a crossing symbolising their entry into a new life. Wedding guests and the bride and groom stay in a special wing of the hotel, which has its own garden and beach areas, and is adjacent to the Conrad's highly regarded Jiwa Spa and Salon—perfect for pre- and post-nuptial pampering. All these offerings come with reassuringly attentive service. The restrained luxury shows that the Conrad Bali Resort & Spa may be big, but it is not too big for its guests.

ROOMS
283 rooms • 14 suites • 1 Presidential Suite

FOOD
Spice: Asian and Middle Eastern • Suku: primitive-modern fusion • Eight Degrees South: casual beach café • Azure: pool bar with light fare

DRINK
Azure: pool bar • Suku: lounge restaurant with DJ • East: lounge-bar

FEATURES
Jiwa Spa and Salon • Infinity • beach children's club • library • private fitness centre • pools • retail village • tennis

BUSINESS
6 meeting rooms • Grand Ballroom • business centre • event planning • private offices • secretarial services

NEARBY
Pura Luhur Uluwatu • beaches • lounge-bars • nightclubs • shopping • sport fishing • surfing

CONTACT
Jalan Pratama 168, Tanjung Benoa, Nusa Dua, Badung 80363 • telephone: +62.361.778 788 • facsimile: +62.361.773 888 • email: baliinfo@conradhotels.com • website: www.conradhotels.com

four seasons resort bali at jimbaran bay

...bringing the charm of Bali beach bungalows to the world of five-star resorts...

This resort is well known for its beauty and receives rave reviews in travel publications around the globe. One of Bali's most beloved hotels, it was also one of the first to adopt the now-popular all-villa format. Its designers and renowned tropical dream team, Grounds Kent, succeeded in bringing the charm of Bali beach bungalows to the world of five-star resorts when they made the Four Seasons Resort Bali at Jimbaran Bay. It was a pioneering approach at the time, and the hospitality world has never been the same since. The gardens, by Bali's design doyen, Made Wijaya, similarly opened people's eyes to the whimsical appeal of local landscaping style. Starting from scratch, on an arid and stony hillside, Made created a beautiful tropical garden, which has matured well over the years.

Many consider the Four Seasons Resort Bali at Jimbaran Bay to be the best expression ever of Bali style in a resort format. Conceived to recall traditional villages, it consists of walled compounds containing one villa each, which are entered through Balinese gates with unique hand-painted doors. Inside, as in a traditional Balinese home, living spaces are in separate thatch-roof structures and open-air *bales*. Here, however, unlike typical Balinese homes, they come with air-conditioning and marble bathrooms with porcelain soaking tubs and outdoor showers. All have garden areas, sundecks and plunge pools pouring out towards a gorgeous

THIS PAGE (FROM TOP): *A bale overlooks Jimbaran Bay; the waters of the private pool are clear and inviting.*
OPPOSITE (FROM LEFT): *With doors opening to views of the sea, the bedroom feels airy and cool; the resort's temple faces the sea and offers a serene environment for reflection.*

horizon. The Royal Villas have an additional, larger pool. The Balinese character of the architecture is enhanced by furnishings that include local antiques, artefacts and batik textiles. Some villas offer more privacy than others due to the terraced layout of the property, so guests who require utter seclusion should emphasise this priority when making a reservation.

For the ultimate in comfort, guests can choose one of the resort's nine estate residences, which are adjacent to the main property. These are totally self-contained homes in large walled gardens, with two to four bedrooms per estate. The larger ones extend over 2,000 sq m (21,528 sq ft) and more, with long lap pools, elegant master suites, luxurious living and dining areas, libraries, gourmet kitchens and staff quarters. The style is more contemporary and minimalist than that up at the main resort, but the views, not to mention the service, are just as good, and guests enjoy full privileges throughout the whole property. The excellent restaurants, spa, fitness centre, tennis courts, sandy beach and activities programmes of the main resort are additional perks.

The Four Seasons Resort Bali at Jimbaran Bay is near perfect, with the only possible drawback being its beachside location, which requires a long drive before one can reach the many attractions of Ubud, the mountains or the interior of Bali. But that is actually a desirable problem and one that is easy to solve: guests can divide their stay between the Four Seasons Resort Bali at Jimbaran Bay and the Four Seasons Resort Bali at Sayan, near Ubud, to enjoy Bali in both its beach and forest versions.

ROOMS
139 one-bedroom villas •
6 two-bedroom villas • 2 Royal Villas •
5 three-bedroom estate residences •
2 four-bedroom estate residences •
2 two-bedroom estate residences

FOOD
PJ's: Asian-Mediterranean • Taman Wantilan: Indonesian • Warung Mie: Asian • Pool Terrace Café: light meals

DRINK
PJ's bar • Terrace Bar and Lounge

FEATURES
aqua gym • cooking school • exercise and yoga classes • fitness centre • kayaking • kick-boxing • pools • sailing • spa • t'ai chi ch'uan • tennis • water sports

BUSINESS
24-hour business centre • AV equipment • event planning • high-speed Internet access • meeting rooms • mobile phone rental

CONTACT
Jimbaran Bay, Denpasar 80361 •
telephone: +62.361.701 010 •
facsimile: +62.361.701 020 •
website:www.fourseasons.com/jimbaranbay

grand hyatt bali

...linked by waterfalls, landscaped gardens and lagoons...

THIS PAGE: *The Salsa Bar above Salsa Verde Restaurant looks especially inviting at night.*

OPPOSITE (FROM TOP): *The wet treatment alcove at Kriya Spa; artificial rivers and free-form pools, just like this magnificent one, surround the hotel.*

The Hyatt hotels are well known for their excellence. They consistently get their names into some of the most important hotel lists in the world, such as the *Condé Nast Traveller*'s list of top 100 hotels and *Travel + Leisure*'s list of the world's 500 best hotels. These accolades, in addition to numerous industry awards, give potential guests a good idea of what to expect from a hotel chain that has always delivered excellent service in delightful settings, and with its recent extensive renovations, Grand Hyatt Bali is set to exceed expectations.

Designed as four 'ethnic villages' linked by waterfalls, landscaped gardens and lagoons, the layout overcomes the monotony that can result from having large premises. The prime 'village' is the Grand Club area, which comes with its own pool for the exclusive use of club guests, and a beachfront garden. All of the club services one expects are provided, including a dedicated concierge, butlers and a lounge serving drinks, canapés and more. The entire club

area has been reconfigured, refurbished and redecorated to exacting standards. Its suites are now among the best in Bali in terms of amenities, space and style. Some even have split levels, and all of them have lounging areas and outdoor terraces with views over the water gardens or the sea. Those who are seeking commodious accommodation are encouraged to take a club room here, or even a suite or villa, of which there are several different styles and sizes, including two presidential pool villas and an exclusive beachfront suite.

The most exciting new feature at Grand Hyatt Bali is the Kriya Spa. A designer haven of white stone, its architectural simplicity serves to give tired senses a blissful break. In all, there are 24 treatment villas set in minimalist water gardens, providing private havens for Kriya's wellness rituals. These are more than just treatment rooms. Each villa boasts tandem indoor treatment tables for couples, a private outdoor wet treatment area, a traditional relaxation *bale*, a designer bath, and a plunge pool, all set in an enclosed courtyard with cascading water features. The spa's health-promoting and anti-ageing treatments are rooted in local traditions, which use a wealth of

THIS PAGE: The rooms are furnished in neutral colours, with a day bed for lounging or which can be converted into a sleeping bay for children.

OPPOSITE: Nampu, the new Japanese restaurant, has a distinctive blue-tiled roof and overlooks a water feature.

natural herbs, roots and essences. Therapists and aestheticians tailor programmes to suit each client's goals for rejuvenation, beauty and wellness. Kriya Spa also has its own line of natural, eco-sensitive skin care products, which are used throughout the spa and offered for sale in the boutique. The products are based on natural ingredients, and herbs, essential oils, plant extracts, crushed flowers, roots and barks from around the world.

Nampu is Grand Hyatt Bali's Japanese restaurant. Its innovative design is certain to amaze, evoking the charm of a rustic Japanese country inn in true *izakaya* ('sake shop') style. Excellent teppanyaki selections are artfully prepared in three open kitchens, so that diners can watch the chefs at work. A master chef from Japan oversees every detail to ensure that his rigorous standards of authenticity and quality are met.

While ultra-sophistication is the tone at Kriya Spa and Nampu, Grand Hyatt Bali has a lighter side, too. It is an excellent family hotel. With a river pool that is accompanied by a 50-m-long (57-ft-long) waterslide and a children's club nearby, busy big-city families can be assured that the children will have a great time too. Family time is invaluable, but when the grown-ups need to soothe their frazzled nerves, they can send the little ones to Camp Nusa without a worry in the world. This children's club is well supervised and managed, but it is no babysitting back room. It is fantastically active, with programmes that are fun and educational. When children check into the hotel with their parents, they get a 'passport' for the activities and a programme schedule. The passport gives them access to activities a lot more interesting than a wading pool and a climbing frame. Camp 'counsellors' lead youngsters in an active exploration of Balinese art and crafts, and engage them in activities such as pottery, painting, cooking, Indonesian language, dance, scavenger hunts, kite flying and active sports.

Activities for adults are even more numerous. The Bay Club fitness and health centre is a good place to start, with tennis and squash courts, extensive fitness equipment, a steam room and sauna, a lap pool and aerobics classes. There are good running routes on the vast hotel grounds, a putting and chipping green, and an 18-hole seaside golf course almost at the hotel's doorstep. The water sports centre includes on-the-spot windsurfing, outrigger sailing, snorkelling and ocean canoeing, while scuba diving is available nearby, accessible by boat.

For business visitors, Grand Hyatt Bali has a superb convention centre. Two storeys high, it contains 25 meeting rooms, including two boardrooms and three ballrooms. There is also a business centre that provides all the necessary business services. Making events special through excellent planning, budgeting and managing is a source of pride for the meetings and events team here. They are also masters when it comes to pulling off magical weddings and parties. Grand Hyatt Bali remains one of the most popular wedding and event venues on the island.

This hotel is famous for winning awards in Asia and around the world, including 'Best Theme Venue' from a top MICE journal, and has a top ten rating among Asia's business and meeting hotels, according to *Business Traveller* and *The Wall Street Journal*. And with its four 'villages', each spacious enough to be a big hotel in its own right, all manner of functions can be readily accommodated. At the same time, romantic escapades, family beach holidays, or rejuvenating retreats can be enjoyed undisturbed by others.

ROOMS
607 rooms (including Grand and Club Rooms) • 17 grand executive suites • 16 grand suites • 3 special suites • 1 beachfront suite • 2 presidential suites • 2 deluxe villas

FOOD
Garden Café: international • Salsa Verde: Italian • Pasar Senggol: Balinese night market with cultural entertainment • Nampu: Japanese • Water Court: Balinese

DRINK
Salsa Bar • Pesona Lounge • Pool Bar

FEATURES
Camp Nusa • Kriya Spa • The Bay Fitness and Health Centre • clinic • club lounge • pools • shopping village • squash • tennis • water sports

BUSINESS
25 meeting rooms • AV equipment • business centre and services • event planning • high-speed Internet access

NEARBY
Bali Collection Shopping Centre • Pura Luhur Uluwatu • beaches • deep-sea fishing • golf • restaurants • scuba diving

CONTACT
PO Box 53, Nusa Dua, Badung 80361 •
telephone: +62.361.771 234 •
facsimile: +62.361.772 038 •
email: baligh.inquiries@hayttintl.com •
website: www.bali.grand.hyatt.com

heavenly residence

...'a slice of Heaven on Earth'.

THIS PAGE: Villa 'OMG' offers jaw-dropping views with its exclusive location.

Just a five-minute drive from the world-famous Nusa Dua Golf Club, Heavenly Residence operates three villas that stand out for their construction and setting, both of which never fail to attract curious visitors and inspire awe. The villas are literally perched on the edge of a cliff, virtually unseen from land but spectacular if viewed from the ocean. As a result of their location, sheer privacy and astounding views are assured from any of the villas.

Even in The Asmara, an area now known as the millionaires' row of Bali, there are still very few villas that can rival Villa 'OMG', the largest villa of Heavenly Residence, for sheer splendour. Surely an architectural marvel in itself, the villa is set in steps cascading down the cliff, like rice terraces, and took over 18 months to build. Called Villa 'OMG' for 'Oh My God', it is named after the gasps of involuntary surprise made by those who set foot upon this

villa for the first time. That awe is well deserved—the villa, at 700 sq m (7,534 sq ft), is huge and with 180-degree views available from the villa, it appears as though the Indian Ocean has just been laid at one's feet, wide and endless. The accompanying 25-m-long (27-ft-long) infinity-edged lap pool has its longer sides pouring out towards the sea. The ambience is 'a slice of Heaven on Earth', as the villa's website informs prospective guests.

There is also a long ironwood sundeck, complete with a *bale* and lawn, offering equally splendid views. With a capacity of 50 persons, a more dramatic setting for a glamorous party or wedding would be hard to imagine. But Villa 'OMG' is more than its exterior. To bring the stunning natural location indoors, the dining room walls are white to resemble the limestone cliffs, while fish tanks bring the wonders of the surrounding ocean closer to home.

THIS PAGE: *The infinity-edged pool at Villa 'OMG' definitely has to be seen to be believed.*

OPPOSITE (FROM TOP): *Borobudur-inspired carvings and art can be found in Villa 'O-Wow!'; all the villas feature touches of traditional Balinese culture; day or night, the bale by the pool is an excellent place to watch the ocean or meditate.*

Each of the four bedrooms has an en suite bathroom with marble fittings and Grohe taps and showerheads. Throughout, the generous use of mirrors not only visually expands the spacious look of the place, but also reflects the views endlessly.

The second villa has no lack of surprises either. It is called Villa 'O-Wow!', an exclamation that may well come from guests who are shown how to access it. Entry is via a private lift from the underground carpark, up the cliff face, and the doors open onto a garden in the sky. The décor is Javanese in style, with Borobudur-inspired stone carvings and a floating yoga pavilion. With an area of 600 sq m (6,458 sq ft), it has space to spare. Its layout is a minimalist-modern interpretation of a Balinese compound, with three bedroom suites, a studio-office and a *bale* arranged within landscaped grounds. The centrepiece of the villa is an infinity-edged pool

situated just over a sheer drop to the sea, appearing to pour directly out into the ocean. Views throughout the compound are spectacular, and it feels especially dramatic when enjoyed with a cold drink in hand, floating at the edge of the pool.

Villa 'O-Wow!' is ideal for two or three sophisticated urban couples to share, but would also suit families with children old enough not to be afraid of heights. The newest villa, Villa 'O-la-la', is another three-bedroom villa, but one that comes as luxuriously furnished as the other two. Also equipped with an infinity-edge pool and well-maintained gardens, it offers the same stunning views that turn even a short stay here into a memorable experience.

All three villas have access to a private beach at the foot of the cliff, ensuring that guests will not be disturbed by outsiders. State-of-the-art theatre and audio systems in all three villas mean that guests will never lack entertainment. Service is exemplary too: a 24-hour butler and concierge are available, as are housekeeping services to keep the premises trim and spotless. Breakfast is included and personal security staff can be arranged as well. Complete party and event management services are also available upon request. Heavenly Residence is a place that will please any sophisticated urban traveller who wants to get away and enjoy it all, without sacrificing any of the creature comforts.

ROOMS
Villa 'OMG': 4-bedroom villa •
Villa 'O-la-la': 3-bedroom villa •
Villa 'O-Wow!': 3+1-bedroom villa

FOOD
in-villa chef • in-villa dining

DRINK
service for cocktail or dinner parties

FEATURES
24-hour butler • alarm system • breakfast and afternoon tea • CCTV camera • chauffered limousine • DVDs • high-speed Internet access • home theatre • jacuzzi • private beach • pools • security

NEARBY
beaches • golf • lounge-bars • para-gliding • restaurants • shopping • water sports

CONTACT
Jalan Gunung Payung Sawangan, Nusa Dua, Badung 80361 •
telephone: +62.361.780 1166 •
facsimile: +62.361.780 2266 • email: reservation@heavenlyresidence.com •
website: www.heavenlyresidence.com

indah manis

...a family-friendly villa, but with grown-up glamour and style...

THIS PAGE (FROM TOP): Soft, romantic furnishings complement the touches of Balinese culture; lie back and relax in the bale.

OPPOSITE (FROM TOP): A typical Balinese entrance welcomes all; enjoy the great outdoors while one is sheltered under a bale; the dining room offers views of the pool and its surroundings; the 'viaduct weir edge' pool seems to be jutting out into air.

The extraordinary Indah Manis was created by Erik Gangsted, a prominent figure in regional hospitality circles. Many people dream of building an ideal home in Bali, but few of them have a background like Erik's to help bring their vision to life. Before Indah Manis, he managed the Nusa Dua Beach Hotel and the Banyan Tree Phuket, and established his own city centre inn in Geneva, Switzerland. With Indah Manis, his knowledge of Bali and expertise in hospitality are combined to great effect.

Indah Manis feels like a private boutique hotel. The property's design and the professionalism evident in its management also set it apart from other luxury villas in the area. This two-villa residence consists of a five-bedroom main house and a smaller one-bedroom villa beside it called Villa Bulan Madu. The latter is a honeymoon villa with its own pool and sundeck as well as a *bale*. Both are set in private gardens with separate gated entrances, so they can be let together or separately, offering a range of holiday possibilities for couples, groups or families, and especially for gathering and celebrations. Facilities in this exclusive private residence include everything one finds in a luxury hotel, and more. Of course there are elegant stone-clad garden bathrooms, surround-sound stereo, large-screen TVs, deluxe

amenities, attentive service and delicious meals prepared by a dedicated chef. Guests also have the use of a complete fitness room and a spa with a plunge pool, with massages and reflexology provided by therapists, and can request treatments such as a hair mask or a scalp massage. But there are many other extras which even a big hotel might not have, such as a pétanque arena, games room with billiards, outdoor barbecue and even a children's zone which sleeps up to six and comes complete with books, toys, games and movies for the little ones. Guests can also call on an Indah Manis nanny to supervise them. It is a family-friendly villa, but with grown-up glamour and style, and is especially enchanting at cocktail hour, when guests gather at the poolside bar to watch the sunset.

The architecture and décor of both villas reflect the latest in contemporary Asian style, with standout features such as a 'viaduct weir edge' swimming pool cantilevered over the trees below. Spacious terraces and living pavilions make Indah Manis a splendid choice for weddings and parties, as do the skills of its in-house catering team.

From its hilltop location, Indah Manis offers panoramic scenes that can be enjoyed in several directions from the terraces, pools and pavilions. Vistas of the Indian Ocean as well as Bali's west coast all the way to Canggu and the mountains of Bedugul in the east abound. On a clear day, even the volcanos of east Java are visible in the distance.

ROOMS
1 five-bedroom Grand Pool Villa •
1 one-bedroom Pool Villa

FOOD
chef • cooking classes •
shopping service

DRINK
self-catered • sunset bar pavilion

FEATURES
pétanque • billiards • car and chauffeur • fitness centre • games room • in-house spa and salon • library • pools • wi-fi Internet access • satellite TV

BUSINESS
business and secretarial services on request • event planning

NEARBY
Pura Luhur Uluwatu • beaches • golf • restaurants • resorts • shopping • surfing • tennis • water sports

CONTACT
Jalan Temu Dewi, Banjar Tengah, Desa Pecatu, Jimbaran, Badung 80364 •
telephone: +62.361.730 668 •
facsimile: +62.361.736 391 •
email: info@balihomes.com •
website: www.villa-indahmanis.com

intercontinental bali resort

...reminiscent of a Balinese royal compound, but on a grander scale.

THIS PAGE (FROM TOP): *Wooden floors and window shutters create a warm atmosphere; JG's Bar is a pool bar that allows swimmers to fortify themselves with a drink.*

OPPOSITE (FROM TOP): *A seated Buddha statue at the entrance to the Teppanyaki Room at KO welcomes diners; the main infinity-edged pool is a memorable dining venue; the manicured garden invites one to go for a walk.*

Most travellers want everything to be just right, particularly when visiting a part of the world that is new to them. This is especially true when one is travelling with family, and thoughtful, warm service is highly appreciated when dealing with the logistics involved. The InterContinental Bali Resort provides that and more.

A resort set on Jimbaran Bay, with 500 m (1,640 ft) of open beach, it is home to vast, lush gardens that are meticulously maintained, with dramatic water features incorporating carved stone structures in the style of a Balinese temple. The hotel's facilities also reflect the local architecture and are reminiscent of a Balinese royal compound, but on a grander scale. Spread among its six wings are a wide range of accommodation options. There are three distinct 'brands' within the hotel: Resort Classic, Singaraja and Club InterContinental, which offer different categories of rooms, suites and villas. There are more than enough options to suit almost any kind of holiday or event.

Extensive renovations over a three-year period have given the InterContinental Bali Resort a modern style while retaining its classic Balinese atmosphere. The Resort Classic rooms showcase the best in local design, with an emphasis on indigenous hardwood floors and handcrafted furniture. Particularly suitable for families is the Resort Classic suite, which provides a homey atmosphere. The rooms and suites of Singaraja, named after Bali's former northern capital, come with new stone-clad spa bathrooms and elegant furnishings in a contemporary Asian style, while Balinese artwork and dark woods further enhance the local flavour.

Grandeur in a grand hotel is expected, and the InterContinental Bali Resort delivers, with an enormous pool, luxurious spa, and a soaring *wantilan* style lobby furnished with oversized club chairs to create a comfortable yet exclusive feel. While adults enjoy the spa facilities and fitness centre or indulge in the resort activities along the beach, children are cared for at Club J, a mini-resort created just for them with cultural and sporting activities. There, morning

gymnastics, Balinese art and music, kite-flying and story-telling sessions entertain and occupy the little ones. For adults, facilities for meetings and events are provided as well, with ballrooms, meeting rooms, a business centre and a dramatic open-air stage for performances, celebrations or weddings. Three bars and four restaurants ensure that guests do not lack for drinking or dining options. Couples can also choose to dine under a canopy along the beach for a romantic evening with lit candles and the gentle waves lapping nearby.

What is not always expected in a big resort is warm, personal service. That is the hallmark of InterContinental Bali Resort and it suits the island paradise of Bali particularly well. Guests who have stayed at the InterContinental Bali Resort praise the wonderful service of the staff and their genuine smiles. Families, couples, business travellers, newlyweds and their guests often write to enthuse about the way everyone treated them with genuine care and personal attention. Even the gardeners smile here and clearly enjoy being at the resort. So do the restaurant staff, room attendants and consequently, the guests.

ROOMS
184 Resort Classic rooms and suites •
129 Singaraja rooms and suites •
100 Club rooms and suites

FOOD
Taman Gita Terrace: breakfast •
Jimbaran Gardens: Indonesian
and international • KO: Japanese •
Bella Singaraja: Italian

DRINK
JG's Bar • Saraswati Lounge •
Sunset Beach Bar

FEATURES
Club J • beach • boutiques • fitness
centre • pools • resort activities •
spa • salon • tennis

BUSINESS
1 ballroom • 8 meeting rooms •
business centre • event planning •
high-speed Internet access •
mobile phone rental • multilingual
secretarial services

NEARBY
beaches • golf

CONTACT
Jalan Uluwatu 45, Jimbaran,
Badung 80361 •
telephone: +62.361.701 888 •
facsimile: +62.361.701 777 •
email: bali@interconti.com •
website: www.bali.intercontinental.com

club intercontinental

Designed to offer unprecedented service and hospitality...

THIS PAGE: *The exclusive Club pool invites guests to go for a swim, or seat themselves on the lounge chairs to relax.*
OPPOSITE (FROM TOP): *Surrounded by Balinese artefacts, a pleasurable soak awaits; the Club InterContinental Airport Lounge welcomes guests; classical décor that is sure to delight the guests.*

When royalty and heads of state come to Bali, their experience is very different from other travellers. They are shielded from every possible disturbance and protected within a bubble of discreet service from the moment of arrival. Disembarking from the aeroplane, they are greeted by polite uniformed staff and ushered immediately to private quarters within the airport. There is no need to queue at the immigration counter or wrestle for their luggage at an arrival hall carousel. Efficient staff handle everything on their behalf.

In Bali, this kind of welcome is no longer reserved only for royalty or heads of state. With an exclusive lounge located within the airport, every Club InterContinental guest is treated this way. From the moment one arrives in Bali, premium service shelters one from the minutiae of travelling. Refreshments are offered while the staff attends to the necessary entry procedures and once those are completed, guests are whisked off to the hotel by limousine, Jaguar or private helicopter. Naturally, they do not deal with check-in hassles either; rather, they are escorted to an

elegant private lounge while a butler takes care of everything, perhaps even unpacking and arranging their personal effects. Designed to offer unprecedented service and hospitality, Club InterContinental is a resort within a resort, occupying a special wing of the InterContinental Bali Resort on Jimbaran Bay and benefiting fully from the extensive facilities of this classic grand hotel.

The Club Lounge is a spacious haven of civility and dignity, with a contemporary style evoking the grandeur of Asian capitals and luxury retreats of the 1930s. Breakfast, refreshments, high tea, cocktails and late snacks are served on the house. Club guests also enjoy private indoor and outdoor relaxation areas and a Club pool with sunny terraces for their exclusive use. There is no need to jockey for a well-positioned lounge chair here—all provide excellent views. The gardens are expansive and the beach is within walking distance.

Club rooms and the newly launched 'Suite Collection' are sophisticated sanctuaries of light and space. The palette is crisp cream-white accented by elegant, dark, timber fittings, with meticulous attention paid to the décor. Every suite is designed to provide a luxurious experience for travellers, business leaders and celebrities, from the high class amenities to the specially trained butlers. The most discerning VIPs of all choose the Imperial Villa—a large compound with a residence set in its own grounds, each with a private pool, for the ultimate in comfort.

ROOMS
84 rooms • 16 suites •
2 Imperial Villas

FOOD
Club Lounge • Taman Gita Terrace: breakfast • Jimbaran Gardens: Mediterranean and seafood • KO: Japanese • Bella Singaraja: Italian

DRINK
Club Lounge Bar • Saraswati Lounge • Sunset Beach Bar

FEATURES
24-hour butler service • beach • library and lounge • fitness centre • pools • spa • VIP arrival and transfer service

BUSINESS
1 ballroom • 8 meeting rooms • business centre • event planning • high-speed Internet access • mobile phone rental • multilingual secretarial services

NEARBY
beaches • golf

CONTACT
Jalan Uluwatu 45, Jimbaran, Badung 80361 •
telephone: +62.361.701 888 •
facsimile: +62.361.701 777 •
email: bali@interconti.com •
website: www.bali.intercontinental.com

the istana

...the villa itself is just as splendid as its surroundings.

Located within the spiritual sphere of Pura Luhur Uluwatu at Bali's southern tip, The Istana is a private villa offering five-star perks. Housed on a 5,200 sq m (56,000 sq ft) cliff-top property which offers a stunning, panoramic view of the peninsula, The Istana also brings into proximity white-sand beaches that provide intoxicating salt-tinged breezes, a lagoon filled with corals and marine life, sleekly maintained grounds, as well as spectacular sunsets.

It is not just the guarantee of golden sunsets that distinguishes this property, however. Comprising five suites—one master suite and four bedroom suites, of which two faces the ocean and two have garden views, the villa itself is just as splendid as its surroundings. The spacious interiors are furnished with natural materials such as teak and limestone, while rich fabrics with intricate patterns and weaves add a touch of colour. The villa bears an equal

balance of European influences and Asian aesthetics—the former is manifested in the unwavering attention to luxury and detail, while the latter is visible in the sensitive application of earth tones and natural textures which pay creative tribute to the lush landscape of the area. This homage to Bali's charms is enhanced by pieces of strategically placed Indonesian primitive art which showcases the attractive mysticism of the 'Island of the Gods'.

The main house consists of a living and dining room, an entertainment area and four bedroom suites. A highlight here is the white limestone carving on the living room's right wall. This arresting centrepiece depicts the first arrival of the pioneering priest Pedanda Sakti Wawu Rauh, who travelled to Bali from Java in the 16th century. At the very same spot where he attained his spiritual fulfilment, the sacred Pura Luhur Uluwatu temple was later erected, and it remains revered by the locals today. This history and connection to the spirit of Bali is expressed in The Istana's furnishings and its décor.

Social areas are neatly and generously provided. The dining room, seating 10, overlooks lily-filled ponds on one side and the ocean on the other. A bar is conveniently located here as well and comes stocked with international wines, spirits and mixers. The entertainment area, or Dotcom Room, is where guests will find a massive couch covered with Thai silk pillows,

THIS PAGE (FROM TOP): *Tempting dishes prepared by the chefs; the main pool glistens at night; wooden furnishings add a rustic touch to the rooms.*
OPPOSITE: *Daybeds are laid out on the short sides of the pool, providing plenty of space.*

facing a wide-screen television and a home theatre system. Behind the couch there is a cosy study area with a computer that is conveniently equipped with high-speed Internet access. The master suite is in a separate guest house accessed by a walkway near the main entrance. Among its features are a sheltered deck, swimming pool, outdoor shower, daybeds and a kitchenette. The four bedroom suites are quietly luxurious, with sunken bathtubs and private courtyards that provide both physical comfort and space in which to enjoy it.

Outside, guests will find the extensive grounds spread over two levels. The upper-level garden has a bed of thick, soft grass, with coconut trees and lotus-filled ponds adding a tropical feel. The lower level has a sprawling lawn suitable for holding weddings, cocktail parties or playing a simple game of tag with one's children. The villa's main swimming pool overlooks the ocean and separates the garden from the lawn—a shimmering demarcation.

As can be expected of a private villa, guests are assured of all creature comforts, including tantalising meals. The villa's hospitality team ensures exceptional cuisine and full butler service, which comes in handy if guests are travelling with children. Various set menus are available, along with an à la carte selection and an enticing menu for the young ones. Special diets can

THIS PAGE: *Green gardens contrast with the many blues of the pool, the sea and the sky. In the distance, one can see the cliffs.*

OPPOSITE (FROM TOP): *Some of the best views of the ocean are available from on the cliff; Balinese art and its influence can be seen in every room; the décor of the living room is chic, with an island charm that puts one at ease.*

be accommodated with no fuss as well. All one has to do is make a choice and sit back as the chef whips up a feast. Otherwise, the well-appointed kitchen is at the disposal of the guests should they decide to cook something themselves.

With the range of services and facilities provided, The Istana has made it possible for guests to spend their entire holiday on the villa's grounds. Spa treatments ranging from massages to body scrubs and wraps, facials, manicures and pedicures, and even hair braiding can be arranged at the guest's convenience and are provided in-house. Children are not likely to get bored because in addition to the pool, the Dotcom Room comes equipped with a Sony Playstation and a library of DVDs, CDs and books.

Should guests, however, feel the need to leave this private paradise during the day, a chauffeur is available to drive them to an intimate dinner at any of the restaurants nearby, or to any of Bali's historical and cultural sights. The luxury vehicle is family-friendly and seats seven comfortably. Additional vehicles and drivers can be arranged as well if the need arises. If parents would like to leave the children behind for the day, The Istana's capable staff will gladly keep an eye on them, making sure they are sufficiently entertained and that they stay out of harm's way. This is indeed family-friendly service.

With such attention paid to every little detail and its ability to anticipate its guests every need, The Istana is one of the many reasons why a lot of visitors, especially the discerning ones, are choosing to go the private villa route when heading to Bali.

ROOMS
1 master suite • 4 bedroom suites

FOOD
Indonesian • Western • Asian • vegetarian • special diets

DRINK
fully-stocked bar

FEATURES
pool • Dotcom Room • car and chauffeur

BUSINESS
high-speed Internet access

NEARBY
Pura Luhur Uluwatu • beach • surfing

CONTACTS
Jalan Labuan Sait, Pantai Suluban, Uluwatu, Badung 80361 •
telephone: +62.361.730 668 •
facsimile: +62.361.736 391 •
email: info@balihomes.com •
website: www.theistana.com

jamahal private resort + spa

A huge lagoon pool meanders through the resort...

THIS PAGE: *Daybeds, pavilions and lounge chairs arranged in separate groups by the pool provide plenty of privacy.*
OPPOSITE (CLOCKWISE FROM TOP): *The chocolate treatment restores the skin to peak condition; tribal artefacts and original paintings lend individual character to every room; Jamahal provides serenity for peaceful meditation.*

Inspired by *The Dolphin*, a much-loved book by Sergio Bambaren, a Swiss businessman resolved to follow his dreams. He left the rat race to fulfil a new destiny by creating a home in Bali. This dream blossomed, ultimately becoming Jamahal Private Resort & Spa, a collection of 10 luxurious bungalows and three exclusive villas, nestled in shady gardens in Jimbaran.

A secret hideaway, it is cleverly hidden right in the middle of the resort town and provides exclusive guest access to a luxury beach club across the road. With jungle greenery dripping with flowers, Jamahal is a welcome refuge from the sun's heat. A huge lagoon pool meanders through the resort, accented by natural boulders and a cascading waterfall.

But this resort is much more than just a jungle bungalow complex. Sophistication, unapologetic luxury and urbane artfulness abound. The place feels sexy, with a contemporary but traditional element evident in the interiors: dark woods, big marble bathrooms with bathtubs, jewel-toned fabrics and smooth, luxurious sheets. While this is ideal for honeymoons and romantic escapes, the range of villa configurations suit a variety of holiday agendas.

Garden Villas open onto the central lagoon pool, yet are secluded from view by smart landscaping and garden walls. More private are the Pool Villas, which have decently sized

pools and, as with all villas, are enclosed in courtyards to provide seclusion. The large Frangipani Villa is a complete tropical-modern residence, ideal for a group or a large family, with two grand master suites, a huge pool, a relaxation *bale* and extensive indoor and outdoor living areas, plus a fully equipped designer kitchen. The layout of the villa is also excellent for an elegant cocktail or a private dinner party. The entire Jamahal Estate may also be let for larger gatherings such as weddings, with accommodation that can cater for up to 36 guests.

The Jamahal Spa is spacious and serene, with a wide range of treatments, including special packages for couples. Hot stone massages and facials are popular, and so is the 'Jamahal Experience', which incorporates Aryurvedic treatments. Therapists will also bring portable massage tables to guests in their villas or walled gardens. Plans are also underway to expand the resort with two exclusive state-of-the-art spa villas and a fitness room in 2008.

The intimate size of this resort makes it feel like a private estate, at which every traveller is an honoured guest. It is an individualistic place for people who want something different and who appreciate good value, but without sacrificing luxury.

ROOMS
4 Garden Villas • 3 Pool Villas • 3 Pool Suite Villas • 2 Garden Villas with direct pool access • 1 Jacuzzi Suite Villa

FOOD
Jamahal Lounge: East-West organic fusion

DRINK
Jamahal Lounge • bar in each villa

FEATURES
beach club access • lagoon pool • spa • fitness centre (from mid-2008) • adult-only policy (16 years and above)

NEARBY
beaches • shopping • restaurants • traditional seafood cafés • surfing

CONTACT
Jalan Uluwatu 1, Jimbaran, Badung 80361 •
telephone: +62.361.704 394 •
facsimile: +62.361.703 011 •
email: info@jamahal.net •
website: www.jamahal.net

jimbaran puri bali

...a luxury beach hotel that is simple, unpretentious and supremely relaxing.

THIS PAGE: *Lotus pools and palm trees—the quintessential Bali experience for any visitor.*
OPPOSITE (FROM TOP): *One of the offerings from Tunjung Café; the stylishly furnished rooms offer the best of Bali style.*

There are numerous luxury resorts in Bali. Some, however, are so stylish that they feel flighty, while others overstate minimalism to such a degree that the surroundings feel impoverished. But Jimbaran Puri Bali is neither of those. It is a balm for those who have overdosed on over-conceptualised luxury: a luxury beach hotel that is simple, unpretentious and supremely relaxing.

Jimbaran Puri Bali is part of the Orient-Express group, who are known for providing authentic experiences in exotic locales; their Orient-Express train journeys and 'Road to Mandalay' river cruise trips are travel legends. The same devotion to authenticity, without sacrificing luxury or comfort, applies at Jimbaran Puri Bali.

Old-timers in Bali brag about how great it was back in the 1970s when they first discovered this island. They had simple bungalows along the beach and enjoyed tranquillity, sun, sand and sea in a slow-paced village setting. That's all over now, they proclaim. But in fact, it is not quite over. Jimbaran Puri Bali is a place that offers that authentic 'old Bali' experience, but without the deprivations those early Bali tourists had to endure. A collection of typical Balinese cottages with low, thatched roofs are dotted about under a canopy of tropical

trees. Set discreetly back from the shore, they leave a wide lawn extending towards the sea for all to enjoy. Drinking, dining and spa areas adjacent to the beach are intentionally built light, low and natural to keep the level lawn and pool totally open to the sands of Jimbaran Bay, so that guests can sense the sea right from their bungalows. There is something inherently relaxing about the way Jimbaran Puri Bali is open to the beach, with no barriers, no steps to negotiate, no cliff to climb down, and almost no demarcation at all from the strand to the buildings of the hotel itself. Staying here is like being blissfully stranded on a tropical island with nothing to do but hope rescuers do not come too soon.

Inside the oungalows are luxuries the old-timers did not dare dream of. Marble floors and open-beam ceilings with warm, golden thatched roofs combine with elegant, understated furnishings covered in pure cotton and silk, while floor-to-ceiling windows open onto private walled gardens. Modern comforts such as air conditioning, flat-screen TVs, wi-fi Internet access and sound systems complement the experience, while sunken terazzo baths, rain showers and draped king-size beds complete the roll call of physical luxuries.

The Resort's Nelayan Restaurant (*nelayan* means 'fisherman') is made of bamboo and palm twine, and stretches right out onto the wide beach, with some tables actually sitting on the sand. To dine here by candlelight, on fine local seafood or French Mediterranean specialities, watching as the stars come out, is an especially delightful treat.

ROOMS
32 one-bedroom garden cottages •
8 beachfront cottages •
2 two-bedroom cottages

FOOD
Nelayan Restaurant: fresh local seafood and French Mediterranean • Tunjung Café: Indonesian and Balinese cuisine • breakfast buffet

DRINK
Puri Bar: poolside and service on the beach for drinks and snacks

FEATURES
spa • pool • honeymoon packages • water sports • yoga • t'ai chi ch'uan

BUSINESS
catered functions • secretarial and translation services on request • wi-fi high-speed Internet access •

NEARBY
Jimbaran Bay • Jimbaran Fishing Village • Pura Luhur Uluwatu • golf • shopping • restaurants • surfing

CONTACT
Jalan Uluwatu, Jimbaran, Badung 80361 •
telephone: +62.361.701 605 •
facsimile: +62.361.701 320 •
email: info@jimbaranpuribali.com •
website: www.jimbaranpuribali.com

kayumanis jimbaran private estate

...open to the vista of gently swaying palms.

THIS PAGE: *Tapis restaurant offers different dining environments, with a choice of open pavilions, outdoor seating, or an air-conditioned dining room. All this, and a big lap pool, too.*
OPPOSITE (FROM TOP): *A hammock among the trees is one of the best ways to experience an old coconut plantation; private pool villas were constructed without sacrificing mature palm trees, merging nature and modernity.*

Situated on an old coconut plantation beside Jimbaran Bay, Kayumanis Jimbaran Private Estate is at peace with its environment. Nothing about it is imposing. The architecture is simple and the resort is impeccably finished with the finest natural materials, showing tropical modernism at its best.

There is something intensely pleasurable about the atmosphere in old coconut plantations. The light constantly changes as it angles down through widely spaced trees. A breeze through the palm fronds soothes the mind. The view expands in all directions over a level carpet of grass, and space is measured by the dark lines of tree trunks. It is a perfect setting for this serene boutique hotel, with just 19 villas set in a vast expanse of land, punctuated by shimmering ponds and open to the vista of gently swaying palms.

The villas are described as private pool estates and the description is an apt one. Each sits in its own walled compound of over 500 sq m (5,382 sq ft). A tropical garden, shaded by coconut trees, creates a calming and green environment in which to relax. Within each estate are generous living spaces comprising an open-air living and dining area with a gourmet kitchen, a lavish master suite and a separate 'studio' suite which can serve a variety of purposes. It can be used as a second bedroom, a yoga and spa treatment room, a study or a hideaway for deep meditation. Guests have the freedom to choose.

Personal preferences are of paramount importance to the management and staff at Kayumanis Jimbaran. Guests are encouraged to communicate those preferences in detail prior to their arrival. Dietary regimes, pillow and linen choices, even tastes in décor are all impeccably met. To ensure seamless service, a butler-concierge is selected especially for a guest's stay. As a personal aide and problem-solver who is on hand 24 hours a day, he can organise explorations and outings, find

the best shopping deals, chauffeur guests to their desired destinations and, along the way, explain the cultural context of the surrounding areas. Special requests are also quietly attended to. Need the latest *Vanity Fair* in Italian? A *lomilomi* massage? Looking for a full-moon temple festival? Consider it done.

This level of service is absolutely as good as it gets, particularly since the Balinese butlers have a natural way of adapting to the personal style of their guests, striking the right balance between formality and familiarity. If one chooses to stay in, he is just a quick phone call away, but one's privacy is never disturbed.

THIS PAGE: *Deep peace prevails in each private villa compound after dark. Floating in the pool beneath a canopy of stars is an experience to savour.*

OPPOSITE (FROM TOP): *The cuisine focuses on pure freshness, tempts the palate and restores the body; pools in each villa are long enough for vigorous and satisfying laps; minimalist architecture and utter comfort blend seamlessly in the bedroom.*

Entire days can pass peacefully without having to leave one's personal estate and without lacking anything. Bose media systems are iPod-ready, a large plasma TV can bring the world to guests via satellite, and wireless high-speed Internet access is conveniently available. Indoors or outdoors, guests are unlikely to feel bored. The pool is generous in size, complete with a sun-washed timber terrace, while the kitchen is fully outfitted with all the required appliances, including an espresso machine. A complimentary maxi-bar is stocked according to guests' preferences (alcoholic or otherwise), and gourmet cuisine is offered around the clock. Guests may select from the restaurant menu or request customised dishes to suit their own tastes. Meals can also be prepared by the chef in one's own kitchen, or self-prepared, for those who enjoy expressing their personal culinary talents.

Intimate entertainment in one's estate or on the Kayumanis Jimbaran grounds can easily be arranged. Picture a dreamy dinner under the stars, with white linens and flickering lanterns adorning the garden. A gathering of friends can enjoy an aperitif on the terrace or recline in the gazebo before being graciously seated for dinner by the staff. Delicate tones played in *gender wayang* (an intimate *gamelan* ensemble) by Balinese musicians waft toward one's ears from a moonlit corner of the garden. Dreams like this are made real by the adept staff. Somehow that is not surprising in a place that uses the word 'perfection' in its mission statement.

Catering for small- to medium-size events is expertly overseen by the chef of Kayumanis Jimbaran's restaurant, Tapis. It is more than just a restaurant, actually, it is a restaurant in a villa. The layout of Tapis is like that of the walled estate compounds and equally spacious, with settings to suit almost any whim. Choose from an air-conditioned dining salon with shiny wooden floors or an open terrace with formal and informal table arrangements. Guests may also take a leisurely meal by the pool, lounging in a breezy gazebo.

The kitchen is open to the terrace and guests are encouraged to interact directly with the chef, who has a very flexible repertoire. Indonesian food is a source of pride here and is elevated to a level deserving of the term 'cuisine'. Various styles of cooking from throughout the Indonesian archipelago are represented on the menu, and every dish is prepared with market-fresh ingredients. With the Jimbaran fish market only a stone's throw away, guests can count on getting fresh catch for dinner, flavoured with fresh herbs and spices.

Although Kayumanis Jimbaran is not directly on the beachfront, that is not entirely a bad thing. Being set just a little bit inland means that privacy is assured. No one will be loitering in front of your room trying to sell you a sarong, nor will your aesthetic sensibilities be disturbed by random tourists promenading noisily past. Kayumanis Jimbaran does offer beachfront pleasures very close by though, with a shared luxury beach cabana just down the lane. If preferred, guests can take advantage of its sister property on a white sand beach in Nusa Dua, where Kayumanis guests are welcome to indulge in sunbathing and safe swimming. The butler will escort guests to a waiting limousine, and he can also pack them a gourmet picnic basket.

With its special blend of minimalist style and optimal service, Kayumanis Jimbaran Private Estate sees many returning guests. Its close proximity to the airport makes it ideal for weekend escapes. And the utterly at-home feeling of its spacious villas makes it tempting for one to stay for as long as possible.

ROOMS
19 one-bedroom pool estates

FOOD
Tapis: Indonesian • in-villa dining: chef or self-prepared

DRINK
full bar with wines, spirits and beer

FEATURES
24-hour butler service • access to Kayumanis properties in Nusa Dua and Ubud • beach access • limousine • private pool • spa • wedding planning • yoga

BUSINESS
business services • high-speed Internet

NEARBY
Pura Luhur Uluwatu • beaches • golf • lounge-bars • shopping • surfing • traditional market

CONTACT
Jalan Yoga Perkanthi, Jimbaran, Badung 80364 •
telephone: +62.361.705 777 •
facsimile: +62.361.705 101 •
email: jimbaran@kayumanis.com •
website: www.kayumanis.com

the shaba

...designed for guests who are accustomed to the luxuries of gracious living.

THIS PAGE (FROM TOP): A chandelier and fine sheets in the bedroom add touches of luxury; the courtyard and fountain evoke old-world elegance.

OPPOSITE (CLOCKWISE FROM TOP): Flowers infuse a cool drink with tropical flavour; the lit-up swimming pool looks even more inviting at night; patterned wallpaper helps to recreate the historical mood.

The Shaba was created by interior decorator and owner Zohra Boukhari following her terrific success with Villa Balquisse, located just next door. Unifying the Orient and the Occident, The Shaba brings something unexpected to the heart of Jimbaran. Like riads of the Middle East, it is built around a central courtyard, open to the sky. This private interior garden creates a natural sense of flow and a feeling of space. The elegant sofas here present the perfect spot for relaxing, which one can do while listening to the gentle sounds of the fountain.

The Shaba is an extraordinarily large residence, with just two bedrooms and one suite, designed for guests who are accustomed to the luxuries of gracious living. The master suite's blue accents echo the indigo notes in its silky Moroccan carpet, displayed on a floor of vintage traditional tiles. An elegant en suite bathroom features a classic porcelain bathtub, a handmade mosaic shower, and opens onto a spacious dressing room.

The living room, done in apple-green, is decorated with authentic antiques and has views of the saltwater swimming pool, tiled with natural celadon stone. The green tones add a fresh, exotic feel to the living spaces, which have soaring ceilings. In the afternoons, dappled sunlight dances across the floor of the dining and living rooms, filtered through the trees in the garden outside. An intimate library off the living room is just the setting for a tête-à-tête or some quiet time spent writing personal correspondence. The open-plan, professionally equipped kitchen is a gourmet's delight, allowing avid chefs to prepare their favourite dishes without missing out on conversation over the aperitifs. Cooking classes are also offered by The Shaba's chefs.

Two other bedrooms, accessible through the interior courtyard, are decorated with great taste and charm, and feature lavish bedlinens and romantic touches such as crystal chandeliers over a porcelain bath, and patterned walls evoking an ancient French chateau. All rooms enjoy

modern comforts such as plasma TV screens, satellite TV, iPods and wi-fi Internet access, so that guests will not lack modern entertainment.

With extensive landscaped gardens and lawns, and a long pool with sunny terraces that give access to the house via long rows of French doors, one truly feels at home here. The Shaba is perfectly suited to elegant dinners, poolside parties and larger, catered functions. Guests can relax all the more knowing that indulgences such as Henna Spa and Asam Garam Restaurant are just next door, while superb service from gracious, multilingual staff is always at hand. Such a tasteful blend of Moroccan, French and Indonesian traditions is a refreshing addition to Bali.

ROOMS
1 master suite • 2 bedrooms

FOOD
Asam Garam Restaurant: Asian • Middle-Eastern • Indian • continental and Indonesian • chef

DRINK
Asam Garam Restaurant • shopping service

FEATURES
Henna Spa • bicycles • cooking classes • DVD/CD players • full butler service • iPods • saltwater pool • gourmet kitchen • wedding and event planning • satellite TV • complimentary shuttle bus service • wi-fi Internet access

NEARBY
Jimbaran beach • Pura Luhur Uluwatu • beach resorts • golf • nightlife • restaurants • shopping

CONTACT
Jalan Uluwatu, Gang Gigit Sari, Jimbaran, Badung 80361 •
telephone: +62.361.701 695 •
facsimile: +62.361.703 087 •
email: info@shaba-bali.com •
website: www.shaba-bali.com

villa balquisse

...a combination of many charming scenes...

Villa Balquisse is more like a Moroccan riad, at least in its configuration, rather than a hotel or a villa. Its style is a combination of many charming locations: a colonial plantation, a caravanserai, a country house, a deserted island dream and more. Its owner and creator is Zohra Boukhari, a talented interior decorator with a distinctive Eastern flair. She describes Villa Balquisse as a playground for her ideas, where she constantly creates new atmospheres and designs, and field-tests her latest creations. She feels that since hotels require constant refurbishment and maintenance in any case, why not use the opportunity to experiment and innovate?

This creative approach has been a great success. Villa Balquisse is the antithesis of a purely functional, generic hotel environment. It feels personal, alive, lived in and liveable, with the kind of eclectic interiors that evolve over time in a well-loved country home. Indeed, Zohra calls it a *maison d'hôte*, rather than a hotel, and that is what it is.

This marvellous boutique resort encompasses nine bungalows, with two natural stone swimming pools from which to take languid dips. Common areas and private ones are connected by a fascinating labyrinth of courtyards, passageways, arcades and gardens. The possibilities are endless here. Because Villa Balquisse can change the configuration of its villas, it can provide accommodations for families both large or small, groups of friends, or one large group. Entire wedding parties have even been put up at Villa Balquisse with the right balance of togetherness and privacy for everyone.

Each bungalow is unique, with interconnected spaces spread over different levels, and a variety of contrasting environments. Open pool terraces and an expansive lawn give a feeling of spaciousness. Cosy, intimate nooks and daybeds under garden arcades offer perfect solitude. Every spot on the property exudes its own charm and character. From weathered wood and whitewashed patio

THIS PAGE (FROM TOP): *A sarong, the traditional after-bath garb in Bali, is thoughtfully provided; daybeds are large enough for two to lie down side by side.*

OPPOSITE (FROM LEFT): *The living room is as relaxed and laid-back as a home should be; the bed is raised on a dais.*

seating, to harem-like boudoirs with gold-shot silks in jewel tones and rich draperies, guests can choose a setting to suit their mood. Families love Villa Balquisse: teenagers like the opportunity to mingle and socialise with other guests and parents treasure the seclusion of their own private terraces while not being too far from their offspring.

Asam Garam Restaurant at Villa Balquisse is a congenial space with family-style seating. The menu is a world tour of healthy cuisines, combining Moroccan, Indian, Indonesian and Parisian flavours. Cooking classes and hands-on involvement allow guests to join the culinary caravan. Should guests wish, the staff will also organise barbecue parties.

For other physical comforts, Henna Spa is a haven furnished with Asian and European antiques to create a perfect atmosphere in which to enjoy massages and ritual treatments from ancient island cultures. Skilled therapists help to restore one's spirits. Like the rest of Villa Balquisse, the spa is magically quirky, eccentric, rustic and always enchanting.

ROOMS
9 bungalows

FOOD
Asam Garam Restaurant: Indonesian • Asian • Middle-Eastern and European

DRINK
Asam Garam • minibar

FEATURES
Henna Spa • cycling • Villa Balquisse Living boutique • satellite TV • shuttle bus service • wi-fi Internet access

NEARBY
Pura Luhur Uluwatu • beach • golf • resorts • nightlife • restaurants • shopping • surfing

CONTACT
Jalan Uluwatu 18X, Jimbaran, Badung 80361 •
telephone: +62.361.701 695 •
facsimile: +62.361.703 087 •
email: info@balquisse.com •
website: www.balquisse.com

tirtha luhur

...romantic, beautiful, with a touch of mystery and adventure.

THIS PAGE: *The dramatic setting of Tirtha Luhur makes a wedding here particularly memorable.*

OPPOSITE (FROM TOP): *Scattered tealights in the bathroom create a romantic atmosphere; warm earth tones are used in the master bedroom; attention to small details is an intrinsic part of the Tirtha Luhur philosophy.*

Bali is a favoured destination for weddings. After all, it is the 'Island of the Gods': romantic, beautiful, with a touch of mystery and adventure. It seems ideal for a new beginning.

Organising a stylish wedding is no small feat, however. Even today, with planning services provided by the modern wedding industry at hand, it is still an overwhelmingly complex and expensive undertaking. It requires above-average organisational capabilities, knowledge of fashion trends, excellent interpersonal skills and attention to detail. Luckily, these are talents that the team at Tirtha Luhur possesses in abundance.

Tirtha Luhur is the second wedding venue of Tirtha Bridal, which provides premium wedding services in Bali. The first, Tirtha Uluwatu, was such a success that the owners decided to expand their services and provide couples with a location that is just as stunning and memorable. They created Tirtha Luhur, just three minutes away from Tirtha Uluwatu, built on a cliff-top with an elegant wedding pavilion that offers views of the Indian Ocean. The soaring,

white ceiling frames a scene which combines a 20-m-long (22-yd-long) pool that extends towards the horizon with its myriad hues of blue. The pavilion is large, and capable of seating 100 guests in air-conditioned comfort.

There is also the wedding villa and its master bedroom decorated with teak furnishings, silk wall panels and Egyptian cotton bedlinen for a luxurious touch. Attached to it are two guest suites that can be used as preparation rooms or overnight accommodation for guests, and a gazebo with a daybed, offering uninterrupted views of the ocean.

Tirtha Bridal, with more than 15 years of expertise, takes care of virtually everything involved in the ceremony and celebration, from wedding clothes to gifts. The couple can rest assured that the wedding ceremony will run without a hitch.

On the big day, guests are greeted with chilled scented towels while Balinese dancers welcome them. They are then ushered into a lavish lounge for a drink while they await the ceremony, which takes place amid soft music in the flower-bedecked wedding pavilion.

After the ceremony, guests make their way into the garden for sunset cocktails as the wedding photo shoot takes place. The huge ocean frontage—3,000 sq m (32,292 sq ft) of it—provides a stunning background for these pictures, which can be edited and printed on the premises. The newlyweds then release a pair of white doves into the sky to symbolise their love. This is followed by a grand dinner, held either indoors or in the garden and featuring exquisite Asian and French dishes prepared by Chef Hikaru Take.

As dinner ends, there is dancing and entertainment provided by a band. And when the speeches conclude and the reception comes to a close, fireworks burst brightly in celebration.

FACILITIES
wedding pavilion for 100 • 3-bedroom wedding villa • dining pavilion • gazebo

FOOD
Asian and French

DRINK
bar • vintage wine cellar

FEATURES
florist • gifts for guests • hair and make-up services • entertainment • limousine service • pool • guest lounge • photographer • outdoor and indoor dining • sommelier

NEARBY
Bulgari Resort Bal • Pura Luhur Uluwatu

CONTACT
Jalan Uluwatu, Banjar Dinas Karang Boma, Desa Pecatu, Badung 80364 •
telephone: +62.361.847 1151 •
facsimile: +62.361.847 1160 •
email: info@tirtha.com •
website: www.tirthabridal.com

tirtha uluwatu

...devoted to bringing out the magic and romance of a tropical wedding in Bali.

For those who know and love Bali, there is a wedding venue that is particularly memorable for its beauty: Tirtha Uluwatu. The word *tirtha* in ancient Sanskrit translates as 'holy water'. Water performs an essential ceremonial function in traditional Hindu weddings, and its importance is reflected in the beautiful architecture and décor of Tirtha Uluwatu, which is located not far from the revered Pura Luhur Uluwatu in Bali's south.

Created by architect Glenn Parker, this striking venue is devoted to bringing out the magic and romance of a tropical wedding in Bali. The bridal packages are styled for both Asian and Western preferences, but can also be customised to offer a creative fusion of both worlds and to fulfil every possible wedding fantasy. Couples are assured of personalised service with a wedding planner on hand to help the couple through this most special occasion with nothing less than absolute peace of mind, knowing all their needs will be met.

The period of preparation begins with a warm welcome and a ferried ride from one's hotel to the venue. Organising pre-nuptial essentials is a breeze thanks to the on-site bridal boutique, gift shop and wedding studio. Couples are then entertained in the day suites, which offer romantic views of the gardens, ocean and private pool, until an agreed time. Following a brief meeting in the reception lounge, the bride and groom are ushered over an elevated walkway and into the stylish and modern wedding atrium, with an altar constructed from mother-of-pearl. The atrium itself is a dazzling A-line construction of white steel, glass and triangular sails, symbolising dreams about to take flight. The setting is further accentuated by an abundance of flowers, such as orchids, in the chapel.

Afterwards, the wedding party adjourns to the dining room for the reception and post-ceremony festivities. This room features teak wood and Chinese silk, with table settings that include exquisite chinaware, crystalware, silverware and generous floral arrangements to brighten up the place. The food complements the décor perfectly. A gourmet dinner of Asian- and French-inspired dishes is served behind floor-to-ceiling windows that offer views of the landscaped gardens and the Indian Ocean stretching out across the horizon. Couples can also choose to hold the festivities in a more relaxed open-air pavilion where the wedding party can enjoy dinner and dancing under the night sky.

THIS PAGE: *Set upon a pool of water, Tirtha Uluwatu is an ideal place for stunning wedding photos.*
OPPOSITE (FROM TOP): *A beautiful venue for a tropical wedding; a white marble path marks a new beginning in life; flowers, such as orchids and other tropical blooms, fill the chapel with gentle scents.*

FACILITIES
1 wedding atrium • 3 private dining rooms • 5 day suites • 1 open-air dining pavilion

FOOD
Asian and French

DRINK
liquor and wines

FEATURES
guest lounge • florist • indoor and outdoor dining • outdoor dance floor • wedding gown boutique

NEARBY
Bulgari Resort Bali • Pura Luhur Uluwatu

CONTACT
Jalan Raya Uluwatu, Banjar Dinas Karang Boma, Desa Pecatu, Badung 80364 •
telephone: +62.361.847 1151 •
facsimile: +62.361.847 1160 •
email: info@tirtha.com •
website: www.tirthabridal.com

warisan casa

...providing endless possibilities to create a unique look in one's home.

One of the most enchanting aspects of travelling is encountering different cultures and living environments. These encounters are particularly memorable in Asia, where hotel and resort decorators have a rich cultural heritage to work with. But the striking interiors that one sees are not mere imitations of tradition. Often, designers and interior decorators pay a lot of attention to adapting the best of local culture to suit modern settings, often to the extent that guests dream of recreating the look of an Asian luxury resort in their own homes.

But where can one find the myriad elements that make these places so special? It is not easy to achieve an artful combination of furniture, lighting and accessories, or to find quality materials and finishes. Those in the know head for one place: Warisan Casa.

Warisan Casa is the flagship retail outlet of Warisan, a company that has been producing high-quality solid wood furniture in Indonesia for more than 20 years, offering the best designs and quality finishes in the business. In recent years, Warisan has expanded into lighting,

THIS PAGE: *Touches of Asian art and artefacts enhance the exotic feel of a bedroom.*
OPPOSITE (FROM TOP): *Red adds a festive touch to the simple, yet classy look of the living room; the dining set and soft lighting create an intimate mood for a meal with loved ones.*

accessories, soft furnishings and works of art. The company has built a sterling reputation among resort developers and interior designers for quality, responsive service and excellent in-house design talent. Now, its products are available to the public directly through its store.

Warisan's signature collections were developed to please many tastes. At Warisan Casa, furniture comes in a range of styles—classic, colonial, Oriental, rustic, primitive, minimalist and modern, providing endless possibilities for a unique look at home, especially by mixing pieces from the different collections. Warisan Casa also offers accessories that round out a room's décor, including artwork for walls or tables, ceramics, antiques and selected artefacts from around the Indonesian archipelago, as well as lighting and other small ornaments.

In addition to furniture, Warisan Casa provides a range of soft furnishings. Those available here remind one that Warisan is accustomed to dressing exclusive resorts: every piece is produced to international standards, with top-quality materials, including quick-dry foam for outdoor use and fabrics by Sunbrella, Jim Thompson, Donghia and other leading names in the textile industry. Locally woven cloth is also available.

Warisan Casa is an excellent source of inspiration for anyone who dreams of bringing the luxury of tropical living home with them. With its broad range of furniture, accessories and lighting, the Warisan look is not limited to island homes. Individual pieces and collections work well in almost any setting, creating a tropical Asian feeling in a city dwelling, a mountain lodge, a country farmhouse or even a classic chateau.

PRODUCTS
antiques • indoor and outdoor furniture • home accessories • art and artefacts • lighting • soft furnishings

FEATURES
artwork • custom work • design consulting • use of reclaimed and sustainable materials

NEARBY
Jimbaran Bay • Nusa Dua • Kuta • airport • luxury resorts • restaurants • shopping

CONTACT
Jalan Raya Bypass Ngurah Rai, Kedongan, Jimbaran, Badung 80364 •
telephone: +62.361.701 081 •
facsimile: +62.361.701 634 •
email: casa@warisan.com •
website: www.warisan.com/stores.htm

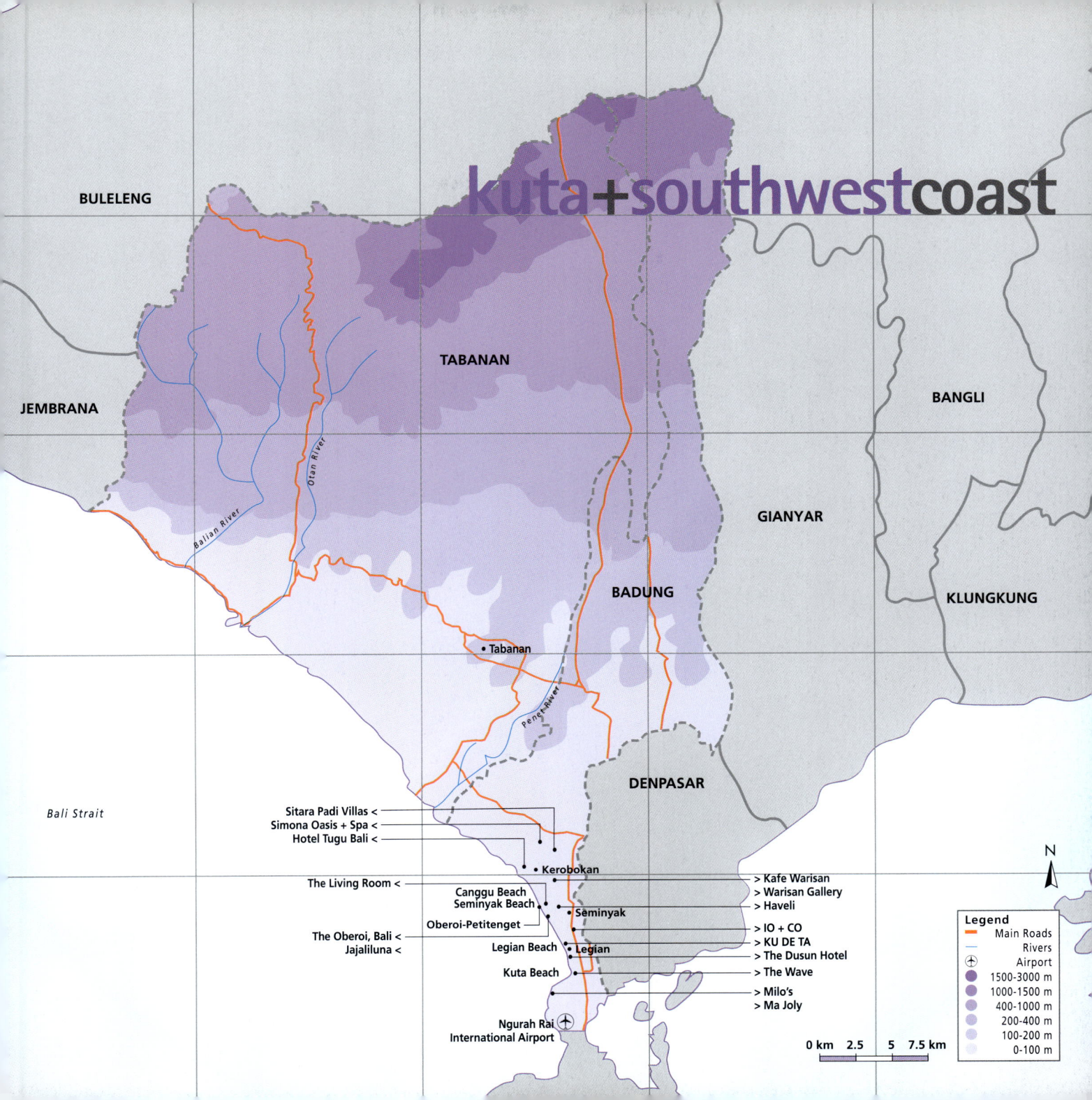

the migration of coastal cool

Bali's international airport sits on the shore in Tuban, with its runway on top of a coral reef. A wide beach begins at this exact point, curving northwards in a gentle arc to embrace an open bay. From the airport to Cemagi point in Canggu lie 16 km (10 miles) of almost uninterrupted sand. The migration of Bali's cool crowd for the past 35 years has followed this curving strand from south to north.

In the 1970s, Kuta was the place to be, down south near the airport. Beyond it were nothing but coconut groves, rice fields and muddy footpaths. Bali's hippies hung out in Kuta until mainstream tourism invaded their private paradise, and then they headed out, building bungalows and businesses further afield. Legian, Kuta's neighbour to the north, was colonised by the trendy set in the 1980s. A decade later, when it was deemed too hot to handle, the ultra-cool migrated up the coast to Seminyak.

The race is on to find prime places to unwind in the lands beyond: Umalas and Canggu. Follow the curve of the coast: from red-hot Kuta to the indigo-cool of Seminyak and beyond, there's a full spectrum of fun on Bali's southwest coast.

a line in the sand

The busiest districts of this trendy coast are linked by one main artery, Jalan Raya (Indonesian for 'main street'), which runs parallel to the beach from Kuta to Seminyak. The road is pretty narrow and gets very congested during the high season in August. But no matter, because there is so much to see and do along the way—who wants to travel quickly while on a leisurely holiday?

Jalan Raya is lined from one end to the other with shops and restaurants of every imaginable kind. It is jam-packed with fantastic stuff to buy, eat, drink and wear for a full 5 km (3 miles). Cheap beads, glamourous fashion, batik and bikinis abound, and more upscale shops are strewn randomly throughout it all, showing the creations of Bali's innovative designers and artisans. Rave wear with random zippers, cut-outs and cosmic graphics, insanely high platform sandals, blindingly bright beaded bags,

PAGE 192: *Frangipani blossoms floating in a blue-tiled pool evoke that tropical holiday feel.*

THIS PAGE: *The scene on the beach at Legian is a congenial mix of locals, expatriates and travellers.*

OPPOSITE: *A peaceful horseback ride at dawn is one of the most pleasant ways to enjoy the beaches of Canggu, Seminyak and Legian.*

It is a non-stop carnival with a kitsch appeal.

leather apparel in a rainbow of colours and silver jewellery in fantastic shapes—it is all on offer. Walking along this street is never a bore. From high fashion to street fashion, and from handicrafts to handmade homeware of international quality, there is a universe of shopping options here.

Less than 40 years ago, Jalan Raya was just a path through coconut plantations, where cows nibbled the turf and one could spot a rich farmer by the fact that he had one clove cigarette in his mouth and an extra one tucked behind his ear—only tycoons sported spare cigarettes on both ears. Pony carts, pedestrians and the occasional motorcycle that plied the Kuta–Seminyak track eventually wore through the grass and it became a ribbon of bumpy sand. Finding the smoothest line through it was often a topic of some debate in the bamboo shacks of Kuta, where the area's early expatriates held court. Now, Kuta is a round-the-clock bazaar of the beautiful and bizarre. To stroll through the entire strip is an ambitious undertaking, recommended only for the most hardcore of shopaholics.

kuta: a crazy carnival city with a beach

Jalan Raya starts in the heart of Kuta, Bali's craziest beach town. It is a non-stop carnival with a kitsch appeal. Kuta has always been funky, but now its flavour is getting richer. What began as a cluster of surf shacks and cafés soon became an urban maze of amusing mayhem. Then, tragedy struck Kuta in 2002, when terrorist bombs killed over 200 people. The fizz went flat and Kuta fell on hard times. Now, there is a renaissance under way and the parts of town that were 'downmarket' are rising again on a wave of new investment.

The flavour of Kuta is being reformulated in a way that is modern and cosmopolitan. Streets once in shambles are now home to multi-storey shopping centres housing global brands. The beachfront boasts the world's first Hard Rock Hotel, a large

THIS PAGE: *Beachfront parties and clubs in Seminyak, Legian and Kuta keep the crowds dancing until dawn.*
OPPOSITE: *By day, colourful kites decorate the skies or compete for prizes in the annual Kuta Carnival.*

THIS PAGE (FROM TOP): *Plenty of cheap and cheerful souvenirs are piled high in the sidewalk stalls of Kuta and Legian; residents and tourists come together to release baby sea turtles raised in a hatchery—their numbers are threatened by illegal culling for their meat and body parts.*
OPPOSITE: *The street scene in Kuta, although crowded and chaotic, has a funky charm all its own.*

Starbucks and a stylish, three-storey entertainment complex with a view of the setting sun. Nearby is a modern mega-mall called Discovery Shopping Mall, beside Musro, a big-city club with Las Vegas-style cabaret shows, live bands, DJs 'til dawn, and private karaoke rooms with sexy hostesses.

Yes, Kuta has gone global in a big way. It is still lots of fun, but with big clubs, big names and big hotels. It still has the big surf that got everything going in the first place and a big beach that is as beautiful as it ever was. Surfers and sunbathers still cavort on the sand, where passing vendors sell temporary tattoos, beaded hair-braiding and fake Rolexes. Only now they have fake Franck Mullers and Suuntos, too. Indeed, even the funky beach scene of Kuta has gone global.

Vestiges of local charm survive in Kuta's side streets, however. Narrow lanes from the beach to the main street hide alluring spots unchanged by the tide of plate glass and stainless steel sweeping the high street. Poppies Bali is one of them. A Bali institution, Poppies began in 1973 as a little café cooking banana pancakes for hungry surfers. In 1975, the owners put up a few thatch-roofed bungalows. It has hardly changed in over 30 years, but the scene around it certainly has. When the bungalows were built, they were surrounded by acres of coconut trees, with a view straight through to the beach. Now, you can hardly find Poppies; it is completely engulfed by the city around it. Made's Warung in Kuta has a similar story. It, too, is a Bali institution with its original flavour intact. TJ's Mexican Restaurant, another pleasant oasis, has stayed almost the same since the 1980s when it opened. There are still scraps of old Kuta hidden away, and a stroll through the small streets can lead to atmospheric locations, but one has to get out of the car and walk.

gotta love legian

When Kuta was transformed from a bohemian backwater to a bona fide tourist destination, the hip crowd moved up to Legian. In the 1980s and 1990s, they built bungalows here in big, shady gardens, and the world's knowledgeable travellers

Vestiges of local charm survive in Kuta's side streets, however.

joined them. Legian sprung to life at a time when nomadic spirituality was in fashion, and the beautiful people took to it in droves. This was the era of house music, rave culture and a general global love-in that chose as its party zones Goa, Ibiza and Bali. People raved by night and during the day practised Osho, Vipassana, yoga, satsang and shopping. The enlightened glitterati who took over Legian in those days gave it a certain glamour that had been lacking in Kuta.

Amidst Legian's few thoroughfares is a network of little lanes and paved paths that start and end on a whim. Most are not passable by car, yet they snake their way through to the hundreds of villas and bungalows that sprung up like mushrooms when

Legian first took off. It is all rather random, an organic outgrowth of the cosmopolitan crowd that colonised it. The labyrinths of Legian are still mostly residential and quiet, with pockets of green land left vacant for no discernible reason. One suspects the lack of road or path access is to blame. Still, the green bits are a blessing.

Besides the big beach hotels, accommodation in Legian is still quite cheap and of the bungalow variety, with some classy villas popping up here and there. One senses an inevitable move upmarket, however, heralded by the Outrigger, a glamourous apartment block on Blue Ocean beach.

The focal point of Legian was, and still is, Blue Ocean Boulevard, a brief bit of road that runs right along Legian beach. Blue Ocean is a popular hangout, with a row of cafés, a great mix of people, and lounge chairs on the sand. There is a surfing school there by day and a booming club scene all night.

Blue Ocean cafés fill up at sunset with a diverse crowd. What first got this strip going was a club called Double Six, which still rages on until dawn seven nights a week. Its owner won the land it sits on by throwing a double six on the dice, hence its name. This is the only nightclub in the world with its own bungy jumping tower above a big swimming pool, run by A. J. Hackett, the New Zealander who made bungy jumping popular. Clubbers can take a jump anytime if the dance floor's not thrilling enough.

Double Six has an elite lounge in an annexe to the main club, formerly known as Paparazzi, now relaunched as Syndicate. It draws a better-dressed crowd, as does its sister club down the road, Bacio. At all three, not least in Bacio, the ratio of slinky Indonesian women to tourists is high. *Bacio* is Italian for 'kiss'. Since Legian began booming, it has been awash with love and kisses—universal love and the carnal kind, air kisses and illicit ones. It is all part of Legian, and one just has to love it.

THIS PAGE: *Bacio is one of the slickest nightclubs on the beach in Legian.*
OPPOSITE: *Surfers discovered the waves of Kuta, Legian and Seminyak in the 1970s, and today, a whole new generation is rediscovering them, along with the breaks of Canggu and Seseh further up the coast, which are growing in popularity.*

all the talk is about seminyak

Since refugees of the building boom and booming bass beats of Legian started shifting to Seminyak, the town has taken off like a rocket to the stratosphere of cool. Like Bali's hip coast as a whole, Seminyak has a north to south gradient, getting hipper the further north you go. In the south is Jalan Dhyana Pura, a strip of nightclubs and bars that is always in a state of flux. The summit of chic is the northern part of Seminyak, with prime beachfront stretching from The Oberoi and KU DE TA up to Petitenget.

For shopping, sleeping, seeing and being seen, nowhere in Bali beats Seminyak. Just as Legian came after Kuta and upped the glamour ante, so Seminyak followed on from Legian and raised the stakes higher still. Seminyak's prices have gone up, too. One often gets what one pays for, and Seminyak delivers the goods. Hotels and villas here are the last word in luxury; the area's boutiques are bursting with the best local styles; and the restaurants and nightspots are legendary.

Seminyak is such a phenomenon that it even has its own magazine, *The Yak*, a local lifestyle bible for the *Wallpaper* generation. Sold in trendy venues for the stylish traveller, this publication covers the Seminyak scene from end to end. Its founder, Sophie Digby, whirls like a top from one exciting party to the next, keeping tabs on Seminyak society and sniffing out trends. There is some decent writing in there between the many glamourous advertisements. So if it is in *The Yak* it is probably a fact—at least in Seminyak.

the fickle face of fabulousness

Not all of Seminyak is a screaming success. Some of it is in need of town planners and the style police. Ripe for rehabilitation is the formerly fabulous Jalan Dhyana Pura, also known as 'the Gaza Strip'. Before the Kuta bombing it was Bali's most booming nightlife zone. Lined with lounge-bars, clubs and discos, it was a raucous free-for-all every night. The intense concentration of Westerners made some say it 'smelled' like a bomb target and that pushed the crowds away. An air of increasing debauchery also turned people off. Finally, the local community pulled the plug on some of the street's excesses. Clubs closed, reopened with different names, then closed again. Jalan Dhyana Pura is shape-shifting now, with some nightclubs looking ripe for rebirth, but as what, no one knows. Chic retail is coming in quickly and opportunity knocks.

Further north, Seminyak's hippest area, the Oberoi–Petitenget district, has established itself firmly on an elite level. Getting there from Jalan Dhyana Pura though

THIS PAGE: *Private villas have been popping up in Seminyak and the scenic districts beyond it, drawing an increasingly elite crowd who rent or buy the palatial properties.*
OPPOSITE: *Exclusive beach villas and hotels in Seminyak offer levels of serenity, privacy and elegance rarely found anywhere else.*

is no easy feat. This points out a problem plaguing Seminyak—the roads. They are completely inadequate for a growing population, especially one that is accustomed to Rodeo Drive or Via Montenapoleone. The most direct drive from Jalan Dhyana Pura to The Oberoi is a narrow lane—with 13 sleeping policemen—so brutal it will shake your Chanel shades off your nose on the way. It is called Jalan Sarinande, or Sari Dewi, pointing out another headache in Seminyak. Roads have multiple names and numeric addresses are creative rather than sequential.

Jalan Sarinande is symptomatic of Seminyak's lack of planning. It is the focus of intensive luxury villa development, but still too narrow for cars coming in opposite directions to pass. This is madness, of course, causing face-offs that have ended in fisticuffs. In exasperation, Sarinande's most stylish complex, The Elysian, put radio-toting flagmen on the street to manage the flow and avoid confrontations. What happens next is anyone's guess. Ironically, Oberoi–Petitenget's best retail and restaurant street is in the worst condition of all. Jalan Laksmana, as it is officially known, is a moonscape of potholes, its narrow tarmac blocked by rogue vehicles randomly parked and taxis cruising at a snail's pace.

the inner sanctum of chic

The clogged and chaotic Jalan Laksmana runs from Seminyak's main street to the beach, arriving where The Oberoi sits sedately beside 'party central', KU DE TA. The road was once called Jalan Oberoi, after the hotel, until the government rechristened it Jalan Laksmana. As Seminyak boomed, it suddenly sprouted a row of popular restaurants and was nicknamed 'Eat Street'. High-end retail boutiques soon followed and new ones are opening at a dizzying rate. Accordingly, *The Yak* and locals now call it 'Boutique Street'. No matter what you call it though, Jalan Laksmana is a phenomenon, a dynamic shopping and eating environment like no other in Bali.

The Oberoi–Petitenget area, for the moment, is the most desirable district. It is defined by a stretch of road starting at Jalan Laksmana, following Jalan Petitenget, and looping back along Jalan Raya Seminyak. This inner circle of chic is a world unto itself, complete with restaurants, lounge-bars, nightclubs, elite retailers, luxury hotels, villas and the best stretch of beach in Seminyak. It began with just a few landmarks: KU DE TA, The Oberoi, The Legian Suites, La Lucciola restaurant and a Greek café called Mykonos. All were beloved only by those in the know. Word got out about five years ago and development exploded. Now, property here is so hot that there's no stopping the boom. Real estate agents have cropped up on every corner and villas are rising from the rice fields at an alarming rate. Some are bona fide luxury residences, while others are glorified ghettos, where miniscule gardens encase plate glass bungalows resembling air-conditioned ATM kiosks.

This district of Seminyak is largely responsible for the 'villa-fication' of Bali. For the migratory global social set that loves Seminyak, staying in a hotel is just not done—it's villas, and villas only. And the Oberoi–Petitenget district is the best address. Access to

THIS PAGE: *Lounge-bars in the ultra-trendy Petitenget area are known for their creative cocktails, equally creative DJs, inviting swimming pools and dreamy gardens.*
OPPOSITE: *KU DE TA has been the mainstay of Seminyak's nightlife—and daytime lounging—for nearly a decade.*

THIS PAGE: One of the world's most scenic golf courses—and a challenging one, too—is found near the temple of Tanah Lot on the coast beyond Canggu.

OPPOSITE: Tanah Lot is best viewed after sunset or at dawn, when the tour buses are gone and total tranquillity returns to the temple, which is set on a rocky outcrop overlooking the Indian Ocean.

KU DE TA, the phenomenally successful beachside club, is key. If one can't shoot a champagne cork from KU DE TA to one's villa, it might be too far away. The popularity of this place means it gets a bit crowded, but there are other nightspots nearby. Just up the road is The Living Room, Hu'u and Luxe Lounge at Sentosa Private Villas and Spa. When the sun comes up, the best breakfasts can be had within stumbling distance at La Lucciola, right on the beach.

Further along Jalan Petitenget is the Bali Catering Company, managed by Kafe Warisan. Besides catering for in-villa parties both large and small, the company sells a tempting range of pre-packaged delicacies and patisserie. The refrigerated pâtés, terrines, soups and sauces are superb, making it easy to impress one's impromptu guests. The company is fast becoming the daily deli stop for discriminating villa dwellers.

canggu beckons

Many of the villa dwellers shopping at the Bali Catering Company are on their way home to the up-and-coming areas north and west of Seminyak. The migration of cool which began in Kuta and rolled north for decades is rolling on. Those who feel Seminyak is urbanising too fast have cast their eyes north and west again. The neighbourhoods of Umalas, Semer and Kuwum are still a bit of a hodgepodge, lacking good roads and filling in fast between what roads there are. There is, however, a very nice riding stable in Umalas, for beach treks and serious riding.

The next nice neighbourhood is Berawa, a beach waiting to be discovered, and beyond it the rolling hills and crashing surf of Canggu. This is the district that looks likely to become Bali's answer to California's Santa Barbara or Ojai. The size of the building lots tends to be bigger here than down in Seminyak, and there are even some beachfront plots still to be had, for a price. Canggu and the towns beyond it benefit from the proximity of Le Méridien Nirwana Golf & Spa Resort, a few miles further along the coast near Tanah Lot. This, and the completion in Canggu of a big international school and a country club, signify where the southwest coast's next hot spot will be.

The migration of cool which began in Kuta and rolled north for decades is rolling on.

the dusun hotel

...service and ambience are natural, normal and never intrusive.

THIS PAGE: *Guests can relax around the 'village' pool, though this one looks more luxurious than most.*

OPPOSITE (CLOCKWISE FROM TOP): *Breakfast is served; enjoy a petal-strewn bath; a poolside seat is just what holidaymakers long for; the rooms contain every amenity for every eventuality.*

Dusun means 'village' in Bahasa Indonesia, and it is a very appropriate name for this boutique hotel, which comprises just 14 thatch-roof villas, each self-contained. There is no lobby or restaurant and no standing on ceremony, making it more like an isolated hamlet than a hotel. Robert Hepworth, The Dusun Hotel's creator, has realised with this property his vision of a new kind of Bali hotel: villas that feel like privately rented residences, but without the problems that come with rentals, and each offering hotel-style service and amenities.

A pioneer in the field, Robert co-founded The Villas, Bali's first development of serviced holiday homes. Then he outdid himself by creating The Dusun, which is in an even better location. The hotel sits squarely in the most desirable neighbourhood in Bali, Petitenget. A short and pleasant stroll away are Seminyak's best beaches, restaurants, spas and

nightspots, including 'Eat Street' (also known as Bali's famous restaurant row) and Bodyworks.

Guests at this hotel have no need for wheels at all. They can easily walk to the shops—from those serving basic needs to the chic boutiques, they are all just a short stroll away. That kind of convenience makes for an exceptionally relaxing stay. Even in this prime spot, The Dusun remains blissfully quiet as it is set in a little lane off the paved road. The flexibility of a private villa allows guests to shop for themselves and cook in their kitchen or order in from dozens of excellent restaurants nearby.

The Dusun takes a friendly, family approach to hospitality in every regard. The service and ambience are natural, normal and never intrusive. Each villa has its own butler, but guests soon find he is more like their best friend in Bali. Requests and questions are handled pragmatically, without any fuss. This approach works well, if The Dusun's guestbook is any indication. It reads more like the guestbook of a private country house than a hotel comment sheet, with personal jokes, sketches and pasted-in photos. Clearly, guests see the staff as their buddies and the hotel as a home away from home.

Don't be fooled by the relaxed attitude, however. This is not just a bunch of beach bungalows. The Dusun is laden with luxury; the villas are spacious and so are their gardens. Pools are generous in size, and the décor is bright and tasteful, in neutral tones, with extras such as satellite TV, free wi-fi Internet access, and complimentary use of a car and a chauffeur. All of these create a combination of informality and lavishness which guests are bound to remember fondly.

ROOMS
7 three-bedroom pool villas •
7 one-bedroom pool villas

FOOD
self-catered • chef upon request •
shopping service • delivery from
nearby restaurants and cafés

DRINK
shopping service • self-catered

FEATURES
spa treatments on call • library • CDs •
DVDs • satellite TV • IDD phones

BUSINESS
business centre • high-speed Internet
access • translation services •
chauffeur • secretarial services
on request

NEARBY
Pura Petitenget • beaches • lounge-
bars • nightclubs • shops •
restaurants • riding stables • surfing

CONTACT
Jalan Kayu Jati 8, Petitenget,
Kerobokan, Seminyak,
Badung 80361 •
telephone: +62.361.734 000 •
facsimile: +62.361.734 100 •
email: reservations@the-dusun.com •
website: www.the-dusun.com

hotel tugu bali

Those with a taste for rich, strong flavours and a sense of mystery will be well served...

THIS PAGE (FROM TOP): *Puri Le Mayeur is a honeymooner's villa built over a natural lotus pond, where guests also enjoy a private dining pavilion; Kamar Samedhi, the meditation room, looks invitingly serene.*
OPPOSITE (FROM TOP): *Scented oils prepared for the use of guests; the rustic-looking outdoor spa is where the traditional treatments are administered.*

Along Canggu beach, where fishermen spread their nets on the sand in the afternoon, lies Hotel Tugu Bali, a surreal surprise of a hotel. Inside, each room and suite has a unique design scheme, inviting guests to immerse themselves in the different settings portrayed. Yet the styles of décor never overwhelm or clash: this is a themed hotel that is never tacky. The antiques are authentic, and so is the spirit of the place.

Created by a Javanese connoisseur of Indonesian culture, history and antiques, Hotel Tugu Bali was bound to be an extraordinary hotel. Those with a taste for rich, strong flavours and a sense of mystery will be well served, as will those who love the peaceful seaside atmosphere.

To enter Tugu, visitors must walk across a polished wooden bridge, past a 300-year-old Chinese temple-turned-dining salon, before arriving in a vast dark space which serves as Tugu's lobby: the appropriately named Great Room. With teak lounge chairs styled as in a private club, it is reminiscent of an ancient lodge or a historic estate that has been turned into a hotel.

The suites in Tugu evoke that escapist mood as well. The Walter Spies Pavilion, named after the German artist who made his home in Yogyakarta in the 1930s, is decorated with Art Deco furniture, stained-glass windows and original memorabilia such as the artist's camera and photographs. The Puri Le Mayeur Villa, a romantic residence built over a lotus pond, commemorates the love story between Belgian painter Adrien Jean Le Mayeur de Merprès and Balinese dancer Ni Polok, and displays items that Ni Polok left to the owner. Other suites, too, gently introduce guests to the rich culture and lush landscapes of Bali.

Even the numerous dining options are designed to instil a sense of adventure in guests. The Balinese Rajadom offers traditional imperial dining once enjoyed by Balinese royalty in the Dutch colonial era. Simpler but no less exotic is the *megibung*, which can be enjoyed in Wantilan Agung or with a Balinese dance performance by the pond in the Bale Agung area.

Those searching for relaxation will find five spa sanctuaries, each named after a traditional form of beauty or spa treatment in Indonesia. The Mantra therapy—unique in Bali—combines the chanting of mantras, which open the chakras, with a special Tugu massage and is one of the most popular treatments. Accompanying Balinese music completes the experience. This hotel is a haven for visitors who dream of an exotic, surreal Java and Bali. For those who feel at home with romance and fantasy, the magic of Hotel Tugu Bali will be irresistible.

ROOMS
1 Puri Le Mayeur Villa (one-bedroom) • 1 Walter Spies Pavilion • 1 two-bedroom suite • 18 one-bedroom suites

FOOD
Bale Agung: seafood, continental • traditional Balinese, Javanese, and Chinese Peranakan • Bale Sutra: Chinese cuisine • Bale Puputan: Dutch colonial smorgasbord and Balinese Rajadom • Black Chamber: Peranakan • Wantilan Agung: *megibung* • Waroeng Tugu: Javanese and Balinese • tropical garden/poolside: casual • beachfront: seafood barbecue • Colony Room: Dutch colonial • lotus pond: breakfast and casual dining

DRINK
Bale Agung • wine cellar

FEATURES
Waroeng Djamoe Spa • dancing, *gamelan* and cooking classes • antiques collection • pool • massages • fitness facilities • cycling • sunset horse-drawn *bendi* rides • tennis • horseback riding • snooker table

BUSINESS
weddings and events for up to 150 in themed environments

NEARBY
Batu Bolong • Cangu village • Tanah Lot • beaches • golf • rice terraces • surfing

CONTACT
Jalan Pantai Batu Bolong, Canggu Beach, Canggu, Badung 80361 • telephone: +62.361.731 701 • facsimile: +62.361.731 708 • email: bali@tuguhotels.com • website: www.tuguhotels.com

jajaliluna

...a sophisticated family residence that feels just like home...

Jajaliluna is an elegant, modern villa located in the most desirable neighbourhood of Bali, the Oberoi–Petitenget area. The benefits of this location are priceless. Just outside the villa are the biggest beaches, the most stylish clubs and a row of the hippest restaurants on the island. This setting is a dream for young socialites and hip urban travellers. But it is not just the young and unfettered who will find Jajaliluna's location a big draw; it is perfect for families too.

Few parents want to be chained to the holiday home during their holiday or tied down by the demands of their children. They want to enjoy posh shopping and gourmet dining, and party with Bali's beautiful people. Unfortunately, with some rental villas, the location leaves these attractions too far away. Dividing time between the lush life and family life becomes a challenge, but not at Jajaliluna. There is no need to spend half the holiday in a car, shuttling kids to their favourite places, or battling back through traffic to check on mischievous teenagers. Jajaliluna sits precisely where the entire family wants to be. The best of Bali for little children, teenagers and savvy parents is right at their doorstep.

And inside the pivoting panel gate of Jajaliluna is a sophisticated family residence that feels just like home—or a dream family home. One enters through a unique Bali-style gate,

THIS PAGE: *The lounge pavilion is the perfect place to unwind in the evenings.*

OPPOSITE (CLOCKWISE FROM TOP): *A poolside siesta for two; a casual picnic lunch by the pool can be arranged; cool breezes waft gently through the doors.*

where the door is a solid panel which pivots at its centre, rather than a traditional two-panel door. The path to the house crosses over a koi pond featuring bowls ablaze with welcoming fire. Innovative design elements such as these enhance every part of the villa's walled garden compound.

Living spaces are set in three pavilions, all located right on the edge of a big, turquoise swimming pool. The main two-storey structure contains a living room, mezzanine and four en-suite bedrooms. All four are the same size and shape, eliminating status battles between members of a group or family. One is

furnished with bunk beds for four kids, and the others with king-size beds. A balcony overlooks the pool, the lawns and the two additional pavilions. There is also an open but formal dining room for taking meals together, and a luxurious space for lounging or yoga.

Big sofas and sunbeds line the pool, so everyone can get comfortable in their own space, and an outdoor picnic table with adjacent barbecue is ideal for casual family meals or a meal by the pool. Throughout Jajaliluna, the interior décor is clean and crisp, a vision of simplicity done in predominantly white and cream, while the grounds have a relaxed design, altogether creating an atmosphere of freshness and tranquillity that calms the spirit.

The staff are numerous and diligent. They keep all the white interiors spotless, do the laundry and take care of the shopping and cooking as well. A full-time villa manager supervises three butlers and maids, four security guards, a gardener and a pool attendant. For groups or families, this arrangement promises a completely hassle-free holiday.

But it will never be a dull one. In addition to the hotspots of Bali in the neighbourhood, Jajaliluna guests have the added benefit of receiving 'gold key' membership cards for the Canggu Club, Bali's most complete sports and country club, about 15 minutes away by car. Sports, recreation and a spacious villa all add up to create a memorable family holiday.

ROOMS
3 bedrooms with king-size beds • 1 bedroom for four children

FOOD
groceries plus service charge • chef • delivery from restaurants and cafés nearby

DRINK
shopping service • catering for cocktail or dinner parties • self-catered

FEATURES
DVDs • IDD phone • pool • spa treatments on request • satellite TV • wi-fi Internet access

NEARBY
Canggu Club • Seminyak beach • surfing • shopping • supermarkets • cafés • restaurants • nightclubs • lounge-bars • riding stables

CONTACT
No. 12A Jalan Laksamana Oberoi, Seminyak Beach, Seminyak, Badung 80361 •
telephone: +62.361.730 668 •
facsimile: +62 361.736 391 •
email: info@balihomes.com •
website: www.jajaliluna.com

the oberoi, bali

...inside its rugged boundary walls, it remains absolutely tranquil and unruffled.

The Oberoi, Bali presents a Balinese version of a 'Grand Hotel' in the great tradition of 'Grand Hotels'. While the dignity and understatement one expects of the world's such establishments is almost palpable here, its flavour is absolutely Balinese. The resort is laid out like a village, with 60 thatch-roof rooms and 14 villas under mature trees, spread out over the vast estate.

The place exudes restrained luxury. The baroque ornamentality of wooden and stone carvings is balanced by the simplicity and spaciousness of the natural setting. Nothing is crowded or contrived. Even the beach feels grand. It is the longest, widest, smoothest beach of any beachfront hotel in Bali, with 500 m (547 ft) of uninterrupted golden sand

First-class frequent fliers adore The Oberoi, as do the frazzled executive elite and honeymooners. In fact, many families have made it a tradition that their members honeymoon at The Oberoi, Bali. This place has been around in one form or another for more than 30 years. That is ancient history in the timeline of tourism development in Bali. When an international businessman built the place as a private club for himself and other globetrotting glitterati, there was still no electricity in the area, and there wasn't until 1986. The Oberoi was still considered to be at the 'back of beyond'. The nearest hint of civilisation was way down in Legian, where bohemian backpackers were just discovering Bali.

Now, The Oberoi is in the middle of the hippest neighbourhood in Bali, a coconut's throw from trendy shopping, restaurants and nightlife. The life of the town has come to it, rather than the other way around. But inside its rugged boundary walls, it remains absolutely tranquil and unruffled. Sprawling over 6 hectares (15 acres), it seems to be a whole time zone away from

THIS PAGE (FROM TOP): *Even after so many years, the resort still manages to draw guests with its quiet, understated charm; guests usually come to think of The Oberoi, Bali as their home away from home.*
OPPOSITE: *A villa with a pool allows guests to dive in anytime they wish.*

the lively scene around it. Guests can party and shop, dance until they drop, then zip quickly back to The Oberoi to recover and regain their spirits in peace.

Some do not bother to go out at all. Why should they? Within The Oberoi, everything one could desire and more is provided. Each of the Lanai rooms has a terrace for outdoor dining and a luxurious bathroom with a sunken bath, while the villas come with a dining pavilion—eight

of them have private, full-size swimming pools—and stately bathrooms that inspired the global Balinese-style bathroom trend. All guestrooms have satellite TV, wi-fi, DVD players and air-conditioning. On the grounds, there is a generous beachside pool, a tennis court, a deluxe spa, a salon and a fitness centre. There is also a gift shop and a gallery frequented not only by guests, but by the cognoscenti of Bali as well. They come to browse the collection, which comprises some of the best creations of Bali's artisans and designers.

Savvy Baliphiles also come for the unpretentious ambience of The Kura Kura, a restaurant in an open pavilion serving fine cuisine; and for Frangipani Café, which is set beside a lily pond and feels more like a beachside umbrella-shaded country club than a café. The chef is famous for his whole live lobster and many other seafood dishes that make full use of the fresh catch available from the sea every day. The menus of both restaurants are well rounded and include Indonesian, continental and Indian cusines.

THIS PAGE: *Details such as Balinese stone carvings and fringed umbrellas by the main pool bring out the exotic flavour of Bali without overwhelming the guest.*
OPPOSITE (FROM LEFT): *The lily pond by the Frangipani Café; there is no need to leave the resort when The Oberoi, Bali looks so welcoming.*

The spa offers a wide range of treatments (Thai, Indonesian, Hawaiian and Ayurvedic) and is superbly managed by the Banyan Tree staff. This spa is especially suited for people new to the spa experience. It is not fussy, and has special expertise in men's treatments and massages. Travel-weary business moguls are particularly pleased with it. Stressed-out, spa-phobic individuals should be sent immediately to The Oberoi's spa on arrival. They will be thankful for the encouragement to overcome that initial anxiety about spas, and at the same time retain good memories from the first-rate treatments administered to them.

The Oberoi can be old-fashioned and relaxed in feeling, like a classic old club for ladies and gentlemen. There is an air of dignity about the place, but it is a 'shoes off' dignity, never officious or rigid, which explains why many dignitaries have stayed here: Kofi Annan, Henry Kissinger and Xanana Gusmão, among others, as well as heads of state from around the globe. The Oberoi is discreet, never flashy, so even new visitors will be comfortable here. It is surprising then, that The Oberoi has built a reputation for style and charm that continues to attract repeat guests and new ones. It also picks up industry accolades with a consistency that newer establishments can only envy, and usually makes the list of top hotels and resorts.

Opinion is unanimous among loyal guests that its staff is one of The Oberoi's greatest assets. Many have worked here for 20 years or more, delivering the genteel, discreet Oberoi style of service. To understand Oberoi service, think 'British butler', then add the natural warmth of the Balinese people. They seem to know exactly when to appear and what with. Polite, intuitive wish fulfilment is their goal. Whether guests desire a secluded candlelit dinner for two under a frangipani tree, or something more complicated, such as an intimate wedding for a small gathering of family and friends, their requests can all be arranged.

In keeping with the aura of dignity, rooms are elegant in a subdued way. Those who take a villa can retreat into a walled garden, enjoying both space and seclusion. Venturing outside in the afternoon, they can enjoy tea and treats served al fresco daily. In the evening, The Oberoi's excellent Balinese dance and musical performances are held in the amphitheatre. These performances are complemented by a traditional Indonesian buffet dinner, which presents the best of Indonesian cuisine. But even food pales in comparison to the on-stage offerings. Performance dinners at The Oberoi are regarded as the best cultural entertainment in the area, and non-Oberoi guests often attend them.

ROOMS
60 rooms • 14 villas

FOOD
Frangipani Café: fresh seafood and light meals • The Kura Kura: Indonesian, continental and Indian

DRINK
Kayu Bar

FEATURES
beach • gardens • pool • spa • tennis • theatre

BUSINESS
business centre • cocktail room for 80 • Internet access • meeting rooms

NEARBY
bars • shops • cafés • restaurants

CONTACT
Jalan Laksmana, Seminyak Beach, Seminyak, Badung 80361 •
telephone: +62.361.730 361 •
facsimile: +62.361.730 791 •
email: reservations@theoberoi-bali.com •
website: www.oberoihotels.com

simona oasis + spa

...built with careful planning and a weighty consideration of aesthetic principles...

There are so many luxury villas in Bali that it can be bewildering to choose one. Scores of new rental properties are launched every year and they offer levels of luxury once unimaginable on this island. Simona Oasis & Spa is among one of the most outstanding.

This is also one of the most beautiful villas yet created in Bali. When it opened in 2007, it raised the bar with its elegance, which distilled the best of villa design. Where some Bali villa designers have given in to the urge to be over-extravagant, Simona Oasis' creators exercised discretion and taste in order to appeal to travellers who value sophistication and subtlety. A Simona Oasis guest is likely to be wearing perfectly cut linen in neutral tones; she or he is someone who finds comfort in the natural beauty of the villa's surroundings, dislikes fuss and ceremony, and is contented to regard the villa as a casual, yet classy holiday home.

Simona Oasis is in Canggu, a coastal community that seems to be developing in a more genteel way than its neighbours to the southeast. The quality, size and architecture of villas in Canggu are noticeably better than the hodgepodge collection of architecture popping up elsewhere. Simona Oasis, built with careful planning and a weighty consideration of aesthetic principles, both typifies and transcends this trend.

Situated on a secluded section of Canggu where two rivers meet, the estate offers accommodation for up to 10, in five self-contained pavilions. Two additional pavilions house living and dining spaces and a complete spa. All are thatch-roof structures, built with carefully chosen natural materials—white limestone, off-white terrazzo and the warm browns of *bingkirai* wood—while a subtle coffee and cream colour scheme prevails throughout for the furnishings and other details. It is the epitome of finesse and quality. Nothing jars the senses or

THIS PAGE: *Bedrooms are perfectly proportioned so that guests feel comfortable and rested here.*
OPPOSITE (FROM TOP): *The outdoor bathtub promises a sensuous and delightful experience; like royalty, guests can relax by the pool under a thatched pavilion, or rest languidly on the daybeds with a drink.*

offends refined sensibilities. Dramatic touches do come into play around the villa, but they are executed with restraint and used appropriately, never in excess.

The pool at Simona Oasis is large, measuring 13 m by 6 m (14 ft by 7 ft) and is another essay in simplicity. It is set amid generous terraces and lawns, with every element in harmonious proportion. Spring-fed ponds grace the gardens, which step gently down to the river. An open lounge pavilion by the pool looks down to the river and another sits right on its banks. Both are draped in signature soft furnishings, and are perfect spots for reading or conversation.

THIS PAGE: *Geometric designs on the lawn outside the living room provide a break from the organic elegance of the Balinese-style interiors.*

OPPOSITE (FROM TOP): *The living room tempts one to while the afternoon away; the villa has an open concept throughout to encourage guests to be as informal as they want.*

In the sleeping pavilions, spacious suites include the features that made 'Bali style' a global trend: platform beds, vast bath and dressing rooms with lounging areas, outdoor bathtubs, garden showers and private garden courtyards. Yet all of this is presented with a sense of proportion, a matching colour scheme and furnishings selected with the utmost care to ensure that they blend in. Bedlinens, curtains and even the simple cushion cover will not be out of place. Outdoor bathtubs are of cream-coloured terrazzo and semi-sheltered by pavilions. Garden showers are open but modern, with big, white, beach pebbles embraced by durable terrazzo and lava stone surfaces. There is none of that dankness or slime that sometimes plagues 'Bali style' bathrooms. In fact, the style has developed and learnt lessons from the global design world, without losing its Balinese spirit.

A feature worth noting and enjoying at the spa at Simona are its two enormous outdoor bathtubs, carved of smooth Java stone in the style of the Majapahit empire. They sit on plinths above a lawn, shaded by tall trees. The effect is elegant, especially at night with candlelit lanterns hanging in the trees. Inside, the spa is similarly fresh and clean, with its interior composed of an intelligent balance of high style and efficiency. Remarkably complete, it boasts professional massage tables, treatment chairs, a sauna, a large jacuzzi and a yoga pavilion. Those looking to rejuvenate their body are assured of expert and caring service. The villa staff of 21, all full-time, include several who are professionally trained bodywork therapists and beauticians. Simona Oasis will go the extra mile for its guests. This is truly an in-estate spa, where treatments can be provided on a whim, be it day or evening.

It goes without saying that Simona Oasis has satisfied all the unwritten specifications required of Bali's best villas. In addition to creature comforts, epicurean and culinary interests are met by a skilled chef, a restaurant-calibre kitchen and a spectacular dining room. Guests can choose to whip up their own meals or have the chef do it. Electronic comforts come from the flat-screen, satellite TVs, high-speed Internet access and iPod docking stations provided. The staff will take on childcare duties and organise anything from cocktail parties to luxury picnics, as well as barbecues, cooking lessons, dance performances, golf tee times and more. The villa is under 24-hour surveillance, ensuring security in the place. A car and a chauffeur are also available whenever guests choose to visit nearby Seminyak and its restaurants and nightclubs.

These amenities, combined with the luxury and beauty that Simona Oasis & Spa provides, are certain to create a delightful stay, and travellers who find their way here are assured of leaving with wonderful memories.

ROOMS
5-bedroom estate (1 master suite, 3 king suites and 1 twin suite)

FOOD
event catering • chef •
self-catered • shopping service

DRINK
event catering • self-catered •
shopping service • minibar •
living room bar

FEATURES
24-hour security • car and chauffeur •
gardens • gourmet kitchen • jacuzzis •
pool • spa • sauna • mountain bikes

BUSINESS
business, translation and secretarial services on request

NEARBY
Seminyak • Tanah Lot • Umalas Equestrian Centre • beaches •
cafés • golf • surfing • restaurants •
water sports

CONTACT
Banjar Padang Linjong,
Desa Canggu Kecamatan,
Kuta Utara, Badung 80361 •
telephone: +62.361.730 668 •
facsimile: +62.361.736 391 •
email: info@balihomes.com •
website: www.simona-oasis.com

sitara padi villas

...it would be hard to find a more congenial setting with so many surprising advantages.

Umalas is an area just north of Seminyak, Bali's elite lifestyle zone, yet it remains a quiet residential community. Once it was rolling countryside, but now it is one of the most sought-after addresses among savvy expatriates, and stylish villas are sprouting up in Umalas' rice fields to cater to them. Sitara Padi Villas is one of these.

Sitara Padi Villas is a collection of three compact courtyard villas and one large estate-like residence called Kahyangan Villa. It is the most outstanding accommodation offered by Sitara. In fact, Kahyangan Villa has become one of the best-kept secrets among some regular visitors to Bali. For a group of friends or a large family, it would be hard to find a more congenial setting with so many surprising advantages.

The features, luxuries and contemporary styling of Kahyangan Villa are equal to that of the other villas, but it is far larger and enhanced by many antique elements. The centrepiece of the residence is a 200-year-old Javanese nobleman's house, painstakingly restored and adapted for modern living. A soaring structure of solid teak, with massive timber columns defining different spaces, it envelops lounging and dining areas, a gourmet kitchen, and a TV room, all furnished with funky touches. The master suite is in an adjoining structure with a timber terrace and glass doors that allow guests to live al fresco or in air-conditioned comfort. Two more luxury bedroom suites are also arranged in separate bungalows on the grounds.

The stylish interior spaces of Kahyangan Villa seem almost trivial compared to what is available outdoors. A sprawling pool with a sundeck is set in rolling lawns that extend out towards rice fields and a wooded brook.

THIS PAGE (FROM TOP): The master bedroom of the Kahyangan Villa overlooks the garden; as twilight approaches, night lights make the pool as alluring as ever.
OPPOSITE (FROM TOP): Antiques in the villas include these figurines in traditional Balinese garb; all the villas boast clean lines and white floors.

The other three villas are smaller, modern Balinese courtyard compounds and have plenty to offer as well. The one-bedroom mini-villa is called Ayodhya, with the kind of style and luxury features one expects only in larger properties. Everything is tucked into a small, private courtyard near the entrance to the Sitara Padi property. It contains a master suite, an open living–dining–kitchen pavilion, timber terrace, tailored garden nooks and a cosy pool. It feels like just the spot for a single traveller who wants to hide away by day and nip out at night to hit the hotspots down in Seminyak, or a young couple whose focus is intimacy and privacy.

Larger in scale is the three-bedroom Astina Villa, which offers a bit more room to unpack and unwind. A landscaped courtyard contains three complete bedrooms suites, each with

THIS PAGE: *The pool and garden at Kahyangan Villa are ready to welcome guests any time.*
OPPOSITE (FROM TOP): *Locally produced pottery adds a rustic touch to the décor; water gushes from a carved head into the wooden bathtub; the open living room and dining space invite easy mingling.*

floor-to-ceiling glass walls and doors that look out to a fair-sized pool, and enough living and garden space to host a few friends for dinner, a cocktail party or a celebration. For a smaller group, there is the two-bedroom Kiskenda Villa, which has its own pool, bedrooms that look out over the water, and the same excellent amenities as the other two: four-poster beds with Egyptian cotton sheets, al fresco bathrooms and poolside loungers. Here, guests are comfortably ensured of privacy as well.

Any one of these villas is a fine base for an extended stay and would work well for someone mixing a bit of business with some corporate networking. All the villas are well-equipped, efficient homes, with a hip, youthful twist. For business purposes, there is high-speed

Internet access, private parking right in front, and a spare bedroom that can be used as an office. On the social side, open-plan kitchens and living spaces, complete with pool views and scenes of rice fields, beg for soirées with close friends.

A path among the trees leads to a footbridge which crosses directly over the stream and leads to the Canggu Club. This is the delightful surprise bonus of Sitara Padi Villas: all guests are given 'gold key' membership cards granting unlimited access to the club for the duration of their stay. Bali's first complete country club, it offers top-notch sports facilities, a library, pub, restaurant and a dining area on an open verandah for taking in the famous Bali sunsets. With a choice of the club's packed calendar of sporting and social activities set before them, guests can mix comfortably with Bali's vibrant resident community. It is like having a ready-made social circle, with plenty of friends to invite for lively dinner parties across the footbridge.

Families adore the Canggu Club, a place where children are never seen as second-class citizens; the children's programmes and supervised play areas let parents relax while the little ones make friends from all over the world. For older children and adults, the sports facilities of this club are unrivalled in Bali: indoor and outdoor tennis are both available, as are squash, aerobics, yoga, fitness, football, cricket, croquet, swimming, billiards and more.

ROOMS
1 three-bedroom Kahyangan Villa •
1 three-bedroom Astina Villa •
1 two-bedroom Kiskenda Villa •
1 one-bedroom Ayodhya Villa

FOOD
self-catered • chef • shopping service • delivery from restaurants and cafés

DRINK
shopping service • self-catered

FEATURES
antiques • books • CDs • DVDs • Canggu Club access • fitness facilities • IDD phones • pools • spa treatments on request • satellite TV

BUSINESS
translation and secretarial services on request • high-speed Internet access • car and chauffeur

NEARBY
Canggu Club • Tanah Lot Temple • beaches • bakery • health food store • French patisserie and café • lounge-bars • nightclubs • restaurants • riding stables • surfing

CONTACT
Jalan Bumbak Kauh, Umalas, Kerobokan, Badung 80361 •
telephone: +62.361.780 0828 •
email: info@sitarapadi.com •
website: www.sitarapadi.com

kafe warisan

...one should not merely eat to live, but live to eat—and with great gusto too.

Whether guests come here for a leisurely meal in the spacious garden, a romantic evening for two on the terrace, or a quick drink and chat with their travel companions by the bar, Kafe Warisan, a French-Mediterranean restaurant in Seminyak, has been known to cast its trendy spell on one and all. It has been doing so since it opened.

As befits a fine-dining establishment, the restaurant lives up to its reputation by maintaining a sophisticated menu and an experienced staff who extend a gracious welcome and provide excellent service. But that is not all that distinguishes Kafe Warisan. Perhaps the most memorable element of the Kafe Warisan experience is the air of creativity that pervades and finds expression not only in the food, but also in the captivating works of art on display.

The signature menu was conceptualised to express the culinary credo that one should not merely eat to live, but live to eat—and with great gusto too. The restaurant has earned its superlative standing through the dedicated efforts and creative passions of French partners Said Alem and Nicolas Tourneville, who launched Kafe Warisan in 1997 with the self-imposed charter of raising the quality of dining experiences in Bali to the highest standard they could.

Chef Nicolas seems to have a natural talent for reconfiguring a simple three-course lunch or a classic dinner menu into a truly gastronomical experience that begs a lingering glass of wine or a cigar at the end, just to prolong the experience. Reviewers seldom fail to acknowledge his genius and even marvel with some degree of wonder at the ways in which he draws inspiration from Bali's local markets, browsing the seasonal produce and fresh ingredients to elicit novel ideas, and the way he

THIS PAGE (FROM TOP): *Chef Nicolas is responsible for the array of dishes that inspire guests to want a little bit of everything; candles add a gentle touch to the romantic atmosphere.*
OPPOSITE (FROM TOP): *A refreshing dessert to round the meal off; guests have a choice of dining indoors or al fresco.*

infuses his creations with a personal energy that is delightful on the palate but hard to pin down in words.

On the plate, Chef Nicolas's signature touch is brilliantly translated via favourites such as Le Foie Gras and Grilled Scallops. Given the wide range of desirable dishes here, even the more regular patrons find it difficult to reduce the menu to just a few favourites. Those who enjoy culinary pleasures in a set package might opt for the Romantic Dinner Menu, which seeks to satisfy both the stomach and the heart. This menu includes the Trio Carpaccio with Red Capsicum Coulis and Spices, Hot Foie Gras with Clear Miso Soup, Pan-Roasted Salmon and Asparagus Saffron Risotto, Grilled Duck Breast with Potato Gnocchi and Cabernet Reduction, and, finally, a Hot Chocolate Soufflé in unhurried succession. Otherwise, taking a chance on something new and unfamiliar will yield just as rewarding an experience.

Though the menu is refreshed regularly, notable dishes to look out for include the Warm Duck Salad with Basilic Mango Coulis, or Les Escargots, consisting of roasted mushrooms stuffed with escargot, for their rich flavours; the Seven Hour Lamb Mechoul served with

Oriental Cousous, or the Grilled Tasmanian Salmon with Basil and Corn Velouté, for a hearty main course; and for dessert, something sweet and surprising, such as the Raspberry Soufflé or the Lemon Meringue Tart.

Kafe Warisan's popularity and exclusive status is the reason why customers need to call in advance for a reservation or make a booking via email. For their efforts, a leaf might be painted with a customer's name on it and placed on the table to acknowledge the reservation. Once successful in securing a place for one's dinner party, diners then have a choice of occupying one of four dining areas: the Upper Galleries, the Garden and Lower Gallery, the Rice Field Patio or the Bar. Each area adds its distinct character to the dining experience.

Dining on the first floor is particularly memorable as guests will enjoy views of the garden and expansive rice fields. It is also here that some of the more talented artists in Bali routinely display their artworks for your viewing pleasure. The garden, covered gallery and bar are also lovely places to dine, especially in the evening when the area is illuminated with candles, adding a touch of romance that complements the rustic surroundings perfectly.

Should the need for an especially intimate occasion arise, guests can request a table on the Rice Field Patio. This covered area is set with tables for two and offers a little more privacy. Here, guests will surely enjoy sampling a good selection from Kafe Warisan's extensive list of French, Australian and Californian wines, with the sounds of light jazz filtering through the air and a flurry of stars lighting up the night sky. Besides a cocktail or preferred beer of choice, there is also the extravagance of a Cuban cigar and cognac to look forward to. What better way could there be to enjoy a tropical evening in paradise?

THIS PAGE (FROM TOP): *Rustic yet formal, with a touch of sophistication and exclusivity—that is the Kafe Warisan style; selections from the menu.*

OPPOSITE (FROM LEFT): *Sitting by the rice fields is certainly a change from other al fresco settings; evenings are an opportunity to sit back, enjoy the night air, and savour good food.*

SEATS
Lower Gallery, Bar and the Garden: 80 • Upper Galleries: 85 • Rice Field Patio: 20

FOOD
French-Mediterranean

DRINK
bar: French, Australian and Californian wines and cocktails

FEATURES
cigars • art displays • vegetarian selections

NEARBY
Warisan Gallery • Pura Petitenget

CONTACT
No. 38 Jalan Raya Kerobokan, Banjar Taman, Kuta, Badung 80361 • telephone: +62.361.731 175 • facsimile: +62.361.732 762 • email: info@kafewarisan.com • website: www.kafewarisan.com

ku de ta

...exudes all the luxury and exclusivity of a private beach club in Europe...

KU DE TA, a beachfront restaurant in Seminyak, has made an inspired investment in modern architecture, classy interior design and an original menu, and this has paid off handsomely. Today, the restaurant attracts an ever-increasing community of enthusiastic patrons, all with the desire to experience KU DE TA's exceptionally fine cuisine and attentive service, and enjoy the sophisticated company within its laid-back tropical surroundings.

Against the unmistakably Balinese backdrop of palm trees and the endless Indian Ocean, French architect Fredo Tafin's eye-catching structure exudes all the luxury and exclusivity of a private beach club in Europe. Whether one is lazing on a custom-made lounger by the white-sand beach, watching the ebb and flow of the waves, or simply waiting for the sun to oblige with a blazing sunset, there is no denying the draw of this five-star, resort-like restaurant, where the staff regularly get asked, 'So, where are the suites?' by appreciative guests.

THIS PAGE: *A restaurant that offers a near-perfect beach to its guests is bound to be special.*
OPPOSITE: *Guests can choose to sip a drink on the daybeds by the shore or partake of fine dining options inside.*

In fact, it would be more appropriate to call KU DE TA an entertainment venue rather than a restaurant because many guests come here to spend a day lazing on the beach, usually arriving in time for breakfast, later indulging in a sumptuous lunch, before cleaning themselves up in the evening and enjoying a leisurely dinner. After dinner, it is time to party to the sounds of visiting international DJs. This venue also regularly hosts private parties, cocktail gatherings and even the odd wedding. A full-time functions team is available to organise every detail, from the flowers to the decorations, the music and, most importantly, the food. With more than 250 staff and six expatriate managers on hand to see to every need, guests find that their experience here is without peer. Many multinational corporations have held events here, including BMW, Cathay Pacific, Credit Suisse, Fashion TV and Singapore Airlines. With such prominent attention, it is no wonder KU DE TA has warranted a mention in *The New York Times*.

The restaurant has no lack of famous customers to boost its reputation either: Anna Kournikova, Kate Moss, Edward Norton, Mel Gibson, Christina Aguilera, Tommy Lee and Bjork are among those who have dined here and left lavish praise behind. And no wonder; it is not just the service or the impressive surroundings, it is the excellent food and the menu that puts the restaurant a notch above the others. Whether it is breakfast, lunch, dinner or supper, Chef Phillip Davenport takes pride in

THIS PAGE: At night, the restaurant shimmers and its distinctive red sunshades gleam like jewels.

OPPOSITE (CLOCKWISE FROM TOP): One of the chef's specialities; a gathering room that is perfect for brunch and lazing the balmy afternoon away; the combination of ocean, wave and greenery is a visual treat.

maintaining a menu that is thoroughly imaginative and flavoursome. The selection of international cuisine features simple but hearty seafood dishes including Baby Lobster Linguini served with tomato, basil and chilli; Tapenade Crusted Dhu Fish with spinach and pine nuts; and Tea Smoked Barramundi Fillet, which comes with a champagne sauce. Most of the seafood is locally caught, thus ensuring it is as fresh as can be. Meat-lovers, have no fear because there is also the Roasted Beef Fillet served with a potato and goat cheese gallette and Prosciutto Wrapped in Veal Cutlet. When it is time for a sweet treat, the delightful Frozen Praline Nougatine with red wine passionfruit sauce and lemon yoghurt sorbet, and the White Chocolate Honeycomb Terrine with strawberry sorbet come highly recommended.

KU DE TA does not fall short when it comes to drinks either. The venue has three bars housing a wide selection of wines from France, Italy, Australia, New Zealand and Chile, and a premium selection of ports, cognacs and liqueurs. It also serves more than 50 types of martinis, cocktails and mixed drinks, which are bound to delight guests.

Decked out in their stylish designer casuals—white linen beachwear for the more conservative, sarongs and bikinis for the less inhibited—and sporting a flawless tan, the merry-makers, each with a drink in hand, will be all set for a night spent partying on the beach until

the wee hours of the morning. They start by mingling patiently while the sun goes down and KU DE TA is transformed from a beach club into an oasis of fine dining. After 11 p.m., the DJ warms up, before letting loose and bringing down the house. Count on celebrity DJs to oblige with a mix of house, ambient, tribal and down-tempo grooves, and watch the partying crowd fill the beach. Notable events which put KU DE TA on the socialite's calendar include the Russian Chic Blesk Krasota party and the Fire Island Jungle party.

There is always a chance guests might get carried away on their first visit, and before they know it, they are squinting at the rising sun the next morning. If that does happen, guests are encouraged to adjourn to the deck and start ordering a scrumptious breakfast. They can choose from a selection of fruit juices and smoothies, then start on the food. Croissants, scones, and pancakes come plain or with fillings, while eggs come with lamb and herb sausages or smoked salmon and are done in different styles—Benedict, omelette and more. Those who wake—or arrive—later can join the brunch crowd, before continuing with their day.

For the guys left to run the show here, things can only get bigger and better. The formula works so well that there has already been talk of exporting it to some of the world's best seaside locales in Europe and Asia. When that happens, it will mean that fans of one of the best beach experiences in Bali will be able to recommend KU DE TA to even more people.

SEATS
200

FOOD
modern international

DRINK
3 bars: extensive wine list, wide selection of cognacs, liqueurs, martinis and cocktails

FEATURES
beach • international DJs • organic produce

NEARBY
Seminyak • Kuta

CONTACT
No. 9 Jalan Laksmana, Seminyak, Badung 80361 •
telephone: +62.361.736 969 •
facsimile: +62.361.736 767 •
email: info@kudeta.net •
website: www.kudeta.net

the living room

...infused with an effortless and natural sexiness.

The Living Room is a beautiful place for beautiful people. Its big, breezy pavilions are bathed in soft light and swathed in flowing draperies and upholstery, with cream being the predominant colour scheme. The effect of this pale setting enhances the appearance of everyone within its premises. The atmosphere feels infused with an effortless and natural sexiness.

It is obvious that Daniel Vanneque, The Living Room's congenial host, wants guests to feel at home, as if they were in their own living room. This explains the name of the restaurant and the ambience he has created, which evokes the atmosphere of a party at home. A savvy set of Bali expatriates treat it just so, regularly inviting their friends here for sophisticated soirees. It's especially popular for after-party gatherings and with groups enjoying an aperitif, some gossip and a bite before moving on to the clubs.

The lounge, on any given night, feels like a chic private party. Its centrepiece is a large *joglo*, which is actually the skeleton structure of a traditional Javanese house, but cleverly re-used here with its posts forming the corners of a four-sided bar. This configuration is convivial, unexpectedly convenient for ordering a second round, and invites mingling among guests. On Friday and Saturday nights, The Living Room's DJs lay down quality house tracks and late night chill-out sounds to keep guests entertained until the wee hours.

The dining room uses an open *joglo* pavilion too, this time decorated in an intimate residential style: deep sofas, Dutch colonial tiles, old teak furniture and lavish flower arrangements that exude romance and glamour. More romantic still is the outdoor dining area, which becomes an enchanted garden by night, with hundreds of candles flickering in glass cylinders everywhere.

THIS PAGE: *The bar is casual yet sophisticated enough for seasoned bar-goers.*
OPPOSITE (FROM TOP): *Long, heavy drapes, lamps and chandeliers create a formal, opulent setting; stylishly served food suits the chic guests of The Living Room.*

This is definitely a place for partying people and intelligent ones too. Such a crowd likes sophisticated food and The Living Room delivers. It offers fine dining, but is not formal. Great food, correctly French, is served with an Asian flourish and fresh local ingredients. Chef I. B. Mardita always slips in a sprinkle of Frenchness, so the dishes may be rich, but never overly so. He emphasises quality over quantity. Favourites include the varied seafood plates, and The Living Room's own version of duck legs confit, Duck Legs Confit 'A L'orientale'. The Pan-Fried Foie Gras on a bed of Ahi tuna carpaccio and gingered sushi rice is a popular choice too. It satisfies the palate without dampening one's enthusiasm for dancing later in the lounge.

SEATS
outdoor: 130 • indoor : 110

FOOD
French-Asian

DRINK
lounge: extensive wine cellar

FEATURES
DJs on weekends • private parties • own label music CD

NEARBY
Pura Petitenget • Seminyak beach • villas

CONTACT
Jalan Petitenget 2000 XX, Kerobokan Kuta, Seminyak, Badung 80361 •
telephone: +62.361.735 735 •
facsimile: +62.361.736 736 •
email: email@livingroombali.net •
website: www.thelivingroombali.net

ma joly

...a culinary beach club for those in the know.

THIS PAGE (FROM TOP): Dining under the pergola allows one to catch the magnificient view; the bar is perfect for watching the sunset with a drink in hand.
OPPOSITE (FROM TOP): The lamb with rosemary is popular with guests; large parties will enjoy the beachside dining option, which comes with a light breeze.

The secret is out: Ma Joly is getting international attention, with reviews coming in from around the world. This fine French restaurant is a hidden treasure. It is set on one of the rare, quiet stretches of sand left in south Bali—Segara beach in the Tuban–Kuta area. Tucked away down a lane that few people take time to explore, it has remained a secret, except among food fanatics, because the chef, Patrick Marty, has a high profile in the gourmet world.

Ma Joly is more than a fine French restaurant, though. One may describe it as a culinary beach club for those in the know. Anyone who eats here—for breakfast, high tea or a full meal—has access to the Ma Joly beach, private pool, lounge beds, showers and dressing room. It is not merely a restaurant but a place to loll about for the day.

In addition to sit-down meals, Ma Joly is earning accolades for its wedding and event planning services. Cocktails for international consuls, press events and private parties held here have delighted those lucky enough to be invited. Weddings at Ma Joly have been described as charming and unique for a number of reasons. Firstly, the food is several levels above normal wedding buffet fare. Next, all Ma Joly weddings exude a certain style and creativity, with elegant beach-themed touches that are artistic and innovative yet appropriate. This is evident in the inspiring floral arrangements that incorporate unusual tropical elements. The result is a romantic mix with well-executed personal touches.

Just beside Ma Joly is Kupu Kupu Barong Beach Resort, part of the same enterprise. A playful, modern and stylish boutique hotel with just 11 suites, it is large enough for a small party. The bridal couple and their guests do not even have to put on sandals to get from the reception to the room. Close enough to the beach and even closer to Ma Joly, it makes an ideal place for a memorable honeymoon too.

For all the attention paid to the surroundings, it is the food that truly draws rave reviews. Fresh seafood is at the heart of the menu. This is not surprising, as Ma Joly sits on Jimbaran Bay, with fresh seafood just a catch away, prepared with exqusite skill by the chef. Bali is embarrassingly well-supplied with excellent French chefs, but Chef Patrick stands out for several reasons. He has won prestigious awards regionally and internationally. He brings a distinctive style to the food, focusing on his home region in the southwest of France, with Mediterranean elements that sit well with the tropical environment of a Bali beach. For example, his Trio de Poissons, a dish made with three kinds of fish, comes with garlic cream and parsley coulis.

Whether one dines al fresco by the sea, in the garden, under the pergola or in the dining room, the food matches the atmosphere perfectly. The Australian Rib Eye with Mountain Herbs goes down well with the sunset over the sea, and French desserts such as Poire 'Belle Hellene', poached pear with vanilla, hot chocolate and Chantilly cream, tastes far better under a Bali moon. Guests are welcome to go for breakfast, armed with a bikini and a book, and end the day with dinner by the Indian Ocean, listening to the waves.

ROOMS
150

FOOD
French with Mediterranean and international influences

DRINK
Beach Bar

FEATURES
beach • boat service to surf breaks • pool • spa • event planning

NEARBY
Discovery Shopping Mall • Waterbom Park • Jimbaran Bay • airport

CONTACT
Jalan Wana Segara,
Tuban, Kuta, Badung 80361 •
telephone: +62.361.753 780 •
facsimile: +62.361.753 781 •
email: reservation@ma-joly.com •
website: www.ma-joly.com

the wave

...a three-in-one total entertainment and dining extravaganza, open around the clock...

THIS PAGE: *The intensely colourful décor of Sailfin Restaurant creates a great setting for fine dining and good conversation.*

OPPOSITE: *The restaurant's lounge has floor-to-ceiling windows that open to the night air.*

In the late 1960s, a handful of wandering hippies showed up in Bali looking for a new kind of Asian vibe. Originally, the established hippy trail ended in India, but a few experience-seekers dared to look further, and they ended up in Bali. Staying with local families, they hung out in Kuta to unwind on the island. According to one early arrival, the road that is now Jalan Pantai Kuta was just a sandy path through a coconut grove. Leaving the main intersection of Kuta village, known as 'bemo corner', he set out down that path in 1970, looking for the beach. After a few minutes, he emerged from a clump of mangroves and found himself on a vast and pristine beach stretching uninterrupted for miles in both directions, with crystal waves curling gently towards the shore. That moment was an epiphany for this American surfer, so he stayed to enjoy it and lives in Bali to this day.

According to the old-timer, the very spot where that path broke through the brush is where The Wave stands today. Back then, on any given day, only half a dozen tourists could be spotted on Kuta beach. Not even the Balinese bothered to visit it, except for a few farmers throwing out nets to supplement the fruits of their land. Those who did come to the shore usually arrived via that same sandy path, and tended to gather where it reached the beach. A little girl named Made sold fruit salad under a tree, and a few local children came to gawk at the foreigners. That girl now owns Made's Warung, a Balinese institution that is about to celebrate 40 years in business. And those children became the first generation of local surfers and Kuta cowboys.

Word got out about the emerging scene in Kuta beach. The path became a road, while homestays became hotels, and surfers

became grandparents. Kuta kept drawing in more people from further away. Its magnetism is still there, and that spot where the path hits the beach is its power centre. Visitors to Bali feel they have not seen the island until they have seen Kuta beach, and when they come, they are always irresistibly drawn to this magic spot, which boasts the most impressive address in Bali: Jalan Pantai Kuta No. 1. It is a good thing that a Malaysian entrepreneur with architecture and high design in his background created The Wave to welcome them in style.

Irreversibly urbanised, Kuta is no longer looking back to its funky roots, but forward and towards high style and higher quality. The Wave is a dramatic example of that progress. It is a three-in-one total entertainment and dining extravaganza, open around the clock. Its dramatic

THIS PAGE: *Enjoy a thirst-quenching cocktail at the bar in Sailfin Restaurant.*

OPPOSITE (CLOCKWISE FROM TOP): *A work of modern art; a seafood platter; the distinctive roof structure is aptly named 'flying roofs'.*

architecture takes its tone from the modern waterfront mansions of movie stars and luxury ocean liners. White limestone stairs sweep up to the arrival deck, with a flying white sail for a roof. Upstairs, Lookout exudes a cool but beach-like feel. From 10 in the morning, the bar at Lookout serves excellent coffee, cakes and light bites to start the day. Beach-lovers can happily hang out here the whole day, enjoying sandwiches, pizzas and light bites, along with its view and chill-out sounds. Friends and families also can begin here, then split up and pursue their own Kuta experiences, with The Wave as an ideal place to regroup later. In the afternoon, there is no better place to rendezvous with the crew for drinks. It is also one of the best vantage points

around for a Kuta sunset. Those who have spent the day at the beach can wind down there, if they wish. But it is the evenings that really take off at The Wave.

The tone goes upscale in Sailfin Restaurant, which serves seafood specialities in an elegant white and purple dining room with floor-to-ceiling windows facing the Indian Ocean. Diners can choose outdoor dining on the deck as well, if they prefer the scent of salty sea air.

Sailfin Restaurant proclaimed the arrival of fine dining at Kuta beach. Australian chef Jesse Lee is especially proud of his Paradise Platter, a hot and cold seafood showcase combining crab, scallops, oysters, prawns, bay bugs, mussels, calamari and catch-of-the-day ocean fish. The variety on this plate must be seen to be believed.

Beneath Sailfin Restaurant, The Club delivers big-city nightclub action, with high technology and cutting-edge interior design. The party gears up at The Club at around 9.30 pm and roars on until the wee hours. Rock and roll, retro, house and hip-hop sounds

seem to shake the building down to the ground thanks to a talented line-up of international and local bands, daring DJs and the mind-blowing Nexo sound system. The active party atmosphere at The Club pulls in the crowd with a vibe that is young, diverse and welcoming to all nationalities and lifestyles.

Music aside, the most arresting feature must be the 48-m (52-ft) marble-topped long bar. No elbowing is needed here; there is plenty of space at this bar for the thirsty. Some elbowing is required, however, when The Wave puts on fashion shows and sexy dance performances, turning the bar top into a catwalk where local talents strut their stuff. At such an event, who would not want to get a better view?

SEATS
Lookout: 130 • Sailfin Restaurant: 160 • The Club: 180 (800 standing)

FOOD
cakes and pastries • coffee • finger food • light meals • pizza • seafood • sandwiches

DRINK
Lookout • The Club • Sailfin Restaurant

FEATURES
dancing • DJs • live music • nightclub • retail boutiques • terrace bar

NEARBY
Kuta beach • Kuta Square • restaurants • shopping

CONTACT
No. 1 Jalan Pantai Kuta, Kuta, Badung 80361 • telephone: +62.361.760 068 • facsimile: +62.361.750 948 • email: info@wave-kuta.com • website: www.wave-kuta.com

haveli

...an ancient caravan had travelled in the most exotic parts...

THIS PAGE: *The warm décor invites customers to slow down and browse, while the riches inside the showroom will surely delight those with an eye for beautiful, distinctive pieces.*

OPPOSITE (FROM TOP): *Bedlinens from The Shahinaz Collection; exclusive tableware and table linens are a speciality at Haveli; the accessories that are needed to recreate luxury and exotic charm can be found here.*

Haveli is a Persian word meaning 'mansion' in northern India and Pakistan. It conjures up visions of dappled sunlight playing on a fountain in the courtyard of a house filled with treasures traded along the old Silk Road: sparkling gold and gems, richly hued textiles and glittering beads. The aroma of exotic spices, resins, sandalwood and rare balms scents the air.

These visions inspired Zohra Boukhari, a long-time resident of Bali, to create her signature retail shop, Haveli, with her business partner Dominique Verdellet. In addition to tableware and accessories, Haveli also offers The Shahinaz Collection, which comprises bedlinens, table linens and cushion covers, all of which are designed and produced in Indonesia and are also used in The Shaba, Zohra's villa in Jimbaran. The style is distinctive, combining the materials and talents of Southeast Asia with inspiration from Europe, the Middle East and Morocco.

Haveli, located on Seminyak's main road, is literally bursting with Zohra's creations and discoveries. In fact, the shop is so full that it has expanded into a second space across the

road and showrooms have been opened at Mozaic restaurant in Ubud and at The Ritz-Carlton, Bali Resort & Spa resort in Jimbaran. One shop was just not enough to hold the entire Haveli range. Upon entering Haveli, shoppers get the impression that an ancient caravan had travelled in the most exotic parts of the world and deposited its riches here. The Shahinaz Collection of bedlinens, cushion covers and drapes uses fabrics that are richly hued and shimmer with shot-through additions in contrasting colours. Floral designs on duvets, bed covers, pillowcases and cushions bring the combined charm and luxury of Asia, Europe and Morocco to the bedroom. Many of the pieces in the collection also feature detailed handwork, such as beading, painting and embroidery. But that is not all. Haveli also offers a range of decorative accessories to complement the bedroom collections, including carved-glass mirrors, brassware, copperware, lamps and lacquerware. Curtains, diaphanous or heavy and rich in colour, create a dramatic or romantic atmosphere as required and help to complete the look of one's boudoir.

Collections for the table-top include unusual glassware, chargers and plates, cutlery and serving pieces. All are complemented by a variety of table linens, which 'clothe' a table rather than merely covering it. Table runners, napkins and placemats are only the beginning. Well-dressed tables must be adorned with trimmings, accessories and jewels, and at Haveli they

are. The twinkling array of innovative bijoux for the table includes beaded napkin rings, candleholders and table garlands, draped artfully among the dishes and trailing from the candelabra and chandeliers. These pieces add a lavish touch without a lavish price tag. It would be tempting to call them party favours and let one's guests go home festooned with the beaded garlands, wearing Haveli's napkin rings as bracelets.

Wholesale enquiries are welcome, if one needs to dress more than one's own home. Homeware and linens ship easily by air or sea, and Haveli and The Shahinaz Collection have online catalogues for remote restocking.

PRODUCTS
bedlinens • curtains • home linens • tableware • table linens • home accessories • lighting

FEATURES
online catalogue • wholesale

NEARBY
Seminyak beach • cafés • restaurants • shopping

CONTACT
Nos. 15 and 38 Jalan Basangkasa, Seminyak, Badung 80361 •
telephone: +62.361.737 160 •
facsimile: +62.361.724 497 •
email: info@havelishop.com •
website: www.havelishop.com •
The Shahinaz Collection:
No. 36 Jalan Kunti, Seminyak, Badung 80361 •
telephone: +62.361.745 0703 •
facsimile: +62.361.724 497 •
email: sales@shahinaz-collection.com •
website: www.shahinaz-collection.com

io + co

...designed to be bold, comfortable, different and surprising.

THIS PAGE: *Shoppers will find that the clothes here are as beautiful as they are comfortable.*
OPPOSITE (FROM TOP): *The variety of accessories allows one to mix and match as necessary; hats, assymetrical hems and the use of black and white blend innovation with elegance; layered dresses and skirts have a breezy, yet classy look.*

IO & CO's products are designed to be bold, comfortable, different and surprising. In its showrooms and shops, IO & CO offers two main product lines for retail and wholesale customers—bodywear and homeware—that exemplify this view. Its popular clothing label, Rebelle Attitude, consists of nine changing collections, with two completely new ones introduced each year.

One of the newest collections, the Adalpur line, features light dresses with fine layers. The muted colour palette gives a bohemian feel, while the same pieces in the alternative bright palette feel far more edgy. The Belier line offers angled cuts, with triangular hems that deconstruct the whole idea of a skirt, putting an end to the battle between mini-skirts and their longer relatives. As in all Rebelle Attitude collections, pieces are cut in free-form ways, allowing the wearer to shape, drape, wrap and tie elements together to create their own personalised look.

Each collection has a distinctive flavour, but all are unified by the label's philosophy and the use of lightweight, comfortable cotton. It is a fabric that can be translucent, but the concept calls for layering to conceal or reveal in any way the wearer wishes. Fit is easy; no need to be bound by a size chart. The wearer is invited to experiment, strapping and wrapping tight to the figure for a new kind of body-conscious style, or leaving the layers loose and floaty. The choice to expose the leg, midriff or shoulder is also up to the wearer. On any given day or at any given moment, one can re-drape, re-wrap or re-layer to suit the mood or the context. This is true fashion freedom. A single collection of six to 10 pieces offer hundreds of looks, because the wearer becomes the designer, combining and layering at will.

A line of co-ordinated accessories makes it easy to pull a look together by adding summery bags and sassy jewellery. Men can enjoy the Rebelle Attitude as well, since IO & CO is expanding into menswear, with a limited range of pieces already available in the showroom.

IO & CO's homeware line exudes a modern, yet earthy ambience. Natural woven items in unusual colours and bold stripes cover storage bins, boxes, frames and accessories. The workmanship is neat, with keen attention to detail. Even the linings of boxes come in matching colours. Quirky cutlery brings a modern yet primitive flavour to the table, alongside laminated wooden serving plates with pop art graphic detailing.

IO & CO uses natural materials such as Indonesian hardwoods and twine in its furniture line, but reshapes them to artful extremes. The line of toys is equally innovative. There is no need to put these toys away after playtime; they are objets d'art in their own right.

PRODUCTS
fashion apparel • furniture • tableware • home accessories • lighting • toys

FEATURES
modern, artistic designs • co-ordinated accessories • use of natural materials

NEARBY
Seminyak beach • shopping • cargo agent services

CONTACT
No. 88 Jalan Sunset Road, Seminyak, Badung 80361 •
telephone: +62.361.847 5824 •
facsimile: +62.361.847 5827 •
No. 361 Jalan Legian Kelod, Kuta, Badung 80361 •
telephone: +62.361.754 093 •
facsimile: +62.361.758 922 •
email: info@ioandco.com •
website: www.ioandco.com

milo's

...an ever-evolving oeuvre of unique tropical fashion.

THIS PAGE: *Bold batik prints make eye-catching clothes, but for true elegance, accessorise them with matching shoes.*
OPPOSITE (FROM TOP): *Handbags woven from straw make use of traditional Balinese materials; large floral prints complement the tropical island atmosphere.*

Fashion designer Milo Migliavacca is a legend in Bali. He's a beloved figure in the island's social circles, having lived here for some 35 years. Unlike many of the bohemian youths who discovered Bali in the 1970s, Milo was a stylish, urbane and determined worker. He came to Bali to create and contribute, not to indulge in a laid-back hippy lifestyle. Having made a career for himself in the fashion world of Milan, working for names such as Fiorucci and Benetton, Milo came to the island with proven talent and experience. He was immediately enchanted by Bali and its attractions and, since then, he has gone on to combine the traditions of Indonesia using his unique vision and skills to create works of sartorial elegance.

Milo's eponymous clothing label presents an ever-evolving oeuvre of unique tropical fashion. Shown in two boutiques in Bali and in the shops of five-star resorts, his designs have been charming visitors for decades. His collections have also gone international; they are sold in boutiques in the capital cities of Southeast Asia and in selected shops at leisure destinations around the world.

Recent collections have a striking graphic appeal, with bold black and white batik patterns on silk chiffon. Complementing these are collections inspired by Milo's love of tropical orchids, with exotic floral colours combined in palettes that are as unusual as those of the most exotic hybrids he grows in his own gardens and orchid farms. Many of the pieces in these collections come richly embellished with beadwork and sequins, and some with Swarovski crystals. Fine handwork is a signature of Milo's designs, and he has cultivated a team of skilled craftspeople in Bali who can do the kind of detailed work one normally finds only in haute couture.

Fabrics are lavish and include silk and silk chiffon as well as an innovative silk jersey that travels well and comes out of a suitcase without a wrinkle. This item is among Milo's bestselling pieces.

Some of Milo's clothing is outrageously sexy, with bared midriffs, translucent sarongs and flirty minis. Worn on the beach, they bring island chic to life. Other styles offer more conservative coverage, such as well-draped palazzo pants, caftans and dazzling evening dresses. Through an ingenious use of patterns and excellent cuts that have the effect of visually slimming and shaping the wearer, these outfits become effortlessly figure-flattering. Milo makes tropical glamour and elegance easy for everyone. Men are not ignored, either. His men's shirts display great panache without sacrificing elegance and dignity. Any man can look attractive in one of his orchid print shirts. These shirts are sought after for their design and quality. The classic cut gives a nod to conservatism, which allows even the most staid gentleman to pull off the tropical look.

Milo's orchid print shirts are wildly popular among Bali's elite. Even the most manly of males wear them proudly, as does Milo himself. They are not only a symbol of being in-the-know in Bali, they are also a symbol of Milo's other great passion: orchids. He is the founder and president of the Bali Orchid Society and has over 1,000 varieties in his home garden alone. He is a noted breeder and designer of new hybrids, cultivated in his dedicated botanical laboratory and orchid farm in north Bali. These form the basis of his inspiration for his orchid-themed shirts, skirts, dresses and accessories.

PRODUCTS
elegant and unique tropical fashion • footwear • handbags • accessories

FEATURES
fine handwork • beading • batik

NEARBY
Made's Warung • beaches • nightlife

CONTACT
studio: Jalan Sarinande 1A, Seminyak, Badung 80361 •
telephone : +62.361.730 410 •
facsimile: +62.361.730 856 •
email: milos@eksadata.com •
website: www.milos-bali.com / www.milosbaliorchids.com

MAIN STORE/SHOPS
Kuta: Milo's & Friends, Kuta Square Blok E1–1A, Kuta, Badung 80361 •
telephone: +62.361.754 081 •
Seminyak: Milo's@Made's Warung, Jalan Raya, Seminyak, Badung 80361 •
telephone: +62.361.731 689

warisan gallery

A must-visit for lovers of Indonesian arts and crafts...

THIS PAGE: *Create a resplendent bedroom with art pieces and furnishings from Warisan.*

OPPOSITE (FROM TOP): *A silver necklace that uses traditional Balinese motifs; a carved stone Buddha head; a wooden chest decorated with colourful, painted panels.*

In 1989, a young couple created Warisan Gallery together to share their love of Indonesian art and artefacts with the world. The word *warisan* means 'inheritance' in Bahasa Indonesia, and aptly describes the shop, which was built on a foundation of deep love for art and culture inherited by owner Dayu Sri from her parents. Her mother once managed a fine art gallery in Ubud. Dayu now hopes to pass that love on to the world.

Warisan Gallery is one of Bali's very first showrooms for antiques, interior design elements and furniture. Located in Kerobokan, just north of Seminyak, Warisan Gallery occupies a custom-built two-storey structure in the style of a Dutch colonial mansion. The location has a romantic feel, with views of rice fields at the back. The vicinity is now filled with antique dealers and showrooms for lifestyle products. But Warisan Gallery still stands out among them.

A must-visit for lovers of Indonesian art, the gallery offers a wide selection of antique furniture, classical and primitive statues, traditional textiles, painting and artefacts. On the ground floor, a niche boutique offers unique clothing and accessories, chosen from the creations of local designers in Bali and Java. Pastel batiks pair delightfully with elegant blouses cut in the tradition of the Indonesian *kebaya*, the national dress for women. Across a terracotta passageway is a larger boutique where unusual artisan jewellery tempt even the most jaded eye. The collections by local designers and artisans combine gold, silver, semi-precious stones and pearls. One collection features finely knotted silk in a rainbow of colours, cunningly intertwined with beads, pearls and stones, managing to be both clothing and jewellery. Another showcase resembles the treasure trove of a maharani, with antique and vintage jewellery from India brought to Warisan Gallery by an itinerant Syrian jewellery trader who returns several times a year with his offerings.

Arranged among the jewellery showcases are collections of furniture, artefacts and carefully selected handicrafts, as well as vintage and contemporary weavings. Table-top accessories fashioned from water buffalo horn and polished to a shine make excellent gifts or souvenirs. They are light, durable, inexpensive yet elegant, and resemble tortoiseshell, so buyers need not shoulder the ethical burden of endangering a rare species.

Above these two boutiques are spacious showrooms that feature Javanese teak furniture from the Dutch colonial period, mixed with quirky vintage pieces and modern creations from Warisan's workshops. Artefacts and decorative curiosities from Bali, Java, Sumatra, Borneo, Sulawesi, Sumba and Timor grace the walls and table-tops. In recent years, the selection of antiques has expanded to include pieces from Myanmar, Laos and China. The range of original and reconditioned Chinese country furniture, ceramic trade jars and porcelain vases are also worthy additions to the ecclectic collection that is available at Warisan Gallery.

PRODUCTS
antiques • clothing • furniture • home accessories • jewellery • primitive art • statues • soft furnishings • tableware

FEATURES
Indonesian and Balinese art • regional artefacts • associated furniture workshop and showroom

NEARBY
Kafe Warisan • Seminyak beach • The Wine House • hotels • villas

CONTACT
No. 68 Jalan Raya Kerobokan, Banjar Taman, Kuta, Badung 80361 •
telephone: +62.361.730 710 •
facsimile: +62.361.730 047 •
email: warisangallery@eksadata.com •
website: www.warisan.com

index

Numbers in *italics* denote pages where pictures appear. Numbers in **bold** denote profile pages.

A

Acuh Tak Acuh, 50
Adnyani, Chef Rai, 102
Agung Rai Museum of Art, 44
Air Bali, 38
Alila Manggis, 32, *39*
Amankila, 32
Amanusa, 143
Anti-Ageing Rejuvenation Clinic, 43
antiques, 25, 49, 110–111, 248–249
Archaeology Museum 45
art galleries 45, 58, 132–133
artefacts 49, 108–109, 132–133
arts, 25, 33, 44-45, 64, 104–107, 108–109, 132–133, 134–137, 248–249
Ary's Warung, **92–95**
Asam Garam Restaurant, 183, 185
Ayung River, 85, 86
Ayung Terrace Restaurant, 70
Ayung Valley Restaurant, 85
Ayurvedic massage, 69

B

Bacio, 40, *201*
Bahasa Indonesia, 15
Balé, The, 143
Bali Aga, 33
Bali Antique Shop, The, *49*
Bali Bird Park, 65
Bali Botanica Day Spa, 43
Bali Cafe, 39
Bali Catering Company, 29, 38, *39*, 206
Bali Deli, 29
Bali Experience, 41
Bali Fashion Week, 41
Bali Golf and Country Club, *142*, 143
Bali Good Food Group, 38
Bali Hyatt, 122
Bali International Medical Centre, 43
Bali Museum, 45
Banyan Tree resort, 145
bars, 40–41, 92–95, 98–99, 102–103, 226–229, 233
basketry, 33, 66
batik, 47, 246–247
Batu Jimbar Estate, *120*
Batu Karu, 30
beaches, 32, 62, *114*, 117, 143, 148, 195, 198, 233
beauty services, 42–43, 69, 74; also see spas
Bedugul, 30
Beduur Restaurant, 87
Begawan Giri, 68
Besakih Temple, see Pura Besakih
Biasa, 47
Biasa Artspace, 45
biking, 65
Bin House, *47*
Bingin Beach, *17*
Bintang, 29
birdwatching, 65
Blanco, Antonio, 59
Blossom Restaurant & Lounge Bar, *41*
Blue Glue, 47
Blue Ocean Boulevard, 201
Bonnet, Rudolf, 83
Boukhari, Zohra, 182, 242–243
boutiques, 25
Boutique Street, 205
Breeze, The, 41
Buddhism, 20
buffalo races, *35*
Bukit Peninsula, 141
Bulgari Hotels & Resorts, 25, *145*
bungy jumping, 201

C

Café Des Artistes, 39, **96–97**
Candidasa, 32
Canggu, 34, 206
Canggu Club, 212–213, 223–225
car rentals, 28
Carlo, 50, **128–131**
Carpenter, Bruce, 132
Carrefour, 29
Casa Luna Cooking School, 39
ceramic art, 51, 66, 107
ceremonies, *14–15*, 18, *21*, 59, 64
Chic Blesk Krasota Party, 233
Chill Reflexology, 43

Christanto, Dadang, 104
cigars, 92–95, 96–97, 226–229
clubs, 40–41, 198, 201, 230–233, 238–241
Club, The, 241
Club Intercontinental, **168–169**
COMO Shambhala Estate at Begawan Giri, 25, 43, **68–69**
Conrad Bali Resort + Spa, **152–153**
country clubs, 26
Cozy, 43
crafts, 33, 64, 66, 248–249
cremation ceremonies, *14*
culture, 14–15, 17, 20, 33, 58

D

dances, *14–15*, 18, 44, *58*
Dancing Dragon Cottages, 39
Dayaks, 20
deLighting, 51
Denpasar, 14
Dewata Lounge, 85
Diatas Pohon Café, 87
DiPutra, Oka, 47
Discovery Shopping Mall, 198
Disini, 50
Dono, Heri, 104
Double Six Club, 40, 201
Dreamland, *147*, *148–149*
Durga, 15
Dusun Hotel, The, **208–209**
Dutch rule, 18–19, 36

E

east Bali, 32–33
Eat Street, 39, 205
Elite Events, 41
Elysian, The, 204
Espace Spa, 43
Esprite Nomade, 38
Etienne d'Souza, 50
Evata Eastern Furniture & Accessories, 50
expatriate community, 14, 16, 60, 66, 117–118

F

fashion, 25, 27, 134–137, 244–245, 246–247

Fichot, Jean-Francois, 48, 113
Fire Island Jungle party, 233
fitness centres, 69, 90, 152–153, 156–159, 164–165, 166–167, 214–217, 223–225
Four Seasons Resort Bali at Jimbaran Bay, *39*, **154–155**
Four Seasons Resort Bali at Sayan, **70–71**
Frangipani Café, 215
Friend, Donald, 118
furniture, 49–51, 128–131, 133, 242–243, 248–249

G

Galeri Esok Lusa, 51
galleries, art, 45, 58, 132–133
Galungan, 19
gamelan, 35, 44, 79, 83
Ganesha Gallery, 45
Garden Terrace Restaurant, 74
Garland, Linda, 23, 51
Gaya Art Space, *45*, 104–105
Gaya Ceramic, 107
Gaya Fusion, **104–107**
Gaya Restaurant, 105
geography, 13–14
Grand Bali Beach Hotel, 118, 122
Grand Hyatt Bali, **156–159**
Gunarsa Museum of Classical & Modern Art, 45
GWK Cultural Park, 149

H

handicraft highway, 66
Hard Rock Cafe, 40
Hard Rock Hotel, 197
Hardy, John, 24, 48, 62–63
Harley Davidson Martini tours, 26, 38
Haveli, 50, **242–243**
Heavenly Residence, **160–163**
Hinduism, 14, 20, 22
Hishem, 50
history, 17–19, 23, 117–119, 147–148
hot springs, 31
Hotel Tugu Bali, **210–211**
Hotel Tjampuhan, 84
Hu'u, 39, *41*, 206

I

Ika Ika, *47*
Indah Manis, **164–165**
Intercontinental Bali Resort, **166–167**
IO + CO, **244–245**
Islam, 18, 20
Island Arts, 49, *132–133*
Istana, The, **170–173**

J

Jajaliluna, **212–213**
Jalan Laksmana, 39, 204
Jalan Raya, 47, 66, 195, 197
Jamahal Private Resort + Spa, **174–175**
Japanese Occupation, 18
Jari Menari, 43
Jatiluwih, 52
Jenggala Keramik, 45, 51
jewellery, 23, 24, 48–49, 112–113, 133, 248–249
Jimbaran Bay, 52, *138–139*, *150–151*
Jimbaran Puri Bali, **176–177**

K

Kafe Warisan, **226–229**
Kamasan, 33
Kawi, 18
Kayumanis Jimbaran Private Estate, **178–181**
Kerremans, Rudy, 96
Kerry Grima, 47
Ketewel, 80
Kirana Spa, 42
Klungkung, 18, *33*
Komaneka Fine Art Gallery, 44, *45*, 74
Komaneka Resort at Monkey Forest, **72–75**
Komaneka Resort at Tanggayuda, 75, **76–79**
KU DE TA, *39*, 41, 52, 205, 206, **230–233**
Kusamba, 33
Kura Kura, The, 215
Kuta, 40, 52, 192–249
Kwizien, 39

L

La Lucciola, 39, 205

index

La Taverna Hotel, 119
Lake Bratan, 30
Lamak Restaurant + Bar, **98–99**
legong (dance form), 62
Lombok, 32
Le Meridien Nirwana Golf & Spa Resort, 206
Le Rasle, Chef Renaud, 87
LED Studio, 48
Legian, 40, 52, 195, 198, 200–201
Legian, The, 41
Legian Suites, The, 205
Limestone, 32, 141
Living Room, The, 41, 206, **234–235**
Luxe Lounge Spa, 43

M
Ma Joly, **236–237**
Macan Tidur, 49, 51, **108–109**
Made Wijaya (also Michael White), 24, 98, 119, 120–121, 154
Made Wianta, 104
Majapahit, 18
Majapahit Beach Villas, **80–81**
Manggis, 32
marine life, 35–36
Markandeya, Rsi, 91
markets, 33, 66, 67
Maru, 48
masked dance, 15
Mason, Victor, 65
MbarGo, 40
Mekar Sari, 50
Michel Harcourt, 47
Migliavacca, Milo, 23, **246–247**
Milo's, 47, **246–247**
Monkey Forest Road, 66
Mount Abang, 31
Mount Agung, 28, 31, 32, 53
Mount Batur, 23, 52
Mount Lempuyang, 32, 53
mountains, 29, 30, 33, 57
Mozaic, 38, **100–101**
Munduk, 30
Murti, Krisna, 104
Museum Puri Lukisan, 44
Musro, 198
Mykonos, 205
mysticism, 21–22

N
Nampu Restaurant, 158
national parks, 30
Naughty Nuri's Warung & Grill, 45
Neka Art Museum, 44, 76
Nelayan Restaurant, 177
Neuhaus, Hans and Rolf, 118
New Kuta, 148
Ni Luh Sutini, Chef, 99
nightlife, 28, 40–41
Nikko Bali Resort & Spa, 143
Nilou, 48
Nirwana Bali Golf Club, 35
north Bali, 35
Nusa Dua, 142–143
Nusa Penida, 80, 122
Nyang-Nyang Estate, 145,147
Nyepi 15

O
Oberoi Bali, The, 205, **214–217**
Oberoi-Petitenget District, 203, 205
OKANE, 47
One World Gallery, 51
Oos River, 78
Orient-Express Group, 87

P
palaces, 32
Palasari, 35
Paparazzi (renamed Syndicate), 40, 201
Paul Ropp's, 47
Pejeng, 65
Penelokan ridge, 31
photography, 52–53
Piment Rouge, 51
Pita Maha Resort + Spa, **82–83**
Poppies Bali, 198
population, 14
Pourquoi Pas, 49
processions, 14–15, 18
Pura Besakih, 31, 87, 88
Pura Dalem, 73
Pura Gunung Lebah, 91
Pura Luhur Ulun Danu, 31
Pura Luhur Uluwatu, 147
Pura Pasar Agung, 32
Pura Pucak Payogan, 88
Pura Taman Saraswati, 73
Puri Ganesha Villas, 39

Q
Q Bar, 40
Quarzia, 48

R
Radiant, 51
Rangda, 15
resorts, 32, 80–81, 82, 86–87; also *see individual listing*
rice terraces, 5, 13, 17, 32, 33, 64
rituals, 20–23, 43
Royal Convention House, 85
Royal Family, 58–59
Royal Pita Maha, The, 62, **84–85**
Royal Villa, 70

S
Sailfin Restaurant, 241
Salans, Chef Chris, 100
salons, 42, 152–153, 214–217
Sanur, 13, 114–137
Saraswati Temple, 58, 59
Seasalt, 39
Selat, 32
Seminyak, 25, 39, 40, 52, 64, 195, 202–206
Seniwati Gallery of Art by Women, 45
Sentosa Private Villas and Spa, 206
Seraya, 32
Shaba, The, **182–183**
shadow puppet theatre, 14, 18
Shalimar, 49
shopping, 27, 46–51
Sidemen, 33
Simona Oasis + Spa, **218–221**
SimpleKonsepStore, 48, 50
Singaraja, 36
Singhosari, 18
Sitara Padi Villas, **223–225**
slave labour, 19
Sobek Bali Utama, 65
Sourcing Bali, 51
south Bali, 28–31, 141
spas and treatments, 28, 42–43, 69, 70, 73–75, 79, 80, 83, 85, 90, 127, 143, 152–153, 156–159, 164–165, 170–173, 174–175, 178–181, 182–183, 184–185, 210–211, 214–217, 218–221
Spies, Walter, 59, 83, 84
Spoiled Hairdressers, 43
Sriwijaya Jewels, 49
Suarti, 48
Sunda Peninsula, 17
superstitions, 21–22
Syndicate, 40, 201

T
Tabanan, 52
Taman Ujung, 32
Tampaksiring, 65
Tanah Lot, 34, 206, *207*
Tandjung Sari, 119
Tanjung Benoa, 142
Tantric Buddhism, 20, 22
Tapis Restaurant, 181
Taro's Elephant Safari Park, 64, 65
temples, 14, 22, 30, 31, 33, 53, 147
Tenganan, 33
Terrace Bali Restaurant, 85
Tirtagangga, 32
Tirtha Bridal, 186
Tirtha Luhur, **186–187**
Tirtha Uluwatu, **188–189**
Tjampuhan Valley, 83
TJ's Mexican Restaurant, 198
Toko Antique, 49, **110–111**
tourism, 14, 25, 32, 36, 57, 59–60, 66, 117, 118, 122, 141, 143, 195, 198
traditions, 20, 33
trance ritual, 15
Treasures, 48, **112–113**
Tropis Equator, 50
Tulamben, 36, 37
Tyler, Carolyn, 113

U
Ubud, 16, 28, 52, 54–113
Ubud Bodyworks Healing Centre, 43
Ubud Hanging Gardens, 63, **86–87**
Ubud Palace, 73
Ubud Readers and Writers Festival, 41, 62
Udayana University, 149
Ultimo, 39
Uluwatu, 147
Uluwatu Handmade Balinese Lace, **134–137**
Unda, 33

V
Vajra Villas, **88–91**
villas, 26, 69, 70–71, 76, 82, 85, 87–88, 124–127, 152–153, 156–159, 160–163, 164–165, 166–167, 174–175, 208–209, 223–225
Villa Balquisse, **184–185**
Villa Casis, *122*, **124–127**
Villa Maya, 80
Villa Nataraja, 80
Villa Samudra, 80
villages, 32, 33, 64
Villa Raj, 80
volcanoes, 52, 64

W
Warisan Casa, **190–191**
Warisan Gallery, 49, *50–51*, **248–249**
Warung Enak Bali, **102–103**
Warung Kudus, 79
Warung Made, 41
water sports, 142
Wave, The, 40, **238–241**
Waworuntu, Wija, 119
wayang kulit (shadow puppet theatre), 14, 18
wedding facilities, 152–153, 156–159, 166–167, 170–173, 186–187, 188–189, 214–217
wellness centres, 69, 77, 79, 85, 90, 127, 218–221
West Bali, 30, 34–35
Wijaya, Made, see Made Wijaya
wine, 92–95, 98–99, 226–229, 233
World War II, 18

Y
yacht leasing 26
Yak, The 26, 38
yoga 69, 75, 85, 91, 160–163, 178–181, 218–221

picture credits + acknowledgements

The publisher would like to thank the following for permission to reproduce their photographs:

Aldo Pavan/Grand Tour/Corbis 66 (top)
Alexander Benz/zefa/Corbis 146 (left)
Alila Manggis 39 (top)
Ary's Warung 92–95
Bacio Bar 201
The Bale 145
The Bali Antique Shop 49 (below)
Bali Catering Company 39 (below)
Bin House + Kay Moreno 47 (below left)
Bruno Barbier/Photolibrary 28
Bruno Morandi/Getty Images 12
Bruno Piazza 49 (top)
Café des Artistes 96–97
Carlo 128–131
Charles O'Rear/Corbis 53 (rice paddies)
Club InterContinental 168–169
COMO Shambhala Estate at Begawan Giri front cover (below left), front cover (top right), back cover (below right), back cover (treatment room), 2–6, 24 (below), 25, 29, 68–69
Conrad Bali Resort + Spa 152–153
Dallas + John Heaton/Free Agents Limited/Corbis front cover (metallophone), 35
Dana Edmunds/Photolibrary 67
David Katzenstein/Corbis 15
Duane Rieder/Getty Images 200
The Dusun Hotel 208–209
Erick Danzer/Onasia 19, 32 (below), 198 (top)
Four Seasons Resort Bali at Jimbaran Bay front flap (top, centre + below), 42 (top), 43 (top), 151, 154–155
Four Seasons Resort Bali at Sayan 43 (below), 57, 70–71
Gary Brettnacher/Getty Images 123
Gaya Fusion 45 (top + below right), 104–107
Glowimages/alt.TYPE 138
Grand Hyatt Bali front cover (below right), 156–159
Guido Alberto Rossi/TIPS Images 33
Haveli 242–243
Heavenly Residence 160–163
Hiroshi Watanabe/Getty Images 114
Hotel Tugu Bali front cover (spa ingredients), 210–211
Hu'u 41 (below left), 205
Ika Butoni 46, 47 (below right)
Indah Manis 164–165
InterContinental Resort 166–167
IO + CO 244–245

Island Arts 132–133
The Istana 170–173
Jajaliluna 212–213
Jamahal Private Resort + Spa 174–175
James Pomerantz/Corbis 197
Jason Hosking/zefa/Corbis 192
Jean Chung/Onasia front cover (wayang kulit puppet), 18
Jean du Boisberranger/Getty Images 140
Jean Du Boisberranger/Photolibrary 13, 20
Jean-François Fichot 48 (below)
Jenggala 150 (below)
Jeremy Horner/Corbis 66 (below)
Jerry Redfern/Onasia back cover (top right), 196
Jim Watt/Photolibrary 37
Jimbaran Puri Bali 176–177
Joe Beynon/Getty Images 32 (top)
joSon/Getty Images 21, 31
Joson/zefa/Corbis 30
Justin Guariglia/National Geographic 17, 148–149 (top)
Kafe Warisan 226–229
Kayumanis Jimbaran Private Estate 27, 178–181
Komaneka Gallery 44, 45 (below left)
Komaneka Resort at Monkey Forest 72–75
Komaneka Resort at Tanggayuda 76–79
KU DE TA back cover (below left), 38, 204, 230–233
Lamak Restaurant + Bar 98–99
The Living Room 41 (below right), 234–235
Ma Joly 236–237
Macan Tidur 108–109
Made Nagi/epa/Corbis 198 (below)
Majapahit Beach Villas 80–81
Margie Politzer/Getty Images 22
Mark A. Johnson/Corbis 147
Mark Webster/Getty Images 141
Martin Westlake/alt.TYPE 54, 206
Martin Westlake/Getty Images 202
MASH/Getty Images 116
Michael Freeman/Getty Images 207
Michael S. Yamashita/Corbis 56
Mike McQueen/Corbis 8
Milo's 246–247
MIXA/Getty Images 42 (below)
Mozaic 100–101
Neka Art Museum 120 (below)

The Oberoi, Bali 214–217
Paul A. Souders/Corbis 64
Paul Kennedy/Getty Images 148 (below)
Paula Bronstein/Getty Images 61
Peter Charlesworth/Onasia 142
Phil Schermeister/National Geographic 194
Philip Lee Harvey/Getty Images 52, 53 (silhouette)
Pita Maha Resort + Spa 82–83
Remi Benali/Corbis 14
Rio Helmi front cover (daybeds), back cover (top left), 53 (festivities), 53 (Mount Agung crater), 58–60, 118–119, 144, 146 (right), 150 (top)
Rony Zakaria/Onasia 199
Roy Bery/AFP 34
The Royal Pita Maha 62 (top), 84–85
Sentosa Private Villas + Spa 41 (top), 43 (pavilion)
The Shaba 182–183
Simona Oasis + Spa back cover (bedroom), back flap (top + centre), 26 (below), 203, 218–221
SimpleKonsepStore 47 (top left)
Sitara Padi Villas 222–225
Sonny Tumbelaka/AFP 65, 195
Sriwijaya Jewels 48 (top)
Terry Williams/Getty Images 23
Tim Hall/Getty Images 117
Tim Laman/Photolibrary 36
Tim Street-Porter 121
Tirtha Luhur 186–187
Tirtha Uluwatu 188–189
Toko Antique front cover (masks), 26 (top), 110–111
Treasures back cover (jewellery), 24 (top), 47 (top right), 62 (below), 112–113
Ubid Hanging Gardens 63, 86–87
Uluwatu Handmade Balinese Lace 134–137
Unknown photographer 120 (top)
Vajra Villas 88–91
Villa Balquisse 184–185
Villa Casis 122, 124–127
Vladimir Rys/Getty Images 143
Warisan Casa 190–191
Warisan Gallery 50, 51 (top + below), 248–249
Warung Enak Bali back cover (Balinese cuisine), 102–103
The Wave 40, 238–241
Zubin Shroff/Getty Images front cover (top left), 16

directory

HOTELS

Club InterContinental (page 168)
Jalan Uluwatu 45, Jimbaran 80361
telephone : +62.361.701 888
facsimile : +62.361.701 777
bali@interconti.com
www.bali.intercontinental.com

COMO Shambhala Estate at Begawan Giri (page 68)
PO Box 54, Ubud, Gianyar 80571
telephone : +62.361.978 888
facsimile : +62.361.978 889
es@cse.comoshambhala.bz
cse.comoshambhala.bz

Conrad Bali Resort + Spa (page 152)
Jalan Pratama 168, Tanjung Benoa,
Nusa Dua, Badung 80363
telephone : +62.361.778 788
facsimile : +62.361.773 888
baliinfo@conradhotels.com
www.conradhotels.com

The Dusun Hotel (page 208)
Jalan Kayu Jati 8, Petitenget Kerobokan,
Seminyak, Badung 80361
telephone : +62.361.734 000
facsimile : +62.361.734 100
reservations@the-dusun.com
www.the-dusun.com

Four Seasons Resort Bali at Jimbaran Bay (page 154)
Jimbaran, Denpasar 80361
telephone : +62.361.701 010
facsimile : +62.361.701 020
www.fourseasons.com/jimbaranbay

Four Seasons Resort Bali at Sayan (page 70)
Sayan, Ubud, Gianyar 80571
telephone : +62.361.977 577
facsimile : +62.361.977 588
website : ww.fourseasons.com/sayan

Grand Hyatt Bali (page 156)
PO Box 53, Nusa Dua, Badung 80361
telephone : +62.361.771 234
facsimile : +62.361.772 038
baligh.inquiries@hayttintl.com
www.bali.grand.hyatt.com

Heavenly Residence (page 160)
Jalan Gunung Payung Sawangan,
Nusa Dua, Badung 80361

telephone : +62.361.780 1166
facsimile : +62.361.780 2266
reservation@heavenlyresidence.com
www.heavenlyresidence.com

Hotel Tugu Bali (page 210)
Jalan Pantai Batu Bolong,
Canggu Beach, Canggu,
Badung 80361
telephone : +62.361.731 701
facsimile : +62.361.731 708
bali@tuguhotels.com
www.tuguhotels.com

Indah Manis (page 164)
Jalan Temu Dewi,
Banjar Tengah Desa Pecatu,
Jimbaran, Badung 80364
telephone : +62.361.730 668
facsimile : +62.361.736 391
info@balihomes.com
www.villa-indahmanis.com

InterContinental Bali Resort (page 166)
Jalan Uluwatu 45,
Jimbaran, Badung 80361
telephone : +62.361.701 888
facsimile : +62.361.701 777
bali@ interconti.com
www.bali.intercontinental.com

The Istana (page 170)
Jalan Labuan Sait, Pantai Suluban,
Uluwatu, Badung 80361
telephone : +62.361.730 668
facsimile : +62.361.736 391
info@balihomes.com
www.theistana.com

Jajaliluna (page 212)
No. 12A Jalan Laksamana Oberoi,
Seminyak Beach, Seminyak,
Badung 80361
telephone : +62.361.730 668
facsimile : +62 361 736 391
info@balihomes.com
www.jajaliluna.com

Jamahal Private Resort + Spa (page 174)
Jalan Uluwatu 1, Jimbaran,
Badung 80361
telephone : +62.361.704 394
facsimile : +62.361.703 011
info@jamahal.net
www.jamahal.net

Jimbaran Puri Bali (page 176)
Jalan Uluwatu, Jimbaran, Badung 80361
telephone : +62.361.701 605
facsimile : +62.361.701 320
info@jimbaranpuribali.com
www.jimbaranpuribali.com

Kayumanis Jimbaran Private Estate (page 178)
Jalan Yoga Perkanthi,
Jimbaran, Badung 80364
telephone : +62.361.705 777
facsimile : +62.361.705 101
jimbaran@kayumanis.com
www.kayumanis.com

Komaneka Resort at Monkey Forest (page 72)
Jalan Monkey Forest,
Ubud, Gianyar 80571
telephone : +62.361.976 090
facsimile : +62.361.977 140
sales@komaneka.com
www.komaneka.com

Komaneka Resort at Tanggayuda (page 76)
Banjar Tanggayuda,
Kedewatan Ubud, Gianyar 80571
telephone : +62.361.976 090
facsimile : +62.361.977 140
sales@komaneka.com
www.komaneka.com

Majapahit Beach Villas (page 80)
Jalan Ida Bagus Mantra, Pabean
Desa Ketewel, Sukawati, Gianyar 80571
telephone : +62.361.730 668
facsimile : +62.361.736 391
info@balihomes.com
www.majapahitbeachvillas.com

The Oberoi, Bali (page 214)
Jalan Laksmana, Seminyak Beach,
Seminyak, Badung 80361
telephone : +62.361.730 361
facsimile : +62.361.730 791
reservations@theoberoi-bali.com
www.oberoihotels.com

Pita Maha Resort + Spa (page 82)
PO Box 198, Jalan Sanggingan,
Ubud, Gianyar 80571
telephone : +62.361.974 330
facsimile : +62.361.974 329
sales@pitamaharesorts-bali.com
www.pitamaha-bali.com

The Royal Pita Maha (page 84)
Desa Kedewatan, Ubud, Gianyar 80571
telephone : +62.361.980 022
facsimile : +62.361.980 011
sales@pitamaharesorts-bali.com
www.royalpitamaha-bali.com

Simona Oasis + Spa (page 218)
Banjar Padang Linjong, Desa Canggu
Kecamatan, Kuta Utara, Badung 80361
telephone : +62.361.730 668
facsimile : +62.361.736 391
info@simona-oasis.com
www.simona-oasis.com

Sitara Padi Villas (page 222)
Jalan Bumbak Kauh, Umalas,
Kerobokan, Badung 80361
telephone : +62.361 7800 828
facsimile : +62.361.977 140
info@sitarapadi.com
www.sitarapadi.com

The Shaba (page 182)
Jalan Uluwatu, Gang Gigit Sari,
Jimbaran, Badung 80361
telephone : +62.361.701 695
facsimile : +62.361.703 087
info@shaba-bali.com
www.shaba-bali.com

Ubud Hanging Gardens (page 86)
Desa Buahan, Payangan,
Ubud, Gianyar 80571
telephone : +62.361.982 700
facsimile : +62.361.982 800
reservations@ubudhanginggardens.com
www.ubudhanginggardens.com

Vajra Villas (page 88)
Banjar Sebali, Desa Keliki, Tegalalang,
Ubud, Gianyar 80571
telephone : +62.361.730 668
facsimile : +62.361.736 391
info@balihomes.com
www.villavajra.com

Villa Balquisse (page 184)
Jalan Uluwatu 18x,
Jimbaran, Badung 80361
telephone : +62 361 701 695
facsimile : +62 361 703 087
info@balquisse.com
www.balquisse.com

Villa Casis (page 124)
No. 3 Jalan Mertasari,
Sanur, Denpasar 80238
telephone : +62.361.270 521
facsimile : +62.361.270 540
mail@villacasis.com
www.villacasis.com

RESTAURANTS

Ary's Warung (page 92)
Jalan Raya Ubud, Gianyar 80571
telephone : +62.361.975 053
facsimile : +62.361.978 359
aryswarung@dekco.com
www.dekco.com/aryswarung

Café de Artistes (page 96)
Jalan Bisma 9x, Ubud, Gianyar 80571
telephone : +62.361.972 706
café_desartistes@hotmail.com
www.cafedesartistesbali.com

Kafe Warisan (page 226)
No. 38 Jalan Raya Kerobokan,
Banjar Taman, Kuta,
Badung 80361
telephone : +62.361.731 175
facsimile : +62.361.732 762
info@kafewarisan.com
www.kafewarisan.com

KU DE TA (page 230)
No. 9 Jalan Laksmana,
Seminyak, Badung 80361
telephone : +62.361.736 969
facsimile : +62.361.736 767
info@kudeta.net
www.kudeta.net

Lamak Restaurant + Bar (page 98)
Monkey Forest Road,
Ubud, Gianyar 80571
telephone : +62.361.974 668
facsimile : +62.361.973 482
info@lamakbali.com
www.lamakbali.com

The Living Room (page 234)
Jalan Petitenget 2000 xx,
Kerobokan Kuta, Seminyak,
Badung 80361
telephone : +62.361.735 735
email@thelivingroombali.net
www.thelivingroombali.net

directory

Ma Joly (page 236)
Jalan Wana Segara, Tuban Kuta,
Badung 80361
telephone : +62.361.753 780
facsimile : +62.361.753 781
reservation@ma-joly.com
www.ma-joly.com

Mozaic (page 100)
Jalan Raya Sanggingan, Ubud,
Gianyar 80571
telephone/facsimile : +62.361.975 768
info@mozaic-bali.com
www.mozaic-bali.com

Warung Enak Bali (page 102)
Pengosekan Road, Ubud, Gianyar 80571
telephone : +62.361.972 911
facsimile : +62.361.972 922
info@warungenakbali.com
www.warungenakbali.com

The Wave (page 238)
No. 1 Jalan Pantai Kuta,
Kuta, Badung 80361
telephone : +62.361.760 068
facsimile : +62.361.750 948
info@wave-kuta.com
www.wave-kuta.com

SHOPS

Carlo (page 128)
No. 22 Jalan Danau Poso, Sanur,
Denpasar 80228
telephone : +62.361.285 211
info@carloshowroom.com
carloshowroom.com

Gaya Fusion (page 104)
Jalan Raya Sayan, Ubud, Gianyar 80571
telephone : +62.361.979 252
facsimile : +62.361.975 895
gaya@gayafusion.com
website : www.gayafusion.com

Haveli (page 242)
Nos. 15 and 38 Jalan Basangkasa,
Seminyak, Badung 80361
telephone : +62.361.737 160
facsimile : +62.361.724 497
info@havelishop.com
website : www.havelishop.com

Shahinaz Collection
No. 36 Jalan Kunti,
Seminyak, Badung 80361
telephone : +62.361.745 0703
facsimile : +62.361.724 497
sales@shahinaz-collection.com
www.shahinaz-collection.com

IO + CO (page 244)
No. 88 Jalan Sunset Road,
Seminyak, Badung 80361
telephone : +62.361.8475 824
facsimile : +62.361.8475 827

No. 361 Jalan Legian Kelod,
Kuta, Badung 80361
telephone : +62.361.754 093
facsimile : +62.361.758 922
info@ioandco.com
www.ioandco.com

Island Arts (page 132)
Jalan Duyung Gang 1/3x Sanur,
Denpasar 80288
telephone : +62.361.285 713/281 690
facsimile : +62.361.287 042
brucar@indo.net.id

Macan Tidur (page 108)
No. 10 Monkey Forest Road,
Ubud, Gianyar 80571
telephone : +62.361.977 121
Jalan Lesmana 17, Seminyak Beach,
Seminyak, Badung 80361
telephone : +62.361.733 875
toko@macantidur.com
www.macantidurbali.com

Milo's (page 246)
Jalan Sarinande 1A, Seminyak,
Badung 80361
telephone : 62.361.730 410
facsimile : +62.361.730 856
milos@eksadata.com
www.milos-bali.com or
www.milosbaliorchids.com

Toko Antique (page 110)
Jalan Raya Ubud, Ubud, Gianyar 80571
telephone : +62.361.975 979
facsimile : +62.361.978 359
tokoantique@dekco.com
www.dekco.com

Treasures (page 112)
Jalan Raya Ubud, Ubud, Gianyar 80571
telephone : +62.361.976 697
facsimile : +62.361.978 359
treasures@dekco.com
www.dekco.com/treasures

Uluwatu Handmade Balinese Lace
(page 134)
No. 59 Jalan Danau Tondano,
Sanur, Denpasar 80288
telephone : +62.361. 287 638
facsimile : +62.361.287 054
info@uluwatu.co.id
www.uluwatu.co.id

Warisan Casa (page 190)
Jalan Raya Bypass Ngurah Rai,
Kedongan, Jimbaran, Badung 80364
telephone : +62.361.701 081
facsimile : +62.361.701 634
casa@warisan.com
www.warisan.com/stores.htm

Warisan Gallery (page 248)
No. 68 Jalan Raya Kerobokan,
Banjar Taman, Kuta,
Badung 80361
telephone : +62.361.730 710
facsimile : +62.361.730 047
warisangallery@eksadata.com
www.warisan.com

VENUES

Tirtha Luhur (page 186)
Jalan Raya Uluwatu, Banjar Karang Boma,
Desa Pecatu, Badung 80364
telephone : +62.361.772 255
facsimile : +62.361.777 252
info@tirtha.com
www.tirthabali.com

Tirtha Uluwatu (page 188)
Jalan Raya Uluwatu, Banjar Dinas Karang
Boma, Desa Pecatu, Badung 80364
telephone : +62.361.847 1151
facsimile : +62.361.847 1160
info@tirthabridal.com
www.tirthabali.com

DINING IN BALI

Air Bali
Dewa Ruci Building,
Jalan Bypass Ngurah Rai 100X,
Kuta, Badung 80361
telephone : +62.361.767 466
facsimile : +62.361.766 581
info@airbali.com
www.airbali.com/tours-and-
charters/picnic-flight

Bali Café
Jalan Laksmana Sebelah Khaima,
Seminyak, Badung 80361
telephone : +62.361.736 484
facsimile : +62.361.735 957

Bali Catering Company
Jalan Petitenget 45,
Seminyak, Badung 80361
telephone : +62.361.737 324
facsimile : +62.361.737 325
info@balicateringcompany.com
www.balicateringcompany.com

Bali Experience
Jalan Raya Semer,
Kerobokan, Badung 80361
telephone : +62.361.731 772
baliinfo@bali-experience.com
www.bali-experience.com

Bali Good Food Group
No. 29A Jalan Sekuta,
Sanur, Denpasar 80361
telephone : +62.361.285 777
info@baligoodfood.com
www.baligoodfood.com/Catering.asp

Batan Waru
Jalan Dewi Sita, Ubud,
Gianyar 80571
telephone : +62.361.977 528
batanwaru@baligoodfood.com
www.baligoodfood.com

Jalan Kartika Plaza,
Kuta, Badung 80361
telephone : +62.361.766 303

Casa Luna Cooking School
Honeymoon Guesthouse, Jalan Bisma,
Ubud, Gianyar 80571
telephone : +62.361 973 282
info@casalunabali.com
www.casalunabali.com/cooking-classes.html

Damai
Jalan Damai, Desa Kayuputih, Lovina,
Singaraja, Buleleng 81155
telephone : +62.362.410 08
facsimile : +62.362.410 09
fom@damai.com
www.damai.com

Dancing Dragon Cottages
Amed Beach, Karangasem 81155
telephone : +62.363.235 21
info@dancingdragoncottages.com
www.dancingdragoncottages.com

Esprite Nomade
Jalan Resi Markandya, Payogan,
Ubud, Gianyar 80571
telephone : +62.361.976 631
facsimile : +62.361.976 630
info@espritenomade.com
www.espritenomade.com

Hu'u
Gang Gagak 1, Jalan Petitenget,
Kerobokan, Badung 80361
Telephone: +62.361.736 443
Facsimile : +62.361.736 573
huubali@indo.net.id
www.huubali.com

Kwizien
Jalan Raya Singaraja, Seririt,
Kaliasem, Lovina, Buleleng 81114
Telephone: +62.362.42 031
Facsimile : +62.362.42 031
kwizien@balikwizien.com
www.balikwizien.com

La Lucciola
Jalan Laksmana, Pura Petitenget,
Kerobokan, Badung 80361
Telephone: +62.361.730 838
Facsimile : +62.361.730 838

Puri Ganesha Villas
Pantai Pemuteran, Gerokgak,
Singaraja, Buleleng 81155
telephone : +62.362.947 66
facsimile : +62.362.934 33
pganesha@indosat.net.id
www.puriganeshabali.com

directory

Seasalt
Alila Manggis
Buitan, Manggis,
Karangasem 80871
Telephone: +62.363.410 11
Facsimile: +62.363.410 15
manggis@alilahotels.com
www.alilahotels.com

Terazo
Jalan Suweta, Ubud,
Gianyar 80571
telephone: +62.361.978 941
www.baligoodfood.com/terazo.asp

Ultimo
Jalan Laksmana 1004X,
Seminyak, Badung 80361
Telephone: +62.361.738 721
Facsimile: +62.361.738 721
vivi_rusda@yahoo.co.id
www.balinesia.co.id

Warung Batavia
Jalan Kunti Gang 33,
Banjar Taktak, Seminyak,
Badung 80361
Telephone: +62.361.731 641

Warung Made Seminyak
Jalan Raya Seminyak,
Seminyak, Badung 80361
telephone: +62.361.753 039
facsimile: +62.361.761 959
info@www.madeswarung.com
www.madeswarung.com

The Yak
Jalan Kayu Jati 9Y, Petitenget,
Seminyak, Badung 80361
telephone: +62.361.743 1805
facsimile: +62.361.737 413
info@theyakmag.com
www.theyakmag.com

NIGHT FEVER

Bacio
Jalan Arjuna, Pantai 66,
Seminyak, Badung 80361
telephone: +62.361.756 666
facsimile: +62.361.764 466

Bali Experience
Jalan Raya Kerobokan 8X,
Banjar Semer, Kerobokan,
Badung 80361
telephone: +62.361.731 772
facsimile: +62.361.731 771
info@bali-experience.com
www.bali-experience.com

Blossom Restaurant + Lounge Bar
Sentosa Private Villas and Spa
Jalan Pura Telaga Waja, Petitenget,
Seminyak, Badung 80361
telephone: +62.361.730 333
facsimile: +62.361.737 111
info@balisentosa.com
www.balisentosa.com

The Breeze
The Samaya Bali
Jalan Laksmana, Seminyak Beach,
Seminyak, Badung 80361
Telephone: +62.361.731 149
Facsimile: +62.361.731 203
info@thesamayabali.com
www.thesamayabali.com

Double Six Club
Jalan Arjuna, Pantai 66,
Seminyak, Badung 80361
telephone: +62.361.733 067
facsimile: +62.361.745 4265
info@doublesixclub.com
www.doublesixclub.com

Elite Events
Jalan Rayar Semer 883,
Banjar Semer, Kerobokan,
Badung 80361
telephone: +62.361.731 074
facsimile: +62.361.736 391
info@eliteeventsbali.com
www.eliteeventsbali.com

Hard Rock Café
Jalan Pantai Kuta, Banjar Pande Mas,
Kuta, Badung 80361
telephone: +62.361.755 661
gm@hardrock.co.id
www.hardrock.com

The Legian
Jalan Laksmana, Seminyak Beach,
Seminyak, Badung 80361
telephone: +62.361.730 622
facsimile: +62.361.730 623
legian@ghmhotels.com
www.ghmhotels.com

MbarGo
Jalan Legian 998,
Kuta, Badung 80361
telephone: +62.361.756 666
facsimile: +62.361.764 466

Q Bar
Abimanyu Arcade, Jalan Dhyana Pura,
Seminyak, Badung 80361
telephone: +62.361.730 927
facsimile: +62.361.735 414

Syndicate
Jalan Arjuna, Pantai 66,
Seminyak, Badung 80361
telephone: +62.361.756 666
facsimile: +62.361.764 466

BEING BEAUTIFUL IN BALI

Anti-Ageing Rejuvenation Clinic
Jalan Bypass Ngurah Rai 1,
Kuta, Badung 80361
telephone: +62.361.767 543
bali@arcclinics.com
www.arcclinics.com

Bali Botanica Day Spa
Jalan Sanggingan,
Ubud, Gianyar 80571
telephone: +62.361.976 739
info@balibotanica.com
www.balibotanica.com

Bali International Medical Centre
Jalan Bypass Ngurah Rai 100X,
Kuta, Badung 80361
telephone: +62.361.761 263
facsimile: +62.361.764 345
info@bimcbali.com
www.bimcbali.com

Ubud Bodyworks Healing Centre
Jalan Hanoman 25, Padang Tegal,
Ubud, Gianyar 80571
telephone: +62.361.975 720
facsimile: +62.361.975 720
info@ubudbodyworkscentre.com
www.ubudbodyworkscentre.com

Chill Reflexology
The Villas Bali Hotel + Spa
Jalan Kunti 118X, Seminyak,
Badung 80361
telephone: +62.361.730 840
facsimile: +62.361.733 751
contact@thevillas.net
www.thevillas.net/english/chill.htm

Cozy
Jalan Sunset 3 Blok A,
Kuta, Badung 80361
telephone: +62.361.766 762
facsimile: +62.361.766 762

Espace Spa
Jalan Raya Basangkasa 3B,
Seminyak, Badung 80361
telephone: +62.361.730 828
facsimile: +62.361.730 502
espace_bali@yahoo.com
www.espacespabali.com

Jari Menari
Jalan Raya Basangkasa 47,
Seminyak, Badung 80361
telephone: +62.361.736 740
facsimile: +62.361.731 779
jarimenari@jarimenari.com
www.jarimenari.com

Kirana Spa
Desa Kedewatan, Ubud, Gianyar 80571
telephone: +62.361.976 333
facsimile: +62.361.974 888
info-english@kiranaspa.com
www.kiranaspa.com

Luxe Lounge Spa
Sentosa Private Villas and Spa
Jalan Pura Telaga Waja, Petitenget,
Seminyak, Badung 80361
telephone: +62.361.730 333
facsimile: +62.361.737 111
info@balisentosa.com
www.balisentosa.com

Rituals
Jalan Legian 476, Legian, Badung 80361
telephone: +62.361.755 926
facsimile: +62.361.762 336

Spoiled Hairdressers
Jalan Umalas II, Umalas,
Kerobokan, Badung 80361
telephone: +62.361.847 5141

THE ART OF LIFE

Agung Rai Museum of Art
Jalan Pengosekan, Ubud, Gianyar 80571
telephone: +62.361.974 228
facsimile: +62.361.974 229
armaubud@denpasar.wasantara.net.id
www.nusantara.com/arma/

Archaeology Museum
Desa Bedulu Jalan Tampaksiring,
Bedulu, Gianyar 80581
telephone: +62.361.942 347
facsimile: +62.361.942 354
bp3-bali@yahoo.com

Bali Museum
Jalan Mayor Wisnu 1, Denpasar 80232
telephone: +62.361.222 680
facsimile: +62.361.222 680

Biasa Artspace
Jalan Raya Seminyak 34,
Kuta, Badung 80361
telephone: +62.361.847 5766
facsimile: +62.361.730 766
info@biasaart.com
www.biasaart.com

Ganesha Gallery
Four Seasons Resort Bali at Jimbaran Bay
Jimbaran, Denpasar 80361
telephone: +62.361.701 010
facsimile: +62.361.701 020
www.fourseasons.com/jimbaranbay/
attractions.html

Gaya Art Space
Gaya Fusion
Jalan Raya Sayan, Ubud, Gianyar 80571
telephone: +62.361.979 252
facsimile: +62.361.975 895
gaya@gayafusion.com
www.gayafusion.com

Gunarsa Museum of Classical & Modern Art
Jalan Raya Banda 1, Takmung,
Banjar Angkan, Klungkung 80715
telephone: +62.366.222 55
facsimile: +62.366.222 57
museumklasik@dps.centrin.net.id

Jenggala Keramik
Jalan Uluwatu II, Jimbaran 80361
telephone: +62.361.703 311
facsimile: +62.361.703 312
info@jenggala-bali.com
www.jenggala-bali.com

Komaneka Gallery
Jalan Monkey Forest,
Ubud, Giaryar 80571
telephone: +62.361.976 090
facsimile: +62.361.977 140
gallery@komaneka.com
gallery.komaneka.com

directory

Neka Art Museum
Jalan Raya Campuhan, Kedewatan,
Ubud, Gianyar 80571
telephone : +62.361.975 074
facsimile : +62.361.975 63
info@museumneka.com
www.museumneka.com

Museum Puri Lukisan
Jalan Raya Ubud, Ubud,
Gianyar 80571
telephone : +62.361.975 136
info@mpl-ubud.com
www.mpl-ubud.com

Seniwati Gallery of Art by Women
Jalan Sriwedari 2B, Banjar Taman,
Ubud, Gianyar 80571
telephone : +62.361.975 485
facsimile : +62.361.975 485
seniwati@dps.centrin.net.id
www.seniwatigallery.com

ISLAND SHOPPING

Acuh Tak Acuh
Jalan Raya Seminyak,
Seminyak, Badung 80361
telephone : +62.361.737 277
facsimile : +62.361.415 277
info@acuhtakacuh.biz
www.acuhtakacuh.biz

The Bali Antique Shop
Jalan Raya Basangkasa 34X,
Seminyak, Badung 80361
telephone : +62.8191.663 8809

Biasa
Jalan Raya Seminyak 36,
Seminyak, Badung 80361
telephone : +62.361.730 308
facsimile : +62.361.730 766
biasa@biasabali.com
www.biasabali.com

Bin House
Kompleks Made's Warung, Jalan Raya
Seminyak, Seminyak, Badung 80361
telephone : +62.361.733 828
info@binhouse.com
www.binhouse.com

Blue Glue
Jalan Raya Seminyak and Jalan Double
Six, Seminyak, Badung 80361
telephone : +62.361.738
658/+62.361.732 607
www.blue-glue.com

deLighting
Jalan Gatot Subroto Barat 99,
Kerobokan, Badung 80361
telephone : +62.361.412 194
facsimile : +62.361.420 512
info@de-lighting.com
www.de-lighting.com

Disini
Jalan Raya Seminyak 6-8, Banjar
Basangkasa, Seminyak, Badung 80361
telephone : +62.361.731 037
disini_bali@yahoo.com

Etienne d'Souza
Jalan Raya Seminyak, Gang Bima 12,
Seminyak, Badung 80361
telephone : +62.361.730 942
facsimile : +62.361.730 942
info@etiennedesouza.com
www.etiennedesouza.com

Evata Eastern Furniture + Accessories
Jalan Raya Kerobokan 100ZZ,
Kerobokan, Badung 80361
telephone : +62.361.735 541
facsimile : +62.361.735 615
evata@pps.centrin.net.id
www.evatafurniture.com

Galeri Esok Lusa
Jalan Raya Basangkasa 47,
Seminyak, Badung 80361
telephone : +62.361.735 262
facsimile : +62.361.735 262
info@esoklusa.com
www.esoklusa.com

Hishem
Jalan Gunung Athena 10,
Banjar Padang Sumbu Kelod,
Denpasar 80361
telephone : +62.361.734 919
facsimile : +62.361.734 921
info@hishem.com
www.hishem.com

Ika Ika
Jalan Raya Seminyak 29X,
Seminyak, Badung 80361
telephone : +62.361.731 658
facsimile : +62.361.731 658
fashion@indosat.net.id
www.ikabutoni.com

Jean-François Fichot
Jalan Suweta 6, Ubud, Gianyar 80571
telephone : +62.361.972 078
facsimile : +62.361.972 078
www.j-f-f.com

John Hardy
Banjar Baturning Mambal,
Abiansemal, Badung 80352
telephone : +62.361.469 888
facsimile : +62.361.469 899
visit@johnhardy.com
www.johnhardy.com

Kerry Grima
Jalan Raya Seminyak 26,
Seminyak, Badung 80361
telephone : +62.361.736 403
kerrygrima@yahoo.com.au
www.kerrygrima.com

LED Studio
Jalan Bisma 9X, Legian Kaja,
Kuta, Badung 80361
telephone : +62.361.762 329
facsimile : +62.361.757 701
ledzz@denpasar.wasantara.net.id

Linda Garland
Jalan Nyuh Gading, Banjar Nyuh Kuning,
Desa Mas, Ubud, Gianyar 80571
telephone : +62.361.974 028
facsimile : +62.361.974 029
lindag@indosat/net.id

Maru
Jalan Laksamana 7A,
Seminyak, Badung 80361
telephone : +62.361.734 102
info@marugallerybali.com
www.marugallerybali.com

Mekar Sari
Jalan Raya Kedewatan 22,
Ubud, Gianyar 80571
telephone : +62.361.974 269
facsimile : +62.361.974 269

Michel Harcourt
Jalan Raya Basangkasa 1200A,
Seminyak, Badung 80361
telephone : +62.361.731 964
baliboutique@m-harcourt.com

Nilou
144 Jalan Raya Kerobokan,
Kuta, Badung 80361
telephone : +62.361.744 6068
marketing@nilou.net

OKANÉ
Jalan Legian Kelod 329,
Kuta, Badung 80361
telephone : +62.361.751 048
contact@okadiputra.com
www.okadiputra.com

One World Gallery
Jalan Raya Basangkasa 1200B,
Seminyak, Badung 80361
telephone : +62.361.730 498
facsimile : +62.361.730 498
pesamuan@indo.net.id
www.oneworld-gallery.com

Paul Ropp
Jalan Raya Seminyak 39,
Seminyak, Badung 80361
telephone : +62.361.734 208
info@paulropp.com
www.paulropp.com

Piment Rouge
Jalan Raya Seminyak 60X,
Seminyak, Badung 80361
telephone : +62.361.730 432
facsimile : +62.361.847 6120
piment@pimentrougelighting.com

Pourquoi Pas
Jalan Basangkasa 23,
Seminyak, Badung 80361
telephone : +62.361.735 757
pourquoipas_bali@yahoo.com

Quarzia
Jalan Laksmana 3A,
Seminyak, Badung 80361
telephone : +62.361.736 644
marco@quarzia.it
www.quarzia.it

Radiant
Jalan Raya Seminyak 4A, Banjar
Bangkasa, Seminyak, Badung 80361
telephone : +62.361.737 085
marcle@dps.centrin.net.id

Shalimar
corner of Jalan Raya and Jalan Hanoman,
Ubud, Gianyar 80571
telephone : +62.361.977 115
facsimile : +62.361.972 263
shalimar@idola.net.id
www.shalimarbali.com

SimpleKonsepStore
Jalan Laksmana 40,
Seminyak, Badung 80361
telephone : +62.361.730 393
sks@simplekonsepstore.com
www.simplekonsepstore.com

Sourcing Bali
Jalan Gunung Salak 31A,
Kerobokan, Badung 80361
telephone : +62.361.744 8025
facsimile : +62.361.430 683
info@sourcing-bali.com
www.sourcing-bali.com

Sriwijaya Jewels
Jalan Laksmana 17,
Seminyak, Badung 80361
telephone : +62.8123.961 810
sriwijayajewels@gmail.com

Suarti
Jalan Raya Celuk 100X,
Sukawati, Gianyar 80582
telephone : +62.361.298 914
facsimile : +62.361.297 861
sales@suarti.com
www.suarti.com

Tropis Equator
Jalan Goa Gong, Banjar Kangin, Desa
Ungasan, Kuta, Badung 80364
telephone : +62.361.742 6276
facsimile : +62.361.702 128
info@tropisequator.com
www.tropisequator.com